Living
Room

I would define globalization as the freedom for my group to invest wherever it likes, for as long as it likes, to produce whatever it likes, buying and selling wherever it likes, and having to bear the fewest possible constraints as regards labor laws and social convention.

—PERCY BARNEVIK, former CEO of ABB

An unidentified reporter then queried the Secretary as to
whether this plan could fairly be translated as take
down the trees, tear-up the earth, evacuate the urban poor,
and let the people hang, generally speaking.

—JUNE JORDAN, "Poem Towards a Final Solution"

The main targets for neoliberal ire are the fragments of democracy and collective solidarity that exist within the state and whose existence the state guarantees. These fragments of democracy and collective solidarity stem from a mix of social gains secured through tremendous struggle by the oppressed and concessions made by the rulers to maintain social peace. We must protect these fragments of democracy and solidarity.

—ERIC TOUSSAINT,
Your Money or Your Life: The Tyranny of Global Finance

Living Room

Teaching Public Writing in a **Privatized World**

NANCY WELCH
University of Vermont

Boynton/Cook Publishers
HEINEMANN
Portsmouth, NH

Boynton/Cook Publishers, Inc.
361 Hanover Street
Portsmouth, NH 03801–3912
www.boyntoncook.com

Offices and agents throughout the world

The author and publisher wish to thank those who have generously given permission to reprint borrowed material:

Portions of Chapter 1, "A Public World Is Possible," and the Epilogue originally appeared in a review by Nancy Welch of *Women and Children First: Feminism, Rhetoric, and Public Policy*. From *JAC: The Journal of Advanced Composition*, vol. 27, 2007. Copyright © 2007. Reprinted by permission of the publisher.

Acknowledgments for borrowed material continue on p. 176

Library of Congress Cataloging-in-Publication Data
Welch, Nancy
  Living room : teaching public writing in a privatized world / Nancy Welch.
    p. cm.
  Includes bibliographical references
  ISBN-13: 978-0-86709-584-5
  ISBN-10: 0-86709-584-9
  1. English language—Rhetoric—Study and teaching. 2. Report writing—Study and teaching. 3. English language—Rhetoric—Study and teaching—Political aspects. 4. English language—Rhetoric—Study and teaching—Social aspects. 5. Persuasion (Rhetoric). I. Title.

PE1404.W454 2008
808'.04207—dc22   2007041652

Editor: Charles Schuster
Production service: Lisa S. Garboski, bookworks editorial services
Production coordinator: Lynne Costa
Cover design: Joni Doherty
Cover photograph: Muhaideen Batah
Typesetter: Valerie Levy / Drawing Board Studios
Manufacturing: Steve Bernier

Printed in the United States of America on acid-free paper
12   11   10   09   08   VP   1   2   3   4   5

Contents

Acknowledgments

I must start by thanking College Editor Charles Schuster for asking me, at the 2003 Conference on College Composition and Communication, if I had thoughts about a new book. The conference took place at the onset of the U.S. invasion of Iraq, and his question helped me channel dismay into something I could work on. This book further owes its heart and a great deal of its substance to the women of my Spring 2003 senior women's studies seminar at the University of Vermont, especially Danielle Belfiore, Cassie Gillespie, Lauren Jones, Jessica Ann Lugo, Katie Monticello, and Jayme VanNoordt, who gave generously of their time during and after our semester. In the chapters to come, I draw on students' work with their permission and use their actual names at their request.

Living Room has been further nurtured by many enriching conversations with good friends and colleagues, including Mary Ann Cain, Lil Brannon, Beth Carroll, and Michelle Comstock, with whom I presented at conferences early versions of several chapters from this book. Shortly before his untimely death, University of Vermont philosophy professor Will Miller shared with me his archives—nearly forty years of anti-war and social justice activism. In Will, students and fellow activists found just the right combination of Italian revolutionary Antonio Gramsci's "pessimism of the intellect" and "optimism of the will"; I must thank him and my comrades Helen Scott and Peter Spitzform for accompanying me as I unlearned the academic training that would have put me on the sidelines of progressive struggles. I can't imagine, either, this book without the marvelous cover photograph by Muhaideem Batah.

Finally, abundant thanks and gratitude go to my husband, Didier Delmas. Some years ago when he said to me, "Postmodernisn isn't going to answer the questions you have. You need Marx," he probably did not expect I would take his words so much to heart. I appreciate his willingness to live with the consequences—and with such good and loving humor.

Several of these chapters are revised and expanded from essays that appeared earlier: "Taking Sides" in *Teaching Rhetorica*, edited by Joy Ritchie and Kate Ronald (Boynton/Cook 2006); "Living Room: Teaching Public Writing in a Post-Publicity Era" in *College Composition and Communication* 57 (National Council of Teachers of English 2005);

"Ain't Nobody's Business? A Public Personal History of Privacy after *Baird v. Eisenstadt*" in *The Private, the Public, and the Published: Reconciling Private Lives and Public Rhetoric*, edited by Barbara Couture and Thomas Kent (Utah State University Press 2004); and "Who's Afraid of Politics? The Feminist Body in the New World Order" in *College Composition and Communication* 55 (National Council of Teachers of English 2003). A version of the story of the University of Vermont's "Tent City" also appears in my review essay of *Women and Children First: Feminism, Rhetoric, and Public Policy* (edited by Sharon M. Meagher and Patrice DiQuinzio, published by the State University of New York Press) in *JAC: A Journal of Composition Theory* 26 (2007).

1

A Public World Is Possible

> *I need to speak about living room*
> *where the land is not bullied and beaten into*
> *a tombstone*
> —June Jordan, "Moving Towards Home"

Between Shock and Awe

This book was conceived between two events that continue to frame my thinking about the challenges people face when they try to forge voices of significance. The first event was a Thursday evening rally in Times Square, protesting the start of the "Shock and Awe" bombing campaign that launched the second, and ongoing, U.S. war against Iraq. That day, with other attendees of the annual Conference on College Composition and Communication, I'd ridden up and down hotel elevators, transfixed by tiny televisions tuned in to CNN: grainy infrared images of eerily empty Baghdad streets, headlights of a lone car rolling along, and then, in the distance, a streak, a flare, a sudden bright burst. Shortly before 5 P.M., joined by two others, I left the conference and headed in a downpour—the three of us sheltered beneath an inadequate umbrella—to the emergency protest in Times Square. There we entered a sea of black umbrellas filling two city blocks. The sea swelled as streams of bodies, more bobbing black umbrellas, flowed in from side streets. But beyond these two blocks we couldn't expand. Columns of police guarding metal barricades hemmed us in.

One month earlier, when some half a million people converged on New York City to protest an invasion of Iraq, there had been plenty more of these cops, clubs, and barricades. But February 15, 2003, had been sunny if bone-bitingly cold; the crowds had been chanting, and the large group with whom I'd marched overran a barricade and sailed past the police, our cries of "One-two-three-four, we can stop the war!" turning to an exuberant "Whose streets? Our streets!" On this night, however, rain poured on a silent protest, the cops stood firm, and two things seemed depressingly clear: We had not stopped the war; these were not our streets. My two companions and I tunneled through the throng. I found several people with whom I'd marched on February 15. The swelling crowd lifted us up against the barricades. The police beat us back. This time I was in no position to slip through, and these cops were in no mood for explanations. After a minute more of this involuntary push and shove, I ducked out and made my way back to the hotel, arriving soaked, chilled, and just in time to take my place on an evening panel about how to get published in *College Composition and Communication*.

Had that awful evening been my only experience of the first response, the fullest response, of people in the United States to the launching of this war, I might have written a very different book or, more likely, I would not have written any book—not on the topic of teaching public writing. It would have been hard to shake the sobering image of so many dripping black umbrellas, the implacable police, their faces grim behind Plexiglas visors. It would have seemed sounder to conclude that we live in creeping (or full-blown) fascism, that protest has no register, that the sanest thing anyone can do is retreat within tiny shoals of relative safety (homes, classrooms, small affinity groups) where we shore up against a mostly "red state" and "security mom" nation whose people overwhelmingly suffer from what Harriet Malinowitz (2003) has called *stupidification*—that is, an inability to get, or even seek, a critical purchase on such explanatory sound bites as "They hate us for our freedoms" and "We need to fight the terrorists on their soil before they come to ours." Or maybe I would have held firm in the belief that those who huddled beneath umbrellas in Times Square are, in fact, representative of a citizenry that is indeed suffering—but suffering from loss of democratic voice, not loss of brainpower. No matter. With or without our consent, I might have concluded, the war goes on. It has a mind of its own.

There was, however, another defining event for me that week, this one two days later. That Saturday, with twenty-five or thirty conference goers, I left the hotel just before noon for a march down Broadway to

Washington Square. The day was bright, the temperatures reaching into the sixties, and while, as the *Village Voice* put it, it wasn't exactly *glasnost* (Ferguson 2003), police allowed demonstrators—whose column filled forty blocks—to proceed mostly unmolested. What a sea change from two nights before. As political writer Dave Lindorff (2003) observed in the next edition of *Counterpunch*:

> It was an astonishing display. Even as the nation engaged in a ferocious assault on the nation of Iraq, and as the first reports of American casualties in that war were coming in, what was shaping up as one of the largest peace demonstrations in the history of New York was getting set to march through the heart of the very city where this new round of global violence had started. . . . That the march was happening at all was a remarkable testament to the power of protest.

The mood of the march, Lindorff observed, was "upbeat but determined." True, the biggest peace marches the world had seen had not been sufficient to keep this war from starting—the president writing off an estimated 10 million demonstrators worldwide as a "focus group" he could simply ignore—but a distinction still begged to be made between the will of Washington and the will of the rest of us. And, for at least that afternoon, I had no doubt I was marching *with* the will of the people. Aproned restaurant workers stood in doorways and applauded as demonstrators passed. From brownstones draped bedsheets with messages of solidarity for the Iraqi people, calls to impeach George Bush, and the pointed question, "How did our oil get under their sand?" Only at one intersection did I see a small—just three or four people—group of counterdemonstrators. Otherwise I was buoyed along in an ocean of humanity whose intelligence and good sense surpassed that of Congress, including those from the Democratic Party who would later claim to have been fooled by falsified warrants for war. Here were thousands upon thousands of people who for months had been bombarded with a hard sell for "Operation Iraqi Freedom" (or even years, if we remember President Bill Clinton and Secretary of State Madeleine Albright stumping for "regime change"). Despite all the means of persuasion at the disposal of the political and corporate powers, people had refused to buy it.

The helpless despair of that first night following Shock and Awe combines with the unrelenting hope of the Saturday march to inform my approach to the chapters in this book. A book about prospects for teaching public writing can't ignore the regulation and repression used to tamp down the ideas and aspirations of much of the population; nor should it ignore the persistent push back by ordinary people still seeking, and sometimes finding, ways to be heard. Together both perspectives on our present moment have guided my explorations into what we can do to teach writing in a way that supports access, voice, and impact while also acknowledging the formidable constraints that convince most people there's very little they can do, very little that people have ever done, to affect the course of national and world events.

If Memory Serves

Most of my writing and teacherly concerns through the 1990s focused on how to cultivate individual practices of revision—of restless questioning and creative textual improvisations—against social and disciplinary constraint. In recent years, however, I've faced a pileup of rhetorical situations that test the power of individual acts of revision. For instance, the U.S. health care crisis (and the cost-containing managed care obstacles confronting my husband and me when he was diagnosed with kidney cancer) and the Rust Belt devolution of the U.S. middle class (leaving half my family unemployed for the better part of the last decade) aren't problems that can be solved by individual will and creativity. Similarly, the teens with whom I've worked since 1998 at a local youth center have not been able—not through literacy alone—to write and revise their way to college access and livable wage jobs *despite* their considerable linguistic gifts. At rallies and demonstrations I've noted inventive slogans and ingenious street theater—*A PROFIT told Bush to start this war; Thanks for the billions! (Sorry about the kids.) Signed Halliburton*—that do impact public consciousness but can't, through sheer *kairos*, stop two wars spurred on by private interests and global grabs for control of the Middle East's resources and Central Asia's trade routes. It is from the need to grapple with such limit situations—where oppositional writing practices cannot, at least not alone, alter larger social arrangements and yet where the urgency for intervention continues to mount—that I wrote the chapters gathered in *Living Room*.

In particular, I want this book to unite two key conversations among teachers of composition and rhetoric. The first concerns a revitalized interest in teaching public writing. More than just a topic *du jour*, the question of how ordinary people reach and persuade influential audiences has taken on intensified exigence as teachers find that the venues in which students' (and our own) arguments might gain a hearing have become noticeably policed and restricted. Participants in this conversation, guided by such theorists as Nancy Fraser, Jürgen Habermas, Hannah Arendt, and Gilles Deleuze, are primarily interested in how to create "strong publics" or viable "counter-publics" within or apart from the social and economic policies that have privatized public space, decision making, and resources and that have also, via recent "homeland security" measures, raised the stakes for dissent. Into this context of restricted space for public voice and participation, I want to bring a second conversation among writing teachers arising from reinvigorated readings of rhetorical history. In answer to the appeals and examples of Jacqueline Jones Royster and Jean C. Williams (1999), Jane Greer (1999), Anne Ruggles Gere (1994), and Susan Jarratt (1991a), among many others, scholars are locating rhetorical history not only in canonized figures and elite institutions but also among itinerant teachers, lecture-circuit reformers, African American abolitionist and civil rights leaders, and working-class college curricula. From Kathleen Welch's (1990, 1994, 1999) calls, scholars have also broadened the study of delivery to include eighteenth-century pulpits and twenty-first-century blogs—predominantly middle-class forums spotlighting individual rhetors that nevertheless can be further expanded to include the working-class rhetorical arts of the soapbox, picket, sit-down, and strike.

In the chapters that follow, I hope to join our current interests in public writing and rhetorical history to argue that if we're to teach effective, responsive rhetorical practices in an era of shopping malls and Clear Channel, of state-sanctioned ethnic profiling and militarized responses to public protest, of private economic interests colluding to shape public policy on everything from energy and interest rates to access to health care and the airwaves, we must explore the *two* neglected canons that Welch has flagged: delivery *and* memory. By recalling the creative responses of earlier generations to constraints on (or prohibitions against) public visibility and voice, we can learn how individuals and groups, especially those lacking official platforms, have effectively argued for wider participation and greater democratization. Those earlier struggles not only offer important contributions to our understanding of how efficacious arguments can be delivered in the most restrictive circumstances; they also upset, and profoundly enrich, the principles underwriting our classroom lessons in invention, arrangement, and style. After all, in the most consequential arguments of the United States in the twentieth century, we find not (or not only) podiums and pundits but workers shutting down production lines, women facing police outside plant gates, students sitting resolute at segregated lunch counters, veterans marching on the Pentagon, and AIDS-HIV activists "dying-in" on Wall Street crosswalks.

Each of these earlier struggles was taken up by groups excluded from the middle- and ruling-class spheres that have been the focus of much academic theorizing. The issues each group fought to bring to public attention for public change had been heretofore deemed private, matters properly dealt with in the family or ruled by the workplace. Each of these struggles was waged to win the very public rights we now see under siege. If brought to bear on today's public writing conditions and concerns, these vibrant models can help us and our students take stock of our own available means. At the very least, if we know how earlier generations effectively argued and agitated for public provision and rights, through what combinations of *kairotic* appeal and embodied action, we'll have a better sense of how to read, and what it might take to resist, the privatizing rhetoric and private interests intent on rolling back those rights today.

The Social Turn in a Privatized World

Through rhetorical memory, we can further recognize that today's restricted opportunities for public voice and participation aren't strictly a "post–September 11th" development. Indeed, current assaults on public programs, rights, and geographic space began well before the presidency of George W. Bush. Susan Wells (1996), for instance, opens "Rogue Cops and Health Care: What Do We Want from Public Writing?" with a story of police brutality from the early 1990s, when quality-of-life zoning and tough-on-crime rhetoric combined to relegitimize racial profiling, segregation, and harassment in the name of private property protection and rights (see also Williams 1991). Upon learning that the written complaint of an African American Temple University student, picked up and beaten by police, had resulted in citywide shake-ups and reforms, Wells at first basks in this evidence of her writing program's success: "Colbert had probably learned to write a strong narrative in *our* program. . . . And his text had been efficacious: it had turned around a whole police department" (1996, 325–26). Then she notes that this student's complaint had been the twenty-third filed against these two officers and that it was likely the public's outraged response to the L.A. police beating of Rodney King that had finally pushed this investigation ahead. Reassessing her initial feelings of triumph and validation, Wells points out that such a reaction reflects both the urgency of teachers' desires for their students to make effective public arguments and the diminishment of our expectations for what they can achieve by doing so. "I once had stronger hopes," Wells writes, "than helping my students write good complaints if they were beaten by cops" (1996, 326).

What Wells' frequently cited essay brings into view is the central problem that has accompanied composition's *social turn* (Trimbur 1994) since the 1980s: Even as our field has increasingly focused on the public dimensions of students' writing and writing pedagogy, the national turn has been in an opposite direction, toward increasing privatization. At odds with our interest in promoting public discourse is the diminished space for public decision-making voice we and our students actually live within. However, diminished space and expectations are neither the result of cultural postmodernism nor a challenge in public-sphere creation that all classes of people within a society have uniformly faced. Instead, I think we garner the most precise and useful insights when we examine current constraints as specific to our *neoliberal* moment and as impinging most heavily in the United States on groups whose economic and social gains from twentieth-century labor and social movements are neoliberalism's prime targets.

Neoliberalism is, in part, a reassertion of classical economic liberalism's central tenet that major political and social decisions are best decided by the market. What makes neoliberalism more than a return to pre-Keynesian, pre–New Deal arrangements, however, is that it powerfully combines "free market" ideology with the social Darwinist conservatism exemplified by the governments of Britain's Margaret Thatcher and the United States' Ronald Reagan (and also pursued by governments, Republican or Democrat, Conservative or Labour, that have since followed their course). Add to this the internationalization of global finance and deregulation of financial markets overseen by the world's economic powers, especially through the carrots and sticks offered by quasi-public bodies such as the World Bank, International Monetary Fund, and the Paris Club. What we then have are corporate *and* state forces (including, as needed, police and military forces) colluding to privatize public resources and services, raise taxes on the poor, cut taxes on wealth and profit, and liberalize capital flows while holding increasingly impoverished and desperate populations in place with tightened immigration and border restrictions. Reagan's trickle-down theory is still advanced as the major warrant to support what is also called globalization. A rising financial tide ostensibly lifts all boats. But the most comprehensive study to date, conducted by the World Institute for Development Economics Research of the United Nations University, suggests that much of the world's population, including within the United States, are trying to stay afloat with, at best, dinghies and life rafts. As of 2000, only 1 percent of the world's population (two-thirds in the United States and Japan) owned 40 percent of the global wealth; the wealthiest 10 percent controlled 85 percent of world wealth (Davies et al. 2006, 26–27).

The growing wealth gap within as well as between nations is explanation enough for growing insecurity. Yet neoliberalism has also made use of the economic crises and recessions of the twentieth century's final decades to go after the political reforms and social provisions fought for by working classes in Europe in the late nineteenth century, in the United States through key decades of struggle in the twentieth century, as well as in Latin America and other regions through post–World War II liberation struggles. In other words, although neoliberalism was born in the economic crisis (falling profit margins brought on by overproduction and intensifying global competition) that ended the United States' long post–World War II boom, it has proceeded since the mid-1970s, with accelerating speed, whether in moments of economic boom or bust, to roll back a century's worth of public programs and social rights. Under neoliberalism, antipoverty and equal opportunity programs have marked the leading edge of services to be defunded. This disinvestment has been assisted by a reworking and reclassifying of racism, sexism, homophobia, and other forms of discrimination as simply and rightly a private employer's or privatized community's prerogative.

This is not to say that neoliberalism does not grant government a role—it is not the primacy of private corporate interests over and above that of nation states. Rather, we might understand government's role in this moment as increasingly that of the "watchtower" (Collins 2003), the state serving to protect private property and private privilege from public demands. Or if there is an "opportunity" role that neoliberal governments play, it is opportunity for the wealthiest alone, as government officials and agencies intervene (at times with brute military force) in production and trade not to protect the public good but to ensure optimal conditions for the "free market."

With neoliberalism, there is indeed a critical—and, as Harriet Malinowitz (2003) aptly identifies it, a critical literacy—problem facing most people, including people in the United States. The problem we face, however, isn't stupidification. Of course, there is a great deal that comes from the mouths and decisions of top policymakers that does assume or wish for a brain-dead population. Remember Reagan's attempt to rename ketchup a school-lunch vegetable? And now, in today's news, the Bush agriculture department has dropped the word *hunger* from its assessments of the food assistance needs of some 35 million Americans. Yet, as the application for public assistance in my state mushrooms to more than a dozen fill-in-the-blank-and-attach-the-appropriate-documentation pages, critical literacy has become a matter of survival in a country that leads not only in wealth but also, among eighteen industrialized nations, in the percentage of people living in poverty (Toussaint 2005, 47). The problem we face is actually neoliberalism's *stupefying* reach, its rhetorical-bureaucratic covers, its market-logic penetration into virtually every aspect of existence. For example, Education Secretary Margaret Spellings, while denying that she sought a No Child Left Behind policy for higher education, recently argued that universities and colleges need to demonstrate the *value added* to students through four years of education (Norris 2006).

Although there have been crucial challenges to three decades of neoliberalism's social insecurity measures—including the spring 2006 massive marches and strikes for U.S. immigrant rights, which I'll return to at this chapter's end—neoliberal privatization presents a rhetorical conundrum. It does so because among the public goods that have been sold or legislated away are the very rights to public visibility and voice we most need to safeguard all others. Within the urgency and constraints created by neoliberal policy, we face the fundamental tension: an abundant need for people, particularly those lacking official credentials, to engage in public argument; and a dearth of space, opportunity, and freedom for most people to do so.

The chapters to come in *Living Room* don't provide a primer for neoliberal economics, nor do they provide guides to, or even arguments for, partnering public writing classrooms with specific social service and social justice organizations. Instead, my aims are more basic as I first work to draw out and examine the neoliberal logic that reprivatizes a host of vital public issues, placing them outside the realm of what is arguable or tucking them away in the gated domains of credentialed specialists. Next I turn to models, lessons, and questions of twentieth-century struggles for living room—historical case studies in rhetorical action against war, oppression, and exploitation—that not only pluralize but also call into question many of the standard (and mostly middle-class) principles about effective communication we tend to teach. Although composition studies has largely ignored the strategies and tactics of working-class and mass-movement rhetors, it's these histories that have reinvigorated my reading of all five rhetorical canons; these lessons from the past bring an expanded sense of possibility, consequence, and risk to classroom discussions about what it means, and what it takes, for most people to try to go public then and now. In the epilogue to this volume, I offer a final case study of students at my university engaged in consequential—and controversial—rhetorical action. Through this story I hope we can consider that history-making rhetors, working collectively to mitigate risk and amplify voice, put into practice both liberal and illiberal persuasive principles.

Underwriting *Living Room* is also my belief that a majority of our students—not only those who identify themselves as concerned with social justice—would benefit from examining the history of argumentation about reproductive and civil rights, public provision for retirement and unemployment, access to health care and education. Perhaps compositionists have reason to worry about critical or service-learning pedagogies that are too particularly "partisan" (Erwin 2006)—if partisan means advocating for Democratic candidates over Republican (both parties, it must be said, are parties of neoliberalism), castigating students for their consumerism (as tuition skyrockets and federal tuition grants are replaced with private loans, most students are looking at a minimum of $800 each month in loan repayments for their "purchase" of a college education), or placing students with liberal advocacy groups (which still restrict classroom study to middle-class public-sphere activity). On the other hand, I think it can be argued that our classrooms have been far too partisan by orienting only on middle-class and ruling-class spheres for rhetorical participation. Here we need to consider with Keith Gilyard (2003) that a third of our students can expect unemployment or underemployment following graduation. Even a degree from a nationally ranked, competitive-admissions university isn't a guarantor of steady, livable wage work. The University of Vermont's survey of the class of 2005 one year after graduation found that 34 percent of working alums overall held temporary (full-time or part-time) jobs, that 20 percent searched for seven or more months after graduation before finding a job, and that 35 percent of working Arts and Sciences degree holders earned less than $20,000 a year (University of Vermont 2006). Among recent graduates with whom I've stayed in touch, one English and sociology double major is now working one full-time job in human services and one part-time job in retail while also taking community college classes in graphic design in the hope that this skill might bring a better job. A political science major, three years past graduation, is back living with his parents, unable to pay rent on his $9-an-hour pay.

For those students who do find full employment, most—as teachers, nurses, social workers, technicians and engineers, service- and public-sector workers of all kinds—are not looking forward to middle-class autonomy and individual control over the security of their jobs, their conditions of work, and the continuation of health care and retirement benefits. It could well be that, if we have been teaching composition as a "middle-class enterprise" (Bloom 1996), we're out of touch with the conditions and needs of the majority of faculty teaching these classes *and* the majority of students enrolled in them. Here is an opportunity to rhetoricize social class(to shift our definition of working class from a focus on cultural identity to a focus on one's available means for exercising decision-making power within and against privatization's strict limits on public rights and voice, including in the workplace.)

By titling this book *Living Room*—in homage to the late June Jordan and her Reagan-era poetry volume (1985) of the same title—I also hope to situate the privatizing challenges we face within a time line reaching back toward the start of the neoliberal era. Undeniably, encroachments on public rights and visibility have intensified since 2001: the mass detainments and deportations of Arab and Muslim men immediately following September 11, 2001; the COINTELPRO-like surveillance of Quaker and Veterans for Peace meetings; witch hunts of prominent Left academics such as Ward Churchill; the long imprisonment of University of South Florida Professor Sami Al-Arian even after a jury refused to convict him on any of the government's laundry list of charges; and the "disappearing" of people into Guantanamo as well as through Immigration and Customs Enforcement (ICE) raids on factories and farms. This is the period, between 2001 and 2007, in which I drafted this book, a period in which I was keenly concerned about the impact of these events on my students' expectations for public writing and participation. We need a longer time line, however, to understand how these events stand in relation to the preceding two decades of expanding executive and police power, shrinking First and Fourth Amendment rights, increasingly confident assertions of U.S. first-strike and regime-change military prerogatives, not to mention the repeal of welfare, dramatic expansion of the U.S. prison system, and privatization of public resources, institutions, even sidewalks and streets. Without the longer view, we can't take in the full scope of the challenge to civic life that most people face.

Natural Order Is Being Restored?

Although June Jordan's *Living Room* (1985) appeared midway through the Reagan and Thatcher regimes, her poems chronicling their aggressive pursuit of a stripped-down economic and hyper-militarized world order, few of these have lost their currency. "Moving Towards Home" might have been penned after Israel's 2002 razing of the Jenin refugee camp or amid the summer 2006 pounding, with U.S.-shipped bombs, of Beirut: "I do not wish to speak about the bulldozer and the/red dirt/not quite covering all of the arms and the legs." Other poems are chillingly prescient about the consequences of shredding social safety nets. When, in "Poem Towards a Final Solution," a fictive reporter suggests that by defunding public programs, the White House is pursuing a policy of "let the people hang," her statement is dismissed as "misleading and alarmist," hampering "the economic recovery of the nation." Reading this poem twenty years later, we can see where Reagan's "economic recovery," Clinton's "personal responsibility," and Bush's "national security" agendas have led: In post-Katrina New Orleans, we did indeed see "the people hang."

Yet Jordan does not assume a complacent and consumerist American public privileged by rampant racism and sexist, homophobic scapegoating. With the opening poem, "From Sea to Shining Sea"—which begins with the solemn incantation, "Natural order is being restored"— she sets a critical stage for distinguishing between the Orwellian rhetoric of press-conference officials and those suffering, from Queens to Grand Forks, the cost of this new social and economic order. Jordan's work in this poem is to draw together diverse groups of people through both their shared immiseration and their shared potential to disrupt the decidedly *unnatural* order that has been imposed upon them.

At the same time, then, that Jordan's *Living Room* records some of neoliberalism's earliest devastating assaults and stupefying ideological covers, the poems point to an alternative future winnable through the spirit, and logic, of solidarity exemplified in her opening poem's insistence that "This is the best time./This is the only time to come together." In this other possible world, "the land is not bullied and beaten into/a tombstone," "the talk will take place in my language," and "the men/of my family between the ages of six and sixty-five/are not/marched into a roundup that leads to the grave" ("Moving Towards Home"). In the United States between 1980 and 1985, however, signs of such another possible world were tough to find, and *Living Room*'s closing call, "It is time to make our way home," may thus seem like nothing more than a rote benediction by a lone poet who lacks the *ethos*, the public office or private power, to affect history's course. Solidarity, we might conclude, has an old-fashioned charm but fails in get-real political appeal.

Certainly it's true that in the opening years of the 1980s, Jordan and other U.S. activists received few answers to their calls for solidarity and mass action. In fact, the Reagan and Thatcher eras began with what turned out to be very nearly mortal blows to labor solidarity: As Reagan fired PATCO's striking air traffic controllers and Thatcher turned out the military against Britain's miners, the rest of labor ducked for cover. Plaintive calls from workers on the frontlines—most notably from Austin, Minnesota's meatpacking workers whose desperate strike against Hormel is the subject of the Oscar-winning *American Dream* (Koppel 1993)—were heard as calls to mourning rather than calls to action. Immersed in the belt-tightening rhetoric of the Reagan and subsequent administrations, most of the U.S. public, and certainly union officials, overlooked that the same year Hormel demanded a double-digit wage cut from Austin workers, it posted $30 million in net profit. Similarly, under the thrall of today's headlines—concessions demanded amid bankruptcy filings by leading airlines and automakers—and anxiety over stagnant wages and growing family debt, it's easy to miss a headline like this: "US Set for Record Run of Profits" (Guerrera and Wighton 2006, 15). *An injury to one is an injury to all*: That was the slogan raised in the early years of the twentieth century by the Industrial Workers of the World (IWW), which battled police, military, and vigilante lynch mobs as it sought to organize the unskilled, immigrant workers shunned by the exclusive and nativist AFL craft unions. Since the Reagan-Thatcher 1980s, as conditions for unskilled, immigrant, and service-economy workers worsen once more, the IWW's slogan has been nearly undone: An injury to one is simply an injury to one.

Yet consider what also accompanied the 1985 publication of *Living Room*: the escalating agitation that brought down South Africa's apartheid regime accompanied by the sanctuary movement for refugees from the U.S. proxy wars against progressive governments and movements in Central America, demonstrations on U.S. campuses to kick out CIA recruiters, plus urgent public actions by ACT UP to force Washington to provide long-delayed acknowledgment of and relief for the HIV-AIDS epidemic. Here we need to extend the time line forward: from 1985 onward as economic, political, and military globalization has continued its destructive march and also as globalization has created voices of audible, international discontent. If we look forward from the mid-1980s, we cannot miss accumulating instances of confrontation and even, with the collapse of apartheid and the implosion of Soviet state capitalism, foundational change. Add to this the 1989 abortion rights demonstration in Washington DC, the protests against the first Gulf War, and the mass uprising of the Los Angeles Rebellion in the wake of the Rodney

King verdict. The end of the 1990s brought another explosion with the global economic justice movement and its anti-corporate-globalization insistence that "The world is not for sale." In the same city in which the IWW had first fought for the right to public speech and assembly, students, environmentalists, workers, and farmers from Latin America and North America united to oppose neoliberalism's biggest offensive, the North American Trade Agreement, against a century's worth of labor, environmental, and social security gains.

None of these movements has proceeded without interruption and setback. Reagan-Bush-era expressions of dissent receded, for instance, with the election of President Bill Clinton and the hope that the new administration would defend abortion rights, stand up for lesbians and gays, deliver universal health care and a peace dividend too—even if Clinton did run for office on the "tough-on-crime" execution of a mentally handicapped black man and promoted the New Democrats' promise to "end welfare as we know it." (Clinton's 1992 Democratic National Convention speech makes for a rich if disturbing lesson in how a rhetor can construct trust-winning appeal that runs from left to right on the political spectrum.) Cowboy capitalists joined by U.S. and European investors were quick to move into the former Eastern Bloc, and any notion of a peace dividend was set aside as old and new players jockeyed for control in the Balkans and the resource-rich, strategically located former Soviet republics. More recently in the United States, economic justice organizations and national antiwar committees have been ambivalent about responding to the war on Afghanistan and silent on the targeting of Arabs and Muslims.

Looking just at these moments of stand-down and retreat, I might conclude—as I might have concluded on the first night after Shock and Awe—that contempory global capitalism is too powerful, people too duped by *Top Gun* media stunts or divided by demonizing stereotypes. I might form such a conclusion except that evidence of refusal and resistance still abounds. Jordan's call to collective action against neoliberal rollback in *Living Room*'s (1985) opening poem, along with her radical claim to identification with oppressed groups worldwide in the collection's final poem—"I was born a Black woman/and now/I am become a Palestinian"—has found multiple echoes. Here are some examples: in the 1997 UPS strike as full-time and part-time workers banded together to insist "Part-time America doesn't work!"; in 2002 when tens of thousands of protestors gathered simultaneously in Porto Alegre and New York City to hoist banners proclaiming "They are all Enron and we are all

Argentina!"; in 2006 as French and North African students and workers defeated the Villepin government's divide-and-conquer job security rollbacks with the slogan *Workers, students, unemployed, undocumented— let's fight insecurity with solidarity!* Even as by every measure globalization has increased human misery and environmental degradation something else has increased too: the motivation for mass resistance by people who are bound together in, and potentially against, the same "race to the bottom." Solidarity rhetoric has in these moments a material, not only a moral, basis.

Moreover, these are examples of winning solidarity that academics ought to embrace to address our own deteriorating conditions of work. Neoliberal "flexibility" has created in the United States neoliberalized universities with 65 percent of faculty working without the tenure track's (increasingly shaky) job security and academic freedom and with 46 percent of faculty working part time (American Association of University Professors 2006). "Money for the classroom, not the boardroom!" was the slogan of my faculty union's first contract drive, fueled by popular outrage at the World Com and Enron debacles and by frustration with a university administration that had added eighteen new vice presidents while downsizing faculty and staff. Today, however, despite one union covering us all, adjunct and tenure-line faculty at my university are increasingly divided by varying degrees of "privilege" that are in fact varying degrees of vulnerability. Here it might help us to take a chapter from the 1997 UPS strike and its worker-uniting arguments (Kumar 2006). We need the slogan "Part-time higher ed doesn't work" both to connect with other faculty against corporatized administrations and to connect with students, the majority of whom will not be richly rewarded in the new economy and so likewise need strategies for solidarity and resistance (Gilyard 2003, 229).

Though we can't call a strike or launch a social movement from a classroom, we can teach and learn the attitudes, relationships, and practices that are the preconditions for imagining oneself and others as participants in social policy making and agents of social change. Try even just bringing a makeshift soapbox into the classroom—an exercise I'll return to in this book and that Erwin (2006) also describes. Ask your students to step up on it and, for a minute or two, talk—on any topic and in any tone—about what is on their minds. "Don't Be Afraid of That Soapbox Day!" is the single event in all of my classes that students point to, in final papers and course evaluations, as teaching, and even changing, them the most: not because most are likely to

engage in soapboxing again but because for a moment they felt visible, not just in a classroom but with their classmates in shared difficulties and shared potential.

A Public World Is Possible

For much of the time that I worked on this book, I have been unable to say that all we must do is look outside our department meetings and beyond conference hotels to see what our mission and relevance—what a future for public writing—could be. What appeared to be the rising tide of the global economic justice movement rapidly receded with the September 11, 2001, attacks; the intermittent struggles against war and for abortion rights and gay marriage were absorbed into election campaigns by candidates who would openly support none of these causes. Following the November 2004 reelection of George W. Bush, *The Nation* even amputated the famous assertion of Joe Hill, IWW organizer and working-class free-speech defender, who went to his death proclaiming "Don't mourn—organize!" After the election, *The Nation* advised simply, and self-indulgently, "Mourn."

A handful of weeks in the spring of 2006, however, have brought once again into view what massive public contestation against neoliberalism's scapegoating and exploitation can look like. Declaring "We produce, we demand!" Latino workers, with and without papers, led the first mass strikes—shutting down the country's biggest airports and ports—the United States has seen since the 1930s, also joining labor and civil rights solidly together for the first time in U.S. history. The *New York Times* certainly grasped the full potential for order-shaking upset. In a weekend editorial preceding the mass May Day demonstration, it worried that come Monday "The nation will rattle with the emptiness of millions of immigrants not working, not shopping and not going to school," and the editorial ended with this warning: "Sleeping giants can, and should, get moving. But they should tread carefully" ("The Sleeping Giant" 2006).

Never mind this absence of official sanction, May Day's *El Gran Paro*, or Great American Boycott, surged forward, and although—as has been true of all prior significant challenges to corporate globalization and U.S. policy—this surge did not issue from the halls of academe, it had a measurable impact on the available ideas and lifting aspirations on my college campus. In fact, awakened on the University of Vermont (UVM) campus were the first sizable mobilizations in almost twenty years. With the city's newly formed immigrant rights coalition, several

lecturers from UVM's College of Education (who had just received pink slips after ten, fifteen, and even twenty years of service) stood with education students behind the banner "No one is illegal—or disposable." Other students, organizing with staff and custodial workers, launched a "tent city" for livable wages. By pitching pup tents in the shadow of the $61-million, 186,000-square-foot student center under construction, they created a visual image of the great gulf between the center's lavish amenities and the poverty wages to be paid to those who would staff its retail mall and restaurants.

In the absence of official endorsement and moneyed sponsors, these from-below movements are genuinely grassroots. They are also remarkably, and necessarily, inventive as individuals and groups come together not only to raise good slogans but also to figure out how, through mainstream and alternative channels, to make their slogans heard while facing multiple foils. The students at UVM who pitched Tent City, for instance, had originally planned a takeover of the administration building wing that houses offices for the president and twenty-one vice presidents. When they were turned away by a locked door and an armed guard (for the rest of that spring the university kept its administrative wing under lock and guard), they improvised on the space available, the university's green. Here we have a re-presentation of Marx's aphorism: Though not in conditions of their own choosing, these men and women strove to make history.

It is not in conditions of their own choosing either that dissenting soldiers are organizing today with remarkable inventiveness. While *The Nation* cried "Mourn" following the 2004 elections, Navy petty officer Pablo Paredes called a press conference. Wearing his message on a T-shirt— "Like a [Bush] Cabinet Member, I Resign"—Paredes stood in view of his San Diego-based, Iraq-bound ship and explained to reporters why he would face court-martial rather than board. Paredes wasn't acting as a lone rhetor. He organized the press conference with San Diego military counseling, peace and justice, and antiwar veterans groups and through the inspiration of the Iraq War's first soldier to publicly refuse (re)deployment, Camilo Mejía. Inspiration—this time of Vietnam-era GI coffeehouses—also moved Citizen Soldier, a soldiers' and war resistors' advocacy group, to open the Different Drummer Café outside the gates of Fort Drum in Watertown, New York. Because new homeland security measures deter today's war resistance counselors from walking onto a base and talking with soldiers in the commissary, creativity beyond the GI coffeehouses is also coming into play. Vermonter Liam Madden, cofounder of the Appeal for Redress campaign, for instance, has organized with other servicewomen and men to use their active-duty status to deliver "care packages" on half a dozen U.S. bases from Virginia to California (Totten 2006). What's inside these care packages? Baked goods, of course; also *Sir! No Sir!* (a powerful documentary about the Vietnam soldiers' revolt), *The Ground Truth* (featuring members of Iraq Veterans Against the War), plus information on soldiers' rights to dissent.

Academics concerned about our own freedoms for teaching and research should take heart and courage from these members of a wider public standing up despite considerable restriction and threat of reprisal. Particularly for teachers concerned with how people lacking public office and private means find or create an audience, there's much to learn here too. Paredes used a forum, the press conference, that is usually not viewed as among the available means of uncredentialed citizens and noncommissioned officers. Madden "repurposed" the apolitical care package as a means to deliver the ideas, information, and tools soldiers need to organize together against war. Of course, they, like participants in the immigrant rights movement and campus campaigns for livable wages, use new information technologies that many compositionists see as central to our field's future. We should also note how in these key recent movements new information technologies support, but don't supplant, low-tech and traditional means of delivery. From an overpass in Los Angeles on May Day hung a bedsheet banner: "After I growed your food and built your home, why do you treat me like a criminal?" In the middle of Manhattan, uniformed "soldiers" order "civilians" down on the pavement and up against walls—a fully embodied, frighteningly real piece of street theater called "Operation First Casualty" written and performed by Iraq Veterans Against the War to bring home (as participants explain) the truth—war's first casualty—about the occupation of Iraq (Iraq Veterans 2007). Against one of Tent City's pup tents is a piece of plywood spray painted with the words *UVM Can Do Better*. Within the circle of pup tents, someone sets up a plastic milk-carton soapbox. A sympathetic staff member in the university's facilities office supplies a sound system so that what is spoken from the soapbox—music, speeches, poetry, letters of support—can be heard across the green and through the administration building's open windows. In a seminar discussion of these campus arguments and rhetorical means, a senior art student notes that in addition to ignoring the question of livable wages, university expansion plans also omit new facilities and faculty for the overenrolled, space-cramped studio art program. For her final project in a seminar on women's rhetoric, the student organizes a petition drive among art students and faculty and a meeting with the university's president, preceded by a public "paint-in" to show, visually, how limited space pushes students into setting up easels in hallways and stairwells.

What I am describing here is how, for a few weeks, many of us witnessed an expansion, not diminishment, of people's hopes for what public rhetorical practice can achieve. Each is also an incredible demonstration of Wells' (1996) observation that effective public writing in a privatized age—"After I growed your food ... "; "They're our brothers/ they're our sisters/We support war resistors"—is not going to sound (and indeed in any age has *never* sounded) like E. B. White. I don't want to overstate the reach of each of these going-public attempts. Dissenting soldiers have yet to receive the wide broadcast that would be possible if they were supported by a national antiwar movement, and they struggle against severe reprisal including courts-martial, prison sentences, and dishonorable discharges that would strip them of education and health care benefits. The Department of Homeland Security answered the spring 2006 mass demonstrations for immigrant rights with "Operation Return to Sender," particularly cracking down on Latino workers in workplaces, such as meatpacking plants in the Midwest and South, with rejuvenated labor unions. At the University of Vermont, even as education lecturers and students publicly rallied against contract-violating layoffs, union staffers negotiated behind-the-scenes settlements for each, extinguishing their hopes for continued full employment and undermining job security for hundreds of campus lecturers. In these ways and more, the war goes on. That's a perspective we can't avoid if we're to teach public writing in touch with the difficult conditions at hand. But here, in the examples of antiwar care packages and paint-ins for art, and in the pages to come, I hope to offer a much fuller perspective from which we can teach: Yes, the war goes on, but people have—and frequently find ways to assert—minds of their own.

"Your Appeal Has Been Reviewed by the Medical Director"

In a featured session at the annual Conference on College Composition and Communication, sociolinguist James Paul Gee (1999) told this story to a packed ballroom of conference goers:

A graduate student in his department, an Asian woman for whom English was a second language, couldn't find a thesis adviser. It wasn't, Gee emphasized, that this student lacked facility with the English language. Rather, he argued, she lacked mastery of her larger Discourse situation—*Discourse* with a Capital *D*. The student seemed to assume, for instance, that any faculty member she approached was required to accept the adviser's role. Thus she appeared too demanding, not sufficiently solicitous, not tuned in to the academic ritual in which faculty consent ceremonially to serve students once it's been made clear that students are serving them. (Gee did not press his analysis further to consider that underwriting faculty reactions may also have been shades of the expectations that graduate students who are female and Asian will be even more particularly deferential.) This is the Discourse that the student had not mastered, and from this first part of the story, Gee drew the lesson that teachers must do what faculty in his graduate program failed to do: clue students in to the Discourses that wield power in their lives.

Then Gee told his audience the rest of the story: Unable to secure an adviser, the student lost her standing in the program, lost her student visa, and was forced to return to her home country. From this ending, Gee drew a second lesson: We must not only teach students about languages of power but also teach students *the* language of power (or, at least, in the audience discussion that ensued from Gee's talk, "languages of power" instantly became *the* language of power) so they are not deported from the discourse communities they seek to join.

At the time I sat in that ballroom and listened to Gee's anecdote and lessons, I had just come through round one of an argument with my university's managed care health plan. That battle had involved months of studying and attempting to use a particular language of power, months of trying to grasp and manipulate the Discourses my husband and I were tangled within as we sought approval to transfer his treatment for a rare genetic cancer, known as VHL, to a Boston hospital that specializes in this form of the disease. After having made, and lost, every argument I could think of with the seemingly remote and faceless administrators of this managed care plan, I listened to Gee's story with a great deal of interest and also, when it came to the second lesson, a lot of frustration. In fact, I wrote the notes that would become this essay in the half-hour break following his address.

Today, while I still feel some frustration, I also feel something else: sympathy. I feel sympathy because the conclusion—that we need to teach languages of power, that doing so will ensure our students' future empowerment or at least basic inclusion and security—is comfortingly affirmative. We're writing teachers, after all. Manipulating words, mimicking and parodying strange jargons, exploring the constraints and possibilities of different genres, trying out and revising rhetorical forms: We know how to do this; we know how to teach this; and perhaps we also want to believe that it's not only worthwhile to do so but also singularly indispensable, these language arts the foundation on which all else (the ability to get a job, keep a job, slip past bureaucratic foils, stave off deportation) depends. At a time when the future of English studies and the humanities seems precarious, a sociolinguistic justification for attending to and teaching a language standard is also a real comfort. It allows us to relate to, yet claim critical apprehension of, the national standards movement; we can strategically use, and yet also purport to be reasoning beyond, market logic to assert the importance of composition teaching. It is even more comforting—gratifying, in fact—to hear a featured speaker at a national conference emphasize through such a stark cautionary tale the prime importance of what we teach; after all, by material measures such as pay and job security, what compositionists do isn't regarded as very important by most universities at all.

I do not mean to sound simply sardonic in my use above of words such as *comforting* and *gratifying,* and I also don't want to be simply dismissive of Gee's argument and his two lessons. When I sat down to write what would be the first of a dozen letters to our managed care health plan, I, in fact, took great comfort in the idea that once I'd figured out the most persuasive arguments from the articles my husband had researched in our medical school's library, once we had figured out just the right combination of assertion and supplication, a fine balance among logical, emotional, and ethical appeals, approval would surely be forthcoming. Schooled in narrative, I hadn't had much prior experience with writing arguments of this kind, and despite—or maybe because of—the dire circumstances (tumors in the brain, spine, both kidneys), it was a challenge I relished or at least took sustenance from. (I thought of it this way: I couldn't control the spread of the disease, but here on the page, in this letter, were arguments I could line up, make orderly and right.) Similarly, my husband, placed on a vocational track by the French school system despite his wish to one day attend a university and study philosophy, hadn't had much experience with academic research; the challenge of tracking down, comprehending, and explaining to others (including our doctors) those medical journal articles was one in which he took real delight. Although we were concerned about tone, organization, and making good medical, economic, and humanistic sense, I don't think it occurred to either of us that the medical director to whom we sent these requests and appeals would not care a whit about what we said or how we said it. It was a long while before we acknowledged to each other that our research and letters were doing no good: The "response" we received to each appeal—"because these services are available within the established network, your appeal has been denied"—had been prepared in advance.

In *Social Linguistics and Literacies* (1996), Gee writes, "[W]hat *counts* is not simply linguistic features . . . but *who* we are and *what* we are doing" (161, my emphasis). That statement does indeed apply to our correspondence with the managed care plan—or maybe more particularly to our unsuccessful efforts to converse with local doctors about treatment plans and a possible transfer of care for the acute issues to the Boston hospital. As Ellen Barton (1997) has examined, a doctor brings to the consultation scene the literacy of his or her medical education; it is the doctor, not the patient, who makes arguments backed by the latest research. For my husband and me, our growing medical literacy, our news of the surgical procedures now advocated by the National Institutes of Health, didn't blur the boundary between care recipients and care providers; it put us out of acceptable doctor–patient conversational bounds altogether. What continued to count was *who* we were. Local doctors responded to what we were trying to do—create, when they would not actively join us, our own convincing warrants for "out-of-network" treatment—with passive expressions of sympathy and, every now and then, a resistance that was emotionally wrought. "I hear you, but unfortunately with the insurance companies, it's just dollars and cents," my husband's primary care doctor told us, shaking his head. Later we arrived home to hear his two-part message on our answering machine, including, "You can go to some big city hospital but just because the doctors there have big names and reputations doesn't mean they're better than the doctors here in Vermont!"

Meanwhile, the managed care plan continued to print and mail the same impersonal response to each specific, detailed, amply documented request: "[Y]our appeal has been reviewed by the Medical Director and has been denied"; "Thank you for the additional information which has been reviewed by the Medical Director. Regretfully, the decision will be upheld." I have a dozen of these letters; all say the same thing: "has been reviewed," "has been denied," "will be upheld," all by someone known only as "the Medical Director." We were caught in a feedback loop (Boquet 2002), and our telephone calls to the managed care plan's business office produced its own feedback loop. Someone who identified herself as a nurse would listen to our troubles, offer a sympathetic response (which she explained was "just" her "personal feeling"), and then advise us to write another letter to the Medical Director with whom, no, we could not speak because he was not actually there. I began to wonder whether he existed at all. We filed a grievance—it would at least produce a hearing, attended by actual in-the-flesh people—though we worried that resolution would come too late. We updated our wills, signed a medical power of attorney, and sometimes cried. At school tenured faculty voted to reappoint me for two more years, though one colleague wondered why I never smiled and was always on the phone (with doctors, lawyers, and insurance administrators).

Months later, when I attended Gee's talk, I was surprised by the intensity of my frustration, even anger—at his conclusions, at the audience's general approval, the nodding heads all around. After all, in contrast to the story Gee told of the graduate student, our drama came to a happier, if provisional, conclusion. We had filed a grievance against the health plan, panicked that we were fast running out of time, but at the same time I had found a National Institutes of Health website seeking patients with VHL. In exchange for allowing NIH doctors to follow the life course of the disease, the website suggested, patients in the study would receive full, federally funded care and treatment. Although our local doctors had said clearly and firmly that no national studies existed, and although the website requested referrals from doctors, not from patients or their spouses, I called the number. Luckily the person on the other end cared more about what I was doing (telling her of a patient who might fit the protocol's bill) than who I was (not an M.D.). Later the NIH would send a letter to our primary care physician thanking him for the referral. Later the Medical Director of the managed care plan would send my husband a letter congratulating him on being accepted into the study and cautioning that his treatments would not be covered by our insurance. We laughed these letters off; my husband made it through that emergency patch of the disease, and he's received his care at the NIH ever since.

It's a happy ending but a provisional one because this free-of-charge, disease-specific care will last only as long as researchers remain interested in this form of the cancer and receive federal funds to match. (On a recent visit a young man who identified himself as a Price Waterhouse consultant asked whether we would mind answering a few survey questions. For starters, if the NIH started billing for patient care, did we have private insurance and would they be likely to pay?) At some future point, we might be faced with arguing again for referrals and approvals, round two. But meanwhile, I've had the luxury of time to consider my correspondence with the managed care plan and what it might teach me about the limits of, and new directions needed in, my work with students to grasp their rhetorical situations and to deploy language in powerful and genuinely empowering ways.

An obvious conclusion I might reach about this correspondence is that my husband and I were arguing from a set of values too radically different from those held by the managed care plan. For example, even though we had included a brief mention of the long-term cost savings of the Boston treatment plan, perhaps our letters had focused too much on the humaneness of pursuing disease-specific, patient-sensitive treatment. Perhaps such arguments cannot be heard by profit-minded managed care plans. Such a conclusion is what my husband's local doctors urged us toward. What we face, these doctors stressed, is an indifferent economic logic that they too are powerless to counter.

This seems to be a conclusion that a sociolinguistic analysis would also be powerless against: We're talking balance sheets, not d/Discourse, here. But such a conclusion obscures what I now realize is the bigger part of the managed care *Discourse Map* (to borrow Gee's term), at least where we live. As it turns out, we weren't dealing with remote, dehumanizing corporate logic—or at least not immediately. Between us and the for-profit corporate insurer was an independent intermediary, a peculiarly *local* health care entity, known in the industry as a PHO, for Physicians and Hospital Organization, which were created in the 1990s so that local hospitals and doctors could reap some of the big-money rewards of the booming health care industry. This particular PHO was set up by my university's teaching hospital and affiliated doctors, with a board of directors comprised of local doctors plus sundry insurance, accounting, and human resources professionals. In turn, this PHO negotiated fees with corporate insurance providers while also managing (through the bureaucratic maze of referrals, denials, appeals, and grievances) patient use of services. Although it proved enormously difficult to learn more about this PHO beyond its post office box, online email form, and phone number to a call center, I did finally figure out that, yes, the Medical Director had a name and an office—indeed an office just a few buildings over from my own because he was also my ostensible colleague, a member of the University of Vermont faculty. And although the standard-form, passive-voice letters we received suggested some disembodied Oz, I think I can reasonably speculate that this medical director was not remote to my husband's local doctors.

I cannot say whether this particular PHO, like some, provides "incentives" for network doctors to ration care (refusing to authorize specialist referrals or order expensive tests). I do know that, despite their claims of commiseration, these doctors did not follow up with written statements of support to accompany our appeals. Economics comes into this, to be sure: On the other side of the PHO is a massive for-profit corporate insurer that the PHO itself was set up to negotiate with, so that doctors, particularly specialists, and hospital administrators (our hospital being among the highest revenue generators in the country) could gain some leverage. But most immediately, I think what we were dealing with is something even more small-minded and impervious to our logos-based appeals: nepotism, parochialism, professional loyalty, masculinist pride. I think of that astonishing message left on our answering machine by my husband's primary care physician: "You can go to some big city hospital. . . ." Anxiousness about expertise, defense against a perceived threat to status—here would be the start of explaining *that* Discourse Map. I also think the first lesson Gee drew from the story of the graduate student is exactly right: We need to be clued in to such Discourses that wield power in our lives. At the very least, my husband and I needed to be clued in to the need for a new primary care physician.

In his address to writing teachers at the Conference on College Composition and Communication, Gee urged audience members to prepare their students to become "geographers" of language, and as a geographer of this particular Discourse Map, I can see, in retrospect, multiple and instructive ways in which our arguments went so wrong. Where I get tripped up, however, is with Gee's second lesson. Clued in to the Discourse, could we have approached the question differently and would a different approach really have produced a dramatically different outcome? The answer I come to is no—a "no" that is a challenge not only to Gee's argument but also to how I've been proceeding as a teacher over the years. Accept but skillfully parody and carnivalize the subordinate roles the local doctors expected us to assume? Manipulate the situation so that (somehow) these doctors believed that new information about this rare disease really was coming from them? Address and refigure the tension between big city and small, generalist and specialist? These are among the rhetorical strategies I've talked about with students, have taught, have encouraged. These are rhetorical strategies that, mostly in the abstract, have given me comfort—comfort in the belief that I really can wield power in language, that I can empower my students, particularly those subordinated by gender, race, sexuality, and class, to do the same. Today, however, I'm more keenly aware of how much the effectiveness of these rhetorical strategies are contingent upon extralinguistic factors, including social position and credentials. I'm more keenly aware of the burden such strategies place on individuals who, in a moment of extremity or faced with ongoing struggle, have the least resources, the least energy, the least time. (We shouldn't have *had* to make arguments; we should have been able to focus on *getting well*.) A sociolinguistic mapping can increase our awareness of social positions, credentials, routines, and rituals. A sociological mapping can further tell us about the intensified gendered and classed burden of privatized, up-to-the-family solutions to public issues such as health care. These mappings do not, however, easily translate into prescriptions of what to do. Who were my husband and I? Not doctors. What were we doing? Trying to make an argument to a highly bureaucratized system designed to spit out standard-form rejection letters as a matter of routine. There is no way here, no matter how good a geographer of language I might become, not to fail—due to exhaustion at the very least.

And therein lies the danger of Gee's second lesson. That second lesson tells students of language and their teachers to internalize the failure, to assume the fault and the inadequacy. In Gee's telling of the tale, the student is deported *because* she had failed to make the right argument. By the same logic, it was *because* we'd failed to assume the correct position that my husband's requests to the managed care plan were routinely denied. These are conclusions I have to reject, that I want to root out of my teaching, so I can see much more hopeful and grounded rhetorical lessons and directions. Those lessons include recognizing when one is caught within an appeal-and-denial feedback loop and examining in any given situation the potential for *and* material difficulties of getting out of that loop. The lessons include—a prime concern in this book—the privatization of authority (the Medical Director and his interests buried deep from view) *and* advocacy (one's available means for securing needed health care worked up as an individual or family matter). The lessons especially include recognizing a need to learn the fullest, collective rhetorics of power—what will be required if we are to win something like universal, not-for-profit health care. Then, when we study up on market logic and accompanying transcripts of appeal and denial, it won't be to find better ways to accommodate but to consider all it would take—what historically it has taken—to change these scripts.

2

Ain't Nobody's Business?

Take One: The Privacy Generation

For women the measure of intimacy has been the measure of oppression.

—Catherine McKinnon (1989)

Some years ago my mother told me the story of how, when she was twenty years old and the mother of two, she drummed up the courage to ask the family doctor about something called "birth control." *Oh no*, the doctor replied. *Not until you have six children at least.*

"So you were born ten months later, and your brother, fourteen months after that."

"And then?" I asked.

"And then your father learned the word *vasectomy*."

At the time my mother told this tale, I was twenty years old, working in Boston, and had just gotten myself down to the Bill Baird Clinic on Boylston Street to be fitted for a diaphragm. I didn't tell her about my visit to Bill Baird; there seemed little to tell. Between her story of a humiliating exchange and my entirely unremarkable after-work appointment lay the Supreme Court decisions of *Griswold v. Connecticut* (1965) and *Eisenstadt v. Baird* (1972). Like *Roe v. Wade* (1973) soon to follow, these landmark decisions, liberalizing access to birth control information and devices, extended the protections of privacy to (some) sexual practices and decisions. The 125-year-old Massachusetts law that would have shut down the Boylston Street clinic just ten years before in the name of protecting future generations' "virility" and "virtue" had been overturned. When I made my appointment, words like *purity* and *chastity* were as far from my mind as my ninth-grade Cliff Notes–assisted reading of *The Scarlet Letter*. (On my mind instead: Would I have the money for the $35 appointment, the diaphragm, and a tube of antispermicidal jelly, given that my secretary's paycheck was $230 a week *before* taxes?) I didn't have to tell my mother about my appointment or why I needed a diaphragm because I understood such matters to be *private*.

Out of this story (or out of this assertion that, thanks to Bill Baird and the Supreme Court, I, unlike my mother, have no story to tell), I might conclude that I was born into the first generation of women to experience the lucky boon of privacy. I might celebrate the good fortune of being granted the "right to be let alone" (Warren and Brandeis 1890) without even having argued for it. There would be obvious weaknesses in such a conclusion: the Supreme Court's only recently reversed refusal to extend minimal privacy protection to lesbians and gays (*Bowers v. Hardwick* 1986); the use of the privacy argument to rule against state funding for medically required abortions (*Harris v. McRae* 1980); and the erosion of geographic and economic, as well as legal, access to birth control and safe abortions through thirty years of legislative and extralegislative activity including presidential gag orders, parental notification and consent statutes, waiting periods, late-term bans, and clinic closings. I could note these weaknesses—and the ways in which privacy rights have not been uniformly extended to poor women, people of color, immigrants with and without documents, anyone receiving public assistance—and maybe, noting these limits, I might argue that women of my generation and beyond need to come together for renewed arguments, renewed activism.

Except for this catch: How to argue *publicly* for that which has been defined as private, outside rhetoric's realm? The Supreme Court rulings on reproduction between 1965 and 1979 did not, after all, expand women's *spheres of liberty* but instead marked new *zones of privacy*. These rulings weren't aimed at granting women *freedom to* but instead (some amount of) *freedom from*—some amount of freedom from public interference and also, by implication, from public support. Of course I've felt pressed many, many times to join phone banks, stuff envelopes, lift banners, raise my voice. But that's just it: I've felt pressed to defend that which I've been raised to believe should need no defense.

I'm not alone. With the election of Clinton and Gore in the early 1990s, organizations such as the National Abortion and Reproductive Rights Action League (now renamed NARAL Pro-Choice America, both *abortion* and *action* hidden from view) stopped organizing abortion clinic defense lines and started fund-raising for Democrats instead. Through the 1990s the prevailing argument was that we could best defend abortion by writing (if and when we could) a check. No more lifting banners or raising voices. Designated defenders for abortion rights would lobby, quietly, instead. It's an argument I wanted to buy—at first. I didn't want to *have* to defend abortion anymore. As a member of the privacy generation, I've been raised to regard sex, birth control, and abortion rights (for starters) as self-regarding, not other-regarding (to adopt John Stuart Mill's [1863] classic distinction from *On Liberty*)—nobody's business but my own.

Indeed, I had no idea, until my mother told me her story, that the right to birth control—no, the right to *privacy* regarding birth control decisions—had such a recent history, more recent than, say, the nineteenth century.

Do We Have (Too Much) Privacy?

One can agree that privacy is not enough without concluding that the choice of privacy arguments in the Roe context was a setback for women.

—Ruth Garrison (1992)

The common wisdom is that in this hypercommunicative age, the boundaries between private and public are giving way, our sense of privacy and rights to privacy eroding. "[T]here is less privacy than there used to be," write Ellen Alderman and Caroline Kennedy at the start of their critique of contemporary publicity (1995, xiv). If I bracket the question of who has less privacy than before—who, historically, has been granted and who has been denied privacy and according to what racial, gendered, and moneyed markers—I can see plenty of evidence for this claim. At this moment I look up from typing to see the U.S. Attorney General argue for increased wiretapping powers. I check my neighborhood listserv and find a posting, subject heading "Homeland Security," that offers tips for exercising surveillance on our street. I check the rest of my email and find half a dozen action alerts: an antiwar activist interrogated by the FBI for her involvement in the (Nobel Peace Prize–nominated) Women in Black; a library worker suspended for using her university email account to compose a message critical of U.S. foreign policy; a Green Party member prevented from flying from Bangor to Chicago because her name showed up on a "no fly" list. It is October 2001, and each night the news brings us images of long queues at airport security gates, people looking on with tight smiles while guards inspect their shaving kits, peek under a pair of folded pajamas. Confronting these encroachments on individual freedom in the name of public interest, I can agree: There's not as much privacy as there used to be.

Yet even though I see stark examples of privacy under siege, I want to disturb the common wisdom long enough to reveal an opposite and at least equally pressing problem that we—particularly as teachers of writing and rhetoric within a would-be democratic society—need to address: We don't live in a world of too little privacy but, increasingly, too much.

Consider:

- At the same time people lament a loss of privacy, more than 8 million of the wealthiest Americans live in some 20,000 gated communities and "imagineered" cities such as Disney's Celebration, Florida, where not only public spaces are privatized (and policed) but also the social responsibilities of citizenship and government are turned over to private enterprise (Blakely and Snyder 1997).

- This privatizing trend affects virtually all areas of public life—schools, prisons, hospitals, policing, trash collection, transportation—as local, state, and national governments "outsource" public services to private companies, transforming citizens into consumers (Bunker and Davis 2000; H. Giroux 2000).

- Since the 1980s companies have increasingly asserted a "corporate right to privacy" (Gilbert et al. 1994) to justify a growing use of confidentiality agreements in the settlements of sexual harassment, workplace discrimination, and products liability lawsuits (see also Hans 2000, 70–111; Ramsey et al. 1998). Well known, for instance, is the 1985 California court settlement that sealed all evidence of the dangers of silicon breast implants and thus protected manufacturer Dow Corning from publicity while thousands more women were implanted with the potentially toxic device (Gilbert et al. 1994).

- The agents of neoliberal economic policy such as the International Monetary Fund (IMF) have made privatization a key condition for any country seeking economic aid or debt relief. As third world countries have privatized airlines, telecommunications, energy, and even water to meet IMF or World Bank mandates, U.S. and European multinationals have stepped in to scoop up these prizes—converting a country's public resources and services into another nation's private property (Green 1995, 51; Toussaint 2005, 227–253; see also Jonathan Franzen's *The Corrections* [2001] for a farcical and frighteningly true-to-life send-up of neoliberalism run amuck as an entire eastern European country is turned into a fire sale for global investors and local capitalists).

Of course, with these examples it may appear that I'm conflating *privacy* and *privatization*. *Privacy* is a word we typically associate with *personal* and *domestic* realms, realms in which we may feel entitled to freedom from observation and interference. Though the entitlements of private life are certainly subject to periodic debate and dramatic revision—as birth control is renamed from moral menace to private choice; as domestic abuse made an opposite shift from personal prerogative to social issue—we most often think of private life as "self-regarding," that is, outside the public interest. In contrast, we associate privatization with political economy and particularly as one piece of the larger trend of neoliberalism: the quasi free-market economic ideology theorized by Milton Friedman and championed by the Reagan and Thatcher governments plus subsequent governments that have followed their leads of tax and social program cuts; relaxation or removal of trade, labor, and environmental protections; and conversion of public resources and institutions to private ownership and new markets for investment and profit (Toussaint 2005, Chapter 1 *passim*). It would seem to be distinct from our ideas of personal privacy first because neoliberal economic tenets are always presented as impersonal (that so-called invisible hand of the market), and second because, feminism's critique of middle-class "separate spheres" notwithstanding, we're still so schooled to distinguish between the (self-regarding) realm of home and the (other-regarding) realms of market and civic institutions. Given these usual distinctions, it might seem, then, that I'm confusing the problem of growing economic privatization with the separate issue of maintaining personal privacy.

Yet that's precisely my point: The distinctions are confused, as anyone must surely feel driving by a gated community or, maybe more to the point, living in one. The rights of privacy, as I've found growing up after *Eisenstadt v. Baird* (1972), do have some liberalizing potential. It's because of privacy rights that I could choose, as my mother could not, when to bear children or, in fact, whether to bear children. Yet these privacy rights—the right to *exclude* a woman's decisions about reproduction from public guarantees as well as debate—have proved shaky, to the say the least. The right to privacy is not really, it's turned out, the same thing as having full, publicly articulated and publicly defended reproductive rights and full, publicly assisted access to exercising these rights. To the contrary, abortion rights and access in the United States are currently very much tied to a woman's economic standing and geographic location. For instance, although over 85 percent of U.S. counties have family-planning clinics, only 13 percent of counties nationwide have clinics or hospitals that offer abortion services (Henshaw and Finner 2003). As a result, the millions of U.S. women have no place in which they can reasonably exercise a right to abortion even if other barriers, including financial, are removed. Since 1982 the number of doctors performing abortions has decreased by nearly 40 percent (Henshaw and Finner 2003), and, with 72 percent of OB/GYN residency programs offering no training at all in abortion procedures (Almeling et al. 2000), that trend will not be easily reversed. At my university medical school's teaching hospital, a ban on elective abortions has been on the books, without discussion and debate, since 1973—a private move to subvert the public rights pushed for by the burgeoning women's movement and affirmed by *Roe*. There's something very different from that "invisible hand" of the market at work here in severely restricting abortion availability.

What we should see in these statistics and the adoption of anti-abortion policies is the privatization of a public issue. Public debate about reproductive rights is supplanted, for instance, by a board of trustees' closed-door decision to remove abortion procedures from the medical school curriculum or to refuse elective abortion services altogether. Women in the process are repositioned, from agents making decisions about their bodies and health, from advocates for the exercise of rights, to consumers who must shop around and whose rights are not collective but extend only so far as their individual buying power. Doctors are repositioned as well; their roles as service providers are managed not only by private insurance companies but also by hospital boards whose fiduciary duty may be to private shareholders or to a sponsoring religious or university body—sponsors who equate abortion services with negative publicity, rising security and insurance costs, and lost gifts from affluent alumni and patrons. In the quiet, steady erosion of abortion access, what we have, then, is not only the privatization of a public issue but also the penetration of a privatizing economic logic: Questions of social rights and justice get re-presented as a matter of individual and corporate bottom lines.

Overall, we can think of this collusion between the individual and economic privacies this way: Individual privacy rights are meant to exclude some or most (personal) matters from public regulation and debate; neoliberal privatization likewise seeks to exclude some or most (business/market) matters from public regulation and debate. In fact, when it comes to writing out definitions, as Nancy Fraser (1997) points out, domestic and economic privacies wind up sounding much the same. "The rhetoric of domestic privacy," Fraser writes, "seeks to exclude some issues and interests from public debate by personalizing and/or familializing them." Similarly, the "rhetoric of economic privacy . . . seeks to exclude some issues and interests from public debate by economizing them" (1997, 88). The means—familializing, economizing—may be different but the ends—excluding key interests and issues from public debate and public defense—are the same. Hence, as Fraser (1989) has argued, if we want to get a critical purchase on this idea of privacy, we might need a shift in terms from "private" experience to "privatized experience" (135). That shift can remind us that experiences marked as "self-regarding" are not naturally and inevitably outside social jurisdiction but have been placed there, raising the questions of by whom, for whom, with what interests and aims, and against whose interests and aims. By thinking in terms of active, historic privatization, not immutable privacy, we can examine how issues become privatized and thus removed from public debate and, in the case of safeguarding reproductive rights, from the public oversight and contestation needed to stop a major hospital from making the "private" decision to ban all elective (that is, chosen by a woman herself) abortions.

We can also extend Fraser's critique of domestic and economic privacies by considering those uncanny moments when constructions of domestic privacy don't just collude with economic privatization but become indistinguishable from it. These are moments in which our existence suddenly appears so thoroughly economized that what we find under siege isn't privacy but publicity: our rights and access to a public self. Maybe I can dramatize this sort of threat through the following example:

In early October 2001, the public radio program *Marketplace Morning Report* aired a story on the mini financial boom experienced by hearth-and-home stores in the aftermath of the Twin Towers and Pentagon attacks. Amid grim reports of falling stocks and rising joblessness, stores such as Williams-Sonoma reported robust sales. People want to "cocoon" at a time like this (the first day of the bombing of Afghanistan), one interviewee explained. They feel a psychological need to "nest." The story's reporter, Aaron Schacter, went on to speculate that there may be more at work than individual psychology. Perhaps people (people, that is, with spending power) were shopping as an expression of their patriotism, answering the president's call to boost the economy. (Perhaps, I would add, such shoppers had seen the October 15, 2001, cover of *Us* magazine—Laura Bush accompanied by the bold heading *Comforter in Chief*—and understood their own feminized roles to provide domestic comfort rather than attempt to direct or dissent from public policy.) Viewed from this angle, such shopping expresses people's strong desires to *do something*—protecting the "homeland" symbolically with duvet covers and cookie sheets. (After all, ordinary citizens hadn't been invited to join politicians, policy makers, and the corporate media in shaping or debating the military attacks. We were sent off to silent candlelight vigils and then to the malls.) So maybe such shopping isn't about nesting, cocooning, and retreats into privacy at all. Maybe it signals the very opposite: an attempt (one that ought to give any rhetorician pause) at *something like* public voice, *something like* public action—an attempt not only channeled into consumerism but also defined as consumerism from the very start.

A few minutes later a new story aired on the latest threats to our privacy. I didn't listen. I was too busy thinking about a different sort of threat: the threat to our publicity rights, to our sense of being public selves. When I tried to explain this to my husband, who is not a U.S. citizen, he shrugged. "There's nothing new about Americans going shopping," he said.

On the one hand, I want to say there *is* something new about this blunt, unapologetic championing of consumerism as the only sanctioned form of civic participation, the only way to *do something* beside display a flag or give blood. (When I first drafted this chapter, teach-in, rally, and debate were decidedly not among the sanctioned forums in which to *do something*. As I revisit this chapter a final time, Professor Ward Churchill's dismissal from the University of Colorado has been upheld by an academic board, DePaul University trustees have denied Norman Finkelstein tenure, and human rights attorney Lynn Stewart is on her way to prison, all "guilty" of the crime of unpopular speech. The teach-in and rally continue to be risky forums for vulnerable and high-profile individuals.) There *is* something breathtaking and terrifying about the dropping of all pretense: The measure of America isn't democracy but capitalism, the measure of one's citizenship isn't one's participation in public decision-making forums but one's spending in the private retail sector. Breathtaking, terrifying, what dropped to dust in fall 2001.

On the other hand, I think we're too prone to theorize from single snapshots in U.S. history; we're too apt to claim, "Nothing like this has ever happened before," or "Everything changed when the Twin Towers fell," or "The neocons have hijacked American democracy!" (For instance, neoconservatives ideology notwithstanding, there was a material basis for the 2001–2002 call to the malls. In contrast with 1940 America, the United States in 2001 had no use for a patriotic production drive. It had an overabundance of planes, steel, textiles, microchips—an overabundance of products and the means to produce them. Hence the call for patriotic *consumption* instead.) What's needed here is a wider angle of vision and a longer historical time line if we're to see that the formidable challenge we face is a bipartisan Washington consensus regarding neoliberalism that is taking a terrible toll on living conditions worldwide and has been taking this toll for upwards of thirty years now. Or, to rephrase my husband's dismissive remark about American consumerism into a statement with which I can fully agree: There's nothing new about privatization.

Take Two: The Privatized Generation

In order to change the conditions of life, we must learn to see them through the eyes of women.

—Leon Trotsky (1970)

Looking back, I see that my family associated privacy not only with matters of sexuality and reproduction but also with just about every realm of daily experience: religion, politics, family economics, employment, and joblessness. This reign of privacy probably had little to do with the Supreme Court and much more to do with my parents' upbringing in lower-middle-class Yankee families in which morality was measured in the ability to hold one's tongue.

"Who did you vote for?" I asked my parents in 1972.

"Shush," Mom replied. "That isn't polite."

"Are we at war?" I asked.

"No," Mom said. "That has nothing to do with us." Even Vietnam was none of our business.

To be fair, I have to recognize that my parents were also products of the McCarthy era—enough to make entire English departments drop all discussions except those focused on beauty and form—as well as the Cold War dread of privacy rights violations that had produced *1984* and *The Naked Society* (see Hasian 2001, especially 97–100). They were the first in each of their families to move away from the tiny corner of southeastern Massachusetts where Welches, Winslows, Gauntlets, and Shoveltons had subjected one another to daily scrutiny for more than two hundred years.

Now my mother frets that giant grocery store chains such as Kroger's are tracking her purchases through the use of membership cards.

Even my father's choice to be an on-the-road salesman—no shop floor or office cubicle for him—appears bound up in an idealization of individual privacy that's so American, it's a surprise to recall that nowhere is the right to privacy constitutionally guaranteed. (Supreme Court decisions such as *Roe v. Wade* [1973] were argued through the Fourteenth Amendment guarantee of due process and equal protection with privacy understood to be an implied or *a priori* right enabling that guarantee.) When twice in six months, by two different companies in two different states, my father was laid-off, we experienced the other side of privacy, the side not associated with freedom and mobility but (as my mother had experienced in the doctor's office years before) humiliation and shame. *Laid-off* is how the companies put it. *Canned*, my father always said, though whether to emphasize his sense of personal disgrace or to expose what lay beneath corporate euphemism, I don't know because this wasn't a matter for family discussion. Twice in one year my father came home, handed my mother a letter and announced, "I've been canned." Twice we children were sent outside to play, then called back in, with nothing more said about the matter until the day came to pack and move. It was the mid-1970s. We lived in what would soon be known as the Rust Belt. Dozens of families around us had to pack and move too. Still we did not talk about it. We'd have brought up sex at our dinner table, I think, sooner than the word *unemployment*.

In later years—having witnessed the journey of my sister and her husband from Nebraska to New York to Indiana to Ohio in a search of a factory offering full-time, not contract, employment; having listened to my university president announce a faculty downsizing program, then counsel us to learn to live with "anxiety"; having joined with my in-laws in France to cheer what Pierre Bourdieu (1998) later called a "social miracle," legions of unemployed French workers organizing to protest for increased benefits while an overwhelming majority of the country, feeling the insecurity of their own jobs, supported their aims—I would understand, finally, that these are not private, self-regarding matters. Globalization and deregulation. Outsourcing and downsizing. Job flexibility and casualization. Structural adjustment and austerity programs. As Eric Toussaint (2005) points out in his exposé of global capitalism, for women worldwide such terms cannot remain the academic property of a credentialed policy-making few because it's women who must "struggle daily to make up for the difference between decreasing incomes and increasing prices" that have accompanied neoliberal economic "reforms" in both the global South and North (2005, 47). While my sister and brother-in-law work multiple, less-than-livable-wage jobs, it's my mother who provides free-of-charge child care for the grandkids. When a postoperative infection puts my husband out of work for half a year and the bills mount up (co-pays and deductibles for each doctor's appointment, visiting nurse, home infusion, multiple middle-of-the-night emergency room runs), we sell our second car and cut back on our "supplemental" retirement savings. If the extension of privacy rights to (some) women appears to mark a radical break between my mother's generation and mine, the trend of *privatization* binds us all back together in a common and socially produced insecurity.

Privatization: It's a word I think of not only in relation to the dominant economic paradigm since Reagan but also in relation to my own increasingly constricted and privatized world between 1978, when my vocational high school began sending me to work in lieu of classes, and 1986, when a lucky combination of public funding and prominent, public-space advertising brought me to the University of Massachusetts at Boston (whose publicly subsidized, open-admissions programs, a crucial legacy of the civil rights movement, had not yet been infiltrated by the new market logic). By saying that I lived in an increasingly constricted and privatized world until I started college, I'm not invoking the usual tale of liberal education. According to the usual tale, the university transforms the asocial or self-centered individual into a public, civic-minded citizen. What I experienced was very different. My education didn't take me from private to public but instead offered me glimpses into—a critical purchase on—the ways in which I was already socialized and especially socialized to regard virtually everything in my world as strictly personal (and so not discussable) or strictly impersonal (and so not discussable either). For example:

In 1982 when I left my $230-a-week secretarial job for one that paid $265, I handed my boss a neatly typed letter of resignation. (Write a letter, the employment agency I'd visited on my lunch hour had counseled. Keep it vague. Say you're resigning for "personal reasons" and refuse, on the grounds of privacy, to reveal any more.)

"You can't do this," my boss protested. "We paid a lot of money for you."

She was referring to the $230 fee they'd paid to the same employment agency for bringing me to them three months before.

"You have to give a reason," she said. "Otherwise. . . ." She looked me up and down, her eyes coming to rest on my midsection. "Otherwise, we'll have to assume the worst about you."

When still I refused to explain, she concluded, "You can't give notice. Clearly we can no longer trust you. You're fired."

"Whatever you think is best," I said, and then—this is how I would remember that moment in years to come, a *denouement* created more from my reading of Carson McCullers' "Wunderkind" than from actual fact—I took the elevator down forty-seven floors and spun out into the noontime world of fresh air and light.

I've told this story many times over the past twenty years (adding that this boss used to follow me into the ladies' room and dictate telexes through the closed stall door—so much for privacy). It's one of a dozen or so back-when-I-was-a-secretary tales I cart about like battle honors. In each telling, I stress how this woman regarded me as she might a poorly purchased cow, how I'd smiled right back and then broke away—*free! independent! a wily deal maker able to get herself $35 more a week!* I hope the paucity of that pay increase and the ridiculousness, or pathos, of that wily deal maker image of myself is apparent. Consider that Tom Wolfe at this very moment must have been gathering material among Wall Street's billionaire bond barons for his *Bonfire of the Vanities*. Now picture me on the sidewalk outside Boston's Hancock Tower, rifling through my empty briefcase—leather, Aigner, a Katharine Gibbs School graduation gift from my Aunt Joan—and panicking because I couldn't find my monthly T pass. That subway pass cost $22—the first week of my raise, after taxes, already gone.

What I always leave out when I tell this tale is the perplexing question of just why I heeded the employment agency's advice—be vague, don't mention the new job, let her think you're knocked up if she wants to—in the first place. (Of course, I understand why the employment agency gave me this counsel: it wanted to continue business with this company, wanted me to invoke personal privacy as a cover.) Why not say, "I've found a new job that pays more, and you ought to be paying more too"? Why not go back out into the secretarial pool and—instead of silently picking up my briefcase and sneakers—shout, "Everyone! Listen! There's more money out there! Not much but it's a start, and if we just band together . . ."?

The answers to these "Why not?" questions are pretty obvious: my family history joined to New Right Reaganism where employment is a personal matter of self-created success or self-inflicted failure. (For an examination of the Reagan-era semantics recasting social issues into "lifestyle" choices, see Howell and Ingham 2001.) As for shouting out loud, calling on others to rally around—the very thought of this would have overwhelmed me with embarrassment (a feeling I finally had to confront and fight head on when I took a public role in my university's faculty union drive). Though I'd found the final scenes of *Norma Rae* thrilling and the movie *9 to 5* deeply satisfying, the idea of actually joining NOW or the Boston chapter of 9 to 5 ran entirely counter to my Mary Tyler Moore idea of making it through being plucky, pert, and indispensable. Feminism? I had my diaphragm and needed nothing else.

My new boss was the treasurer for what would turn out to be a successful U.S. Senate campaign. He enjoyed hitching his thigh up on my desk, lighting a cigar (because I smoked at my desk, I didn't regard this as rude, just characteristic), then telling me how politics really work: "You pay them, they do what you want."

"So what about me?" I asked. It was an honest question, not cynical or sarcastic. I really wanted to know, really hoped he'd tell me. Somewhere out there was the public world—"just a little inaccessible," as Susan Wells writes, "like live theater or downtown department stores" (1996, 326)—and despite my keen discomfort at the thought of joining anything (what if I accidentally joined the wrong group, like the Hari Krishnas I saw every weekend in front of the Harvard Coop?), I wanted desperately to find it. It's the usual story: I wanted to do something, be someone, belong somewhere. I felt this desire especially when the tall, remote man who would become Massachusetts' next senator came in—sailed in, really, never pausing at my desk, never knocking at my boss's closed door, entirely free from the usual business office rules of entry. (Later I would feel *So there* satisfaction when, for a few months in 2004, this same senator lagged in presidential polls, considered too cold and aloof, unable to offer warm handshakes and hellos to ordinary people.) Sometimes while I was typing my boss's fund-raising letters, I tried to imagine myself as a political candidate and then, failing that, I entertained fantasies that I would become someone by becoming a writer.

"So what about me?" I asked my boss. "What can I do?"

"Ha," he said. "That's funny."

It was about this time that I bought myself a journal. I still have it, one of those cardboard-cover composition books, and it contains a single entry: "I know I want to write but what?"

Rhetorical Questions

> *What is needed . . . is not the abandonment of rights language for all purposes, but an attempt to become multilingual in the semantics of evaluating rights.*

—PATRICIA J. WILLIAMS (1991)

For as long as I've been in the fields of composition and women's studies, the questions of what we and our students should write have been framed as "public" versus "personal." In fact, the first essay I read as a graduate student in composition and rhetoric was S. Michael Halloran's 1982 lament over the "decline" of public discourse in U.S. colleges. In that still widely anthologized essay, Halloran contrasts the Ciceronian ideal of "the civic leader who understood all the values of his culture and used artful speech to make those values effective in the arena of public affairs" (1996, 185) with writing-workshop teaching that does not, in Halloran's estimation, "address students as political beings, as members of a body politic in which they have responsibility to form judgments and influence the judgments of others on public issues" (194).

It was 1988 when I first read Halloran's essay—six years after its initial publication and four years after my stint as a secretary for the campaign of the U.S. Senate candidate who didn't know how to say "good morning," "please," and "thank you." I didn't feel defensive when I read Halloran. I can't say I felt any sense of exclusion in being presented with this gentlemen-only history of rhetoric. I felt no discomfort or disagreement because I had already concluded that I was commencing the study of two fields. One was the field of composition, which spoke to my wishful "I know I want to write but what?" The other was the field of rhetoric, which spoke to me not at all. Years later, in a women's studies senior seminar, students and I would work out a definition of rhetoric on the board. *Persuasion, Aristotle, debate, politicians, argument, lies.* It took a good ten minutes to coax just these few scattered, fitful associations from the class. When I asked, "What does rhetoric have to do with you, with us?", the students looked at me, faces blank, mouths shut. That's how I felt through much of this graduate seminar in rhetorical history: blank, uninvolved.

Two decades of subsequent scholarship have, of course, troubled the strict gendered division I unconsciously accepted between the work—my work—of teaching writing and the work—others' work—of examining public opinion making and policy making. Investigations not only into the practices of individual women rhetors but also into schools, associations, unions, clubs, broad social movements, and countercultural affinity groups as crucial sites for rhetorical training have dramatically expanded our understanding of rhetorical history. If we look at history as the story of widening layers of people contesting their exclusion from public participation and visibility, claiming full public voice and rights—from Hyde Park and Haymarket to Montgomery, Birmingham, and Stonewall—our potential understanding of the available means to make arguments broadens and deepens. Moreover, the history of our field becomes a history of contestation over what is and is not within rhetoric's realm and who will and will not have speaking rights on those debates concerning what is and is not the public good.

These developments in our field notwithstanding, however, Halloran's argument, or certainly the private–public boundary at the heart of his essay, is still very much with us. Consider, for instance, Deborah Brandt's (2001a) and Anne Herrington's (2001) recent appeals for composition researchers to distinguish between personal lives and public concerns. It is not the person writing or being written about, argues Brandt (2001a), who matters. "What matters are the ideas or knowledge that research yields for public use" (42) and is in the "public interest" (44). I don't mean to suggest that Brandt and Herrington merely repeat formulations that have come before, another example of *la plus ça change*. For instance, neither author echoes Halloran's 1982 argument for distinguishing between private and public spheres in order to restore rhetoric's presumed lost status. In fact, by presenting us with what is actually an inverse of Halloran's argument, they reflect the preoccupations of our present moment: Each argues for distinguishing the public from the personal in the name of respecting (a writer's, a researcher's, a research subject's) privacy. Writes Herrington, "[W]e should make the choice as to what of our personal lives we feel should be made public on the basis of our own sense of professional and political purposes" (2001, 48). The trouble is that the line between "personal lives" and "public interest" is taken for granted.

It's tough to argue against the good of writing in the public interest. But in my teaching and writing that's exactly what I've tried to do. Or, more accurately, what I've tried to do is make the classifications of public, private, personal, and social *arguable*. The terms *public* and *private*, as Fraser (1989) underscores, aren't "straight-forward designations of societal spheres" but are "rhetorical labels and cultural classifications"—labels and classifications that function "to delegitimate some interests, views, and topics, and to valorize others" (88). What counts as public interest? (I think of the doctor who informed my mother that bearing six children was her social duty.) Whose interests are protected under the banner of privacy? (I think of my father raised to regard unemployment as a private shame.) What has created our guiding sense of what to include, whom to exclude? (I think of myself crossing politics and rhetoric off my very short list of spheres in which I—no Senator Cicero—might participate.)

Most of my students also run into difficulty when they attempt to exercise that judgment of distinguishing between what is and isn't of public use that Herrington and Brandt call for. Very few of these students share with my old boss that sense of entitlement to shape public realms. Instead, most—male and female—look at the question of what it is they could write that would be in the public interest and conclude that there's very little, or nothing at all. This doesn't mean that they cannot churn out a canned essay on "The Question of Capital Punishment." But they— most of them, male and female—do so with little or no sense that the voices of ordinary people, the voices of people such as themselves, might matter one whit, might demand a bigger place than a brief "Therefore, in my opinion . . ." appended to the end. They do so with little or no understanding that their general sense of exclusion from actual public contestation on these issues is something that can be, ought to be, and historically has been questioned.

In recent years I've sought to turn these exclusions into questions at the center of the classes I teach, and as I've done so, I've also shifted from talking with students about the "politics of the personal" to the "politics of *privacy*." That word *privacy* carries with it a history that the term *personal* simply does not. Bound up with *privacy* are stories of benefit and protection and simultaneously stories of exclusion and denial, including countless examples of how privacy rights have been used to justify the power of a husband over a wife, a master over a slave, a boss over a worker. In the end, I won't join with Catherine McKinnon (1989) in arguing that we should abolish the very idea of privacy: I've benefited too much from the strategic if incomplete privacy arguments that won *Eisenstadt v. Baird* and *Roe v. Wade*. Nevertheless, my own uneasy history and the many stories my students bring to class keep me mindful of what the measure of privacy has too often been. I want that tension between privacy as boon and privacy as bane in my classroom and in my scholarship. We need to become more multilingual not only in the troubling discourse of "rights" advanced from above by most national politicians, by the heads of increasingly consolidated and oligarchic multinationals, and by quasi-public institutions such as the World Bank that through the 1990s oversaw the mass global transfer of public resources into private hands. Here we have the "rights" of workers to labor without a union, the "rights" of corporations to disregard environmental protections, the "rights" of a state university medical school's teaching hospital to ban abortion services without public comment and debate. We also need to become more multilingual in individual and especially collective challenges from below to this privatized world order and to the state officials and global institutions that assist in securing it. Here multilingual can mean unlearning our academic penchant for always pursuing "nuance" and "complication." "The water is ours!" was the straightforward rallying cry of Bolivians in Cochabamba who sent Bechtel and its water privatization scheme packing in 2000. "Free abortion on demand!", the cry of early 1970s abortion rights advocates, is another unabashed slogan proponents of women's liberation ought to reclaim, particularly because "free" and "on demand" have both been so seriously undermined that the only word left standing, abortion, becomes a clear right only for those with money.

For my classes, then, I look for texts offering prime examples of how voices and views get worked up as strictly private. This idea of looking at how things get "worked up" into institutional categories comes from feminist sociologist Dorothy Smith, whose *The Everyday World as Problematic: A Feminist Sociology* (1987) provided me with the inspiration to approach this chapter as I did: using my history as what Smith calls a *point d'appui* for investigating the cultural construction and social regulation of privacy. For my classes, too, I look for both contemporary and historical examples of what Fraser calls "discursive contestation" (1989, 86) over the highly political questions of where (and by whom) public and private boundaries are drawn. For instance:

- Patricia Williams' (1991) critique of the privatization of racism, with racial profiling justified and even naturalized in the name of "safety" and a private property owner's "rights"
- Herbert Kohl's (2005) critical examination of the "Rosa was tired" myth that takes Rosa Parks' public, deliberate, and collectively sponsored act of defiance and turns it into a spontaneous accident of history by a noble but naive private individual
- Dana Frank's (2001) account of the Woolworth's clerks whose headline-making 1937 sit-down strike put a public face on women's participation in the U.S. labor market even as the national press tried to present their store takeover—a formidable and successful challenge to what was the Depression decade's Wal-mart—as a gushing, giggling pajama party
- Martin Duberman's (1994) and David Carter's (2004) portrayals of the men and women—gay, lesbian, bisexual, transgender, and transsexual—who both defended Greenwich Village's Stonewall Inn from the intrusion and thuggery of the NYPD's "vice squads" (who fought, that is, for a right to privacy) and launched a public and militant movement for gay and lesbian rights (fighting for full rights to publicity)

An historical and rhetorical examination of abortion rights and ideas governing sex and reproduction in the United States can also show the changing terms of struggle (see, for instance, Baehr 1990, D'Emilo and Freedman 1997, and Reagan 1998). When, how, and why did slogans and statements surrounding abortion change from *Free Abortion on Demand* of the early 1970s to *Who's Choice—Yours or Theirs?* of the mid-1990s to Hillary Clinton's latest apologia for this "sad, even tragic choice" (qtd. in Healy 2005)? With abortion rights today presented almost exclusively as a *moral* dilemma, how do students make sense of Supreme Court Justice Harry M. Blackmun's reflection on the *Roe v. Wade* decision he penned: "It's a step that had to be taken as we go down the road toward the full emancipation of women" (1994)?

With and through such examples, I also want my students to have the means to examine and contest what's been worked up as merely self-regarding or entirely other-regarding in their own histories. These are, after all, writing classes I teach, and I know from that single journal entry I wrote in the 1980s—"I know I want to write but what?"—that a precondition of writing is the belief that one's experiences, perceptions, and spheres of participation are meaningful and thus discussable. Fulfilling that condition takes an act of double consciousness that I've tried to dramatize in my approach to this chapter and that I try to foreground in my teaching, particularly through invention and revision exercises aimed at filling up margins and backs of pages with both contextual detail and analytic speculation.

One revision exercise, "Reseeing the Argument," for instance, asks a writer to look again at a draft, no matter what the genre and no matter how seemingly "personal" the approach, and to draw out in the margins the arguments this early draft may be advancing or implying. In another (invention) exercise, students make two lists: "I'm an authority on . . ." and "I'm concerned about. . . ." First we consider what for the majority of students is a wide gap between the two lists: The students write that they are authorities on their friends, hometown, this or that leisure activity; they write that they are concerned about what one student recently summed up as "big national and world issues I can't actually say anything about." Then we take one shared "concerned about" topic—global warming, for instance—and place it on the board. Around the topic we write first the usual people and groups we assume to be knowledgeable about and authorized to speak on this topic: environmentalists, a variety of scientists, also governments, insurers, even the shipping industry as the polar ice cap melts and opens up new trade routes. Then we consider who else might have day-to-day knowledge of global warming or feel its effects: Vermonters who are witnessing the steep decline in maple syrup production that has accompanied warm-weather trends, for instance, or, some of the state's poorest residents who live in flood and mudslide zones, the most vulnerable to the extreme-weather devastation that has accompanied climate change.

The point of such exercises is not to move students from "private" to "public" or from "narrative" to "argument" but to dramatize, visibly in the margins or in the gap between an "authority" and "concerned about" list, how experiences and genres we've been taught to regard as personal and private are very much bound up in what is social and public, our positions contested by some groups and shared by others. An exercise such as "Re-seeing the Argument" might lead a student to a revision that does indeed highlight the teased-out argument. It might lead a student to delve into the complexities of context. Regardless of what final product results, I want my students to experience through such an exercise a growing, heady sense of how much social history and public debate is packed into a single rough-draft paragraph—even and especially a paragraph about a matter typically marked as personal. I want them to have a sense of how hard it is to write about such a subject, how difficult to sort out one's possible position and side within the arguments—and how necessary, too. I want for students and for myself the ability to exercise real choices between the *freedom from* intrusion and the *freedom to* articulate. The exercise of such choices in writing isn't enough, obviously, to unseat the dominating logic of neoliberalism and halt the privatization of public services, public spaces, and public issues. Writing alone isn't what made possible, for instance, the social miracles of France in the mid-1990s and Argentina in 2001, when unemployment was transformed from a private problem to a public constituency making strong, collective demands (with workers in France taking over unemployment offices and workers in Argentina going a step further as they reopened closed factories under cooperative control). Much more than classroom work is needed here, drawing teachers and students into the risky realm of making spaces for public argument and (our academic regard for complexity and nuance notwithstanding) choosing a side. But such in-class work in the margins of emerging texts does mark one point of resistance, one way that teachers of writing can refuse to participate in the privatization of experience.

Be Very Afraid. But Stand Up Anyway

When I started this chapter, I had in mind to argue that the much
publicized threats to individual privacy in an Internet age distract us from
the real and growing threats to our democratic publicity rights. Yet the
more I engage in the exercise of reseeing the argument and the more I
unpack my rhetorical terms, the more I recognize that such an argument
is incomplete, that privacy and publicity exist as two sides of the same
coin. For example:

Today among my emails is an ACLU action alert detailing the
latest legislative proposal to defend national security through electronic
surveillance, detainment without due process, and secret searches. (The
USA PATRIOT Act has, of course, with overwhelming and dismaying
congressional support, gone on to become law. One of Vermont's senators
even snapped a photo of George Bush signing the act into law—a
Kodak moment for his personal photo album, I suppose.) The USA
PATRIOT Act has profound and damaging consequences for our rights
of privacy. In a crucial twist, however, what this email alert emphasizes
are the devastating effects these invasions of personal privacy will have
on democratic *publicity*: on people's ability and willingness to assemble,
dissent, be noticed in anyway. The alert ends with this ambivalent call to
public action: "Be very afraid. But stand up anyway."

I read those lines, remember my mother saying, "Shush. That has
nothing to do with us," and I realize that the lesson she imparted wasn't
specific to her own post-McCarthy era but still operates, and must be
resisted, in ours.

Risking Rhetoric

In a seminar for new English teaching assistants, convened just as George Herbert Bush had launched the first Gulf War, the instructor asked that we each tell how we came to academe. I'd just read Mike Rose's newly published *Lives on the Boundary* (1989) and, thrilled by this chance to speak for the first time in a classroom about my own vo-tech education, I patterned my story after his. Vocational school, secretarial school, work, night classes, the discovery of open admissions, the wonder that there could be such a thing as graduate school and assistantships: In one long breath I told this tale and then turned to the classmate on my right. This classmate regarded me for a moment, then turned to the instructor, and said, "*I* do *not* tell stories."

It was to me a stunning moment. What a stance! So certain, so committed! I felt a flash of admiration before I settled into another feeling—shame for having so quickly, so uncritically, seized the invitation to speak. I was an MFA student in fiction writing, wrestling with a gloomy sense that all stories are doomed from the get-go. Increasingly evident, too, was how stories worked as warrants to justify imperialist wars (*Those Iraqis ripped babies from their incubators!*) or prove a reactionary rule (*If Nancy pulled herself up by her vo-tech bootstraps, surely anybody can*). So maybe, if *words* are the problem, one should refuse storytelling altogether. Abstain. Don't participate. Don't add to the mess. Those were my thoughts as I left the seminar, heading outside where a lunchtime speak-out was just beginning. With another student, I stood and listened. For a beat or two, I even tried to join in—*Hey-hey, ho-ho*—but the words caught in my throat. Abstain. Don't participate. Don't add more words to the problem.

Here I can locate a key tension I feel in calling myself a rhetorician. As a rhetorician, I feel compelled to scrutinize a story, an argument, or a protest chant for all its flaws. Yet, particularly in pressured moments, I'm still moved to risk putting out a story. It *is* risky: risky to associate ourselves with rhetoric (knee-jerk and sloganeering); risky in our postmodern, post–Cold War era to insist that radical rhetorics are those that stay bound to political scenes we can point to, name, *and* join. Well before the election of George W. Bush and well before the passage of the USA PATRIOT Act and subsequent witch hunts on left academics, many of us were holding our tongues and minding our academic superegos. Where was the mass response from academics to the repeal of welfare, the demonization of gay marriage, the almost continuous bombing campaign waged through the Clinton years against Iraq, Afghanistan, Sudan, Kosovo? Abstain. Don't participate. This was my training too: to appraise arguments from a safe distance but never really take one up.

I've thought a lot about rhetoric in recent years as, at mass demonstrations, I have taken up slogans and chants: *Hey, Bush, we know you/your daddy was a killer too; Hitler, Sharon, it's the same/the only difference is the name.* Certainly such chants can be faulted for their "lack of nuance"; and, in fact, I was vigorously scolded at a recent conference, where I first sketched these ideas, for perpetuating "violence through language." Yet in their moments—the bombing of Afghanistan, the bulldozing of Jenin—such chants have felt to me far from reductive, have seemed instead a necessary part of our available means that we need to reclaim if we're to expose the flesh-ripping, bone-crushing violence routinely covered over by words such as *liberation* and *security fence.*

A fear beyond academic self-consciousness is, however, what I felt when I realized I'd become visible to a small group of young men on my campus. These men, members of the College Republicans, hung posters proclaiming *Bomb Iraq Now!* They authored blogs devoting considerable space to railing against politically active female faculty. One blogger referred to me as a "stupid bitch" whose "ass" should be "fired." Another young man convinced a columnist from the city's newspaper to run a piece about "extremist faculty" whose antiwar views silence students, naming a colleague and me even though we were both on sabbatical at the time. It was an awakening to realize that I could be so visible to a group of men I could not pick out on the street or identify in a lineup.

Actually I think it's because I had never met these students that their words took on muscle and weight, particularly when I crossed the campus after dark or worked in my office on a Saturday afternoon. I needed to put my fears in perspective: I was not subjected to the witch hunt that resulted in the detainment of more than 1,200 Arab, Muslim, and South Asian men in the fall of 2001 (Nguyen 2006) and that turned Professor Sami Al-Arian out of his job at the University of South Florida ("AAUP Condemns" 2003). I had not been publicly harangued as an "anti-American foreigner" as a friend was by Rush Limbaugh on his nationally syndicated radio program. I had tenure, a union, and a U.S. passport; those faceless bloggers never did come up with words that could really hurt me. Still, their bellicosity had the power to unsettle; the newspaper column was enough to convince my city's police department to (briefly) investigate whether the downtown antiwar committee to which I belonged had crossed any (newly created) lines into illegality. *Bomb Iraq Now, fire her ass*: Maybe these young men didn't have the power to make such words so, but they sought to ally themselves with those who did.

———

On the one hand, I want to tell this story to emphasize the tie between U.S. militaristic violence abroad and reproach (and repression) of visibly deviant bodies at home. I want to acknowledge that words can have a profoundly consequential impact. On the other hand, I'm dissatisfied with this story as it stands now, particularly because by accepting the disembodied, anonymous, and so seemingly omnipotent threat of *Bomb Iraq Now, fire her ass*, I wind up implying that for all of us who are too vulnerable to revel in the role of lone lefty hero, our only recourse is retreat. There is danger in dwelling too much on an utterance divorced from its larger context and from the competing interests the utterance serves or denies. This story's larger context includes, to be sure, the few who have a material interest in bombing Iraq, gutting academic freedom, rolling back civil and abortion rights, and further stratifying this society into the handful who have and the many who have not. The story's larger context also includes the many women and men who have every reason to oppose such an agenda. Bullied by a few men on my campus, I may miss the many who are organizing with women to march against war on all its fronts and who are doing so because these assaults—on Afghanistan, Iraq, and Palestine, on social programs, civil rights, and women's rights—are against their interests too.

Fearful of the few, we may also miss the many people on our campuses and in our towns who would want to join in marching and organizing, too, if they knew where and how, if they did not feel they have no choice but to hole up at home, feeling targeted, feeling vulnerable, feeling that they alone are thinking, "No!" and "Don't bomb Iraq" (or Iran or Lebanon). What might we lose in vulnerability and what might we gain in power through becoming visible together? I think here, for example, of the thousands of Arab Americans and Muslim Americans who turned out in Washington, DC for the 100,000-person-strong Free Palestine rally in April 2002—despite the very real threats of detainment and deportation under the USA PATRIOT Act. What a dramatic example of collective visibility, of refusing to be cowed! The story I've told above needs to include such a possibility of collective visibility, the needed counterweight to individual fear and vulnerability.

———

At a fall 2002 meeting of University of Vermont groups threatened by a bullying campus climate, several of us make this argument for collective visibility and safety through solidarity. Someone or some group has scrawled homophobic slurs on dormitory doors. Posters equating Arabs with terrorism cover campus bulletin boards. One afternoon, following a report of a dormitory robbery, campus police tackle and hold a gun to the head of an African American student. (Later the cops defend themselves, arguing that, like the reported male robber, this female student was wearing a hooded sweatshirt.) In the meeting, when one student notes the racism of the College Republicans' event posters, people around the circle nod. The conversation turns toward ideas for campus progressive groups to join together and project our (much larger) presence at the university. "There are more of us," "We should be out there," "We can send a message together": This is what people around the circle begin to say, students from the Black Student Union inviting those from the Free to Be LGBT Alliance to join them the next afternoon to make some banners and posters together. Then a college dean steps in: "You each need to learn to look out for yourself," she says. "You've got to stop imagining that you can go out and be safe and have anyone stand up for you."

There it is again—Abstain. Don't participate—but in a new context with new and higher stakes: Abstain, don't participate, and do not stand out—not as gay, foreign, feminist, antiwar, Muslim, transgender, or as

Black and wearing a hoodie. There will be no collective solutions. No one will stand up with you and speak up for you. It really is too risky.

———

Postmodern feminism has been my training, particularly that strand of postmodern feminist rhetoric promoting not abstention (as if words are the problem) but instead linguistic play (as if words, an individual's words, can be the answer). Lately, though, I'm not sure how much good either the abstentionist or the experimental strand of postmodern feminist rhetoric can do me or my students. Neither tells me what to do, for instance, when I look at facts such as these: While the number of high school and college graduates in the U.S. workforce increased dramatically between 1979 and 1999, wages declined for nearly three-fourths of them (Lafer 2002, 45, 51). Between 1984 and 1996, the number of people in need of work consistently exceeded the number of full-time job openings 14 to 1 and the number of livable wage jobs 97 to 1 (2002, 36–37). A survey in the 1990s found that what employers most valued in potential employees, over college degrees or technical experience, were the "skills" of punctuality, good attitude, and acceptance of the wage scale (2002, 68). What people require to survive and resist this downward trend, argues Gordon Lafer in *The Job Training Charade* (2002), is "not the discipline demanded by employers but the solidarity required for collective mobilization" (224).

Postmodern theories of political economy dismiss Lafer's solidarity solution as out of synch with today's postindustrial landscape, better suited to yesteryear's industrial worker than today's (largely mythical) telecommuting knowledge engineer. Yet whether our students enter retail, service, or manufacturing sectors, most will share in common the challenges of "lean production" (Moody 1997; Turl 2007). That is, they (and "they" also includes "we" academic workers) will be under constant pressure to invent new ways of taking on more work at less pay and with fewer heads and hands. What we and our students need most to withstand such a harsh economic and political climate is neither the "look out for yourself" counsel of the college dean nor the writerly pursuit of textual fragmentation and generic migration. I do understand the appeal of equating freedom of movement on a page with freedom of movement across political and geographic terrains. That's what so much of my own work has been about—the practices that allow writers, especially those disenfranchised from or at odds with a ruling order, to pursue and gain confidence in their unruly ideas. But individual word work, if we press no further, repeats the "supply-side" logic that Gordon Lafer argues is also behind the most conservative of job-training and welfare-to-work programs: a logic that says the problem isn't in the dearth of livable wage jobs and the record corporate profit margins but in the person who lacks the skills to either fit into or transform his or her particular economic/rhetorical moment (2002, 51–53). It's a logic that—endorsed by educational liberals (James Paul Gee, for instance) as well as conservatives—focuses all attention on the individual, his or her presumed need for ramped-up skills, an expanded literacy toolkit. This supply-side logic would also have us assume a mass U.S. public as the *driving* force behind the wars against Afghanistan and Iraq—leaving dissenters to assume they must be isolated and alone, unable to gauge and imagine acting from their (considerable) collective numbers.

What, then, is the alternative? What can teachers of writing teach if not, on the one hand, the literacy and rhetorical skills for individual compliance with existing (social, political, workplace) requirements, or, on the other hand, radical rhetorical skepticism and/or linguistic play (as if Marx got it wrong and we really can make history in conditions of our own choosing or else opt out—abstain—altogether)? To answer these questions without capitulating to one side or the other, we can pull back and ask some bigger questions. If, for instance, it is collective confidence, organization, and creativity that most people need to create a bullying-free campus or to imagine a livable wage and a livable future on a livable planet, what literacy practices and rhetorical orientations can we match to these needs? If it is collective argumentation and mass persuasive action that won—from the mass strikes and demonstrations of the 1930s to the escalating social movements of the 1960s—the tangible gains so imperiled today, what lessons can we draw from those movements as we seek a responsive rhetorical complement for conditions today?

—

The first time I introduced soapboxing to my students, it was an on-the-spot improvisation. I'd arrived in my U.S. Literacy Politics class to find that most students, for one good reason or another, hadn't completed the day's reading, the "Depression Decade" chapter from Jeremy Brecher's (1997) *Strike!* For a moment I imagined scolding them: Would they like to be the class that forced me, for the first time in more than a decade of teaching, to introduce reading quizzes? I considered canceling the class. Then, luckily, I had what turned out to be a much better idea. In "Depression Decade,"

Brecher describes how Flint sit-down strikers dealt with breaches of strike discipline. When a worker coming and going from the building forgot to carry a pass or failed to show up for a shift, a "court" of coworkers meted out such "punishments" as requiring the delivery of an extemporaneous speech—discipline joined to the promotion of working-class education. In that spirit, I explained to students in U.S. Literacy Politics that we'd also try out the punishment of extemporaneous speaking. I turned over a plastic milk carton that, inexplicably, had been gathering dust in a classroom corner all semester. We had a short discussion about soapboxing's working-class history, from London's Hyde Park to West Coast Wobblies. Then we took a very short amount of time for individual freewriting on what to say—any topic, any genre, any tone.

It was a risk, but one we took together, each of us clutching the piece of paper on which we'd just scribbled, yet most everyone disregarding their free-written speech and instead speaking on the spot, inspired by the story, argument, or question of the soapboxer before. We stood and spoke one at a time, but soon we were developing shared stories, offering additional warrants for or rejoinders to a collective argument. There were worries about friends on their way to Iraq, anxieties about health care, a question of whether to speak up—and risk being fired—about deteriorating conditions at work. At the end of class a clamor went up: "Can we do this again?" It's an activity I have done again. "Don't Be Afraid of That Soapbox Day!" is a part of all the classes I teach, from first-year to graduate seminars, especially because of what one student offered that very first time. When Chris' turn came, I thought maybe he'd shake his head; I'd already decided that if he wanted, he could abstain. It was eight weeks into the seminar and in this class of sixteen students, he had never said a word. But then Chris stood up—and what he had to say has stuck, has convinced me of the potential and need of so many of our students, the many who are not blogging, who are not aligned with forces of aggressive power, and who have never been invited, or permitted, to put a perspective out on the floor:

> This is the first time I've ever been asked in a class to stand up and say something about what's on my mind and I just can't believe I'm actually doing this and how incredible it feels and I don't even know what I'm saying now, but—yeah, that's what I want to say.

3

Taking Sides

Philosophers have only interpreted the world in various ways; the point, however, is to change it.

—Karl Marx

Christ is dead, Marx is dead, and myself, I don't feel so good.

—Graffiti on a wall, Paris, May 1968

We are afraid to appear ridiculous, and this may kill us.

—Slogan from the French Women's Movement

"Pessimism of the intellect" is essential for taking stock of the scale of the neoliberal offensive and the powerful organization of its proponents. At the same time, it would be wrong to overlook the "optimism of the will" that spurs on whole sections of the global population.

—Eric Toussaint (2005)

Going to Activism School

At a meeting of the Feminist Research Network, just before the start of the Conference on College Composition and Communication, Susan Miller remarked that lately, she'd been thinking she shouldn't send her students to graduate school; she should send them to activism school instead. I don't know what prompted her remark. At that moment—late in the day as the room grew warm and the lively discussion about feminist rhetoric had lulled—I was in a kind of haze. Was Miller arguing for a new breed of rhetorician: rhetor-anarchist activists whose voices are trained for the next Seattle? Was she echoing Marx's famous assertion that we must do more than fight phrases with phrases? Or was this less a call to the streets and more an expression of late-day, late-capitalist, preconference weariness? I can't say; I wasn't following the discussion closely enough. What I can say is that her words startled me into attention and stayed with me through that conference and through the whole of the year that followed—a year I think of as having been spent in activism school.

Some necessary background: It's only recently that I've defined myself as a rhetorician at all. Though I was mentored by remarkable women who view rhetoric as central to our enterprise, my studies immersed me in writing as a practice of inquiry, a practice I associated much more with (feminized) composition than with (masculinist) rhetoric. The humble appellation of compositionist seemed better matched to my proletarian credentials—vocational high school, secretarial school; later, a degree from an urban, open-admissions university; a doctorate from a large midwestern land-grant institution. Especially because my first try at college was a nighttime basic writing class, I've pointed to composition as the link between who I was and who I have become. Yet, paradoxically, it's likely that I've preferred composition over rhetoric not for its attachment to workaday scenes and on-the-ground struggles but instead (in classrooms that promote inquiry and downplay argument) for its distance. A one-step distance from daily arguments and daily demands is what that first college class—Monday and Wednesday nights at Boston's YMCA on Huntington Avenue—had offered me. There, after a day of typing other people's words, I found space and encouragement for my own.

Elsewhere I've described such writing classrooms as "critical exile" and "potential spaces" where students can "sideshadow" the dominant narratives that compose their lives (N. Welch 1997, 1998, 1999). At the same time, I've been careful to note my distance from the assumptions of the solitary artist's garret. Here, though, I'll admit that there has been something of the garret in my thinking and in my teaching— understandably, I think, because if you've never had a garret and have been told that you are not cut out for one, it can seem like a very precious thing. The university seemed to me to be one big, beautiful garret. It was a place where I did not have to wear pantyhose and no one would ever say to me, "Nancy, get your [steno] book. Nancy, take a letter." It was (when I shut my eyes to who emptied my wastebasket each night, who taught composition side by side with me, and what my university's board of trustees had in mind when they called for "strategic planning") a realm removed from the major sources of antagonism in my life: bosses, bills, layoffs. I can remember explaining to my father, pink-slipped by a company he'd been with for more than twenty years, the concept of tenure:

"You mean they can't fire you?" he asked.

"Well, there're some technicalities, but no, they can't fire me."

At that he nodded and said nothing. A job for life—how could you argue with that?

It's difficult to unpack all the reasons why I've started to ponder what my relationship to argument might necessarily be. Any summary would have to include events in my workplace ("strategic planning," predictably, meant cutting health care, downsizing faculty, and upping workloads for tenure-track and adjunct faculty alike) and also events countrywide (the repeal of welfare, a hijacked presidential election). A summary would also need to include the obstacles I faced when I sought forums for action (an anarchist network whose insistence on consensus resulted in a group both homogenous and small) and scattered, surprising victories (a union for the University of Vermont faculty, tenure track and adjunct together). Such a summary should also include my husband (with whom I learned the rhetorical pitfalls of arguing with managed care bureaucrats) and my students (those in my Literacy Politics course who asked that future classes focus more on public intervention; my advanced nonfiction writing students who say they're afraid of sounding "pushy" and "like a know-it-all" yet love Jamaica Kincaid and June Jordan for the bite of their words). And so the unpacking would continue, revealing all the ways in which I do not have, and no longer desire, the luxury of distance from the world.

In an essay that aims to mediate between the poles of rhetoric as inquiry (a Platonic search in common for truth) and rhetoric as confrontation (the clash of competing perspectives), Dennis Lynch, Diana George, and Marilyn Cooper trace through the twentieth century a "general effort to expand rhetoric's horizons" (1997, 62). Over the past few years, that's what I've sought to do—expand my understanding and practice of rhetoric. Through antiwar organizing in diverse coalitions of labor activists and university students, religious pacifists and lifestyle anarchists, revolutionary socialists (my own orientation) and wary ex-Marxist-Leninists, I've learned something of what it means to link arms with others in a common fight while arguing out the differences among us. I've learned to run the risk of raising a slogan—something

I'd particularly shied away from since 1991 when, at the start of the first Gulf War, I marched under the deadly compromise "Sanctions, Not Bombs." I've thought a lot about the means of persuasion within fledgling coalitions, and I've come to believe something is at stake in winning particular arguments, such as the argument that our local antiwar coalition not insist upon pacifism (and hence moral censure of armed resistance anywhere and under any circumstances) as a point of unity to which all must adhere. While the dominant trend in twentieth-century rhetorical studies, as described by Lynch, George, and Cooper (1997) and as experienced in my own late twentieth-century education, tended away from confrontation and toward mediation, my recent efforts to expand my studies have been in the opposite direction. Schooled in that rhetoric of inquiry, I'm now trying to learn more, much more, about taking a side.

Yet I'm doing so, I also realize, at a moment when it's considered regressive for a feminist and an academic Leftist to profess a desire to argue at all. Notwithstanding individual voices in the field who argue for a return to what Andrea Greenbaum (2001) calls the "muscularity of argumentative discourse" (154),[1] agonistic rhetoric—so stubbornly gendered as muscular and male—is typically avoided both in the specialized field of rhetoric and in the mainstream discourse of liberals, progressives, and (chastened) radicals. Such rhetoric is doubly disdained as antithetical to a properly feminist stance and as an encumbrance to an appropriately postmodern position that, as Diane Davis puts it, shares with Tomas in *The Unbearable Lightness of Being* the belief that "missions are stupid" (Kundera 1984, 313; qtd. in Davis 2000, 164).

I have to say that much of my own teaching, particularly through revision exercises with names such as "Unending the Ending" and "ReSeeing the Argument," is likewise about opening up sealed-tight conclusions and unpacking assertions. With Arundhati Roy (2001), "I'm all for . . . tentativeness, subtlety, ambiguity, complexity. I love the unanswered question, the unresolved story . . . the tender shard of an incomplete dream. *Most of the time*" (11, my emphasis). Most of the time I relish messy, contradictory ethnographic detail that has the power to unseat this or that general principle. So do my students who are drawn to the open-ended and receptive form of the collage. But I've also observed that my students are reluctant to come to conclusions, and that when they do, they are quick—sometimes too quick—to concede that an opposite conclusion might also be true. They appear to be in agreement with Gary Olson's oddly assertive and thesis-driven argument that we repudiate "thesis-flexing rhetoric" and pursue instead a "more dialogic, dynamic, open-ended, receptive, non-assertive stance" (1999, 14). But at what cost? And how did we reach this place where to argue a position, and particularly a position explicitly linked to current events and material consequences, is to be charged with a lack of sophistication and appropriate politics? How did we come to a place where Miller's counsel that students consider "activism school" is heard as reactionary, not vanguard, advice?

To get at these questions, I'll examine two strands in feminist rhetoric that have shaped the ambivalence about argument I've encountered in the classroom and in activist organizations. Though these two strands—the maternalist, which associates women biologically or socially with peacemaking; the postmodern or "third sophistic," which eschews any solid ground on which to stake a claim—appear worlds apart, they share a deep distrust of fixed positions and first principles that is born, for adherents to both feminisms, from the problems of New Left social movements in the 1960s. Before I examine the shared tenets and history of these rhetorics, I want to sketch the context—particularly the United States' recovery from its defeat in Vietnam and efforts, through both economic and military means, to assert singular, seemingly uncontestable dominance in the post-Soviet world order—that has profoundly shaped both. It's a context that has also changed and charged my teaching and that brings me now to the urgent belief that we musn't repudiate assertion, musn't relinquish our willingness to take a stand.

Cool Colonialism and the Diffident Left

It is November 2001, and on my desk is a CD featuring a new game for Macintosh users called *Tropico*. In *Tropico* (2001), the CD's jacket explains, "you take a trip to a third world island AND RULE!" Promising "pure, dictatorial fun," the jacket depicts a verdant island, its beach densely dotted with churches and houses in sumptuous colonial style. A jet hovers overhead, while cruising out of the lagoon is a large yacht, or battleship; it's hard to tell. When my husband first dropped this CD in my lap, I was watching TV. In one part of the world, U.S. warplanes shell a country already decimated by two decades of war; in another, teams of fit, athletic Americans compete to cross deserts, climb mountains, and claim a million-dollar prize. Even amid the bombing of Afghanistan, it remains unfashionable among most academics to speak of imperialism except with a wry tone and arched brow. "We have to stop it with all this knee-jerk talk of imperialism," one cultural studies scholar tells me, "or else no one will take us seriously." I cannot think, however, of any other word that fits.

Apparently, neither could the *Wall Street Journal* and the *New York Times*, which during this same period—as the United States wrapped up for the moment its assault on Afghanistan and turned its sights on Iraq— ran op-eds and articles trumpeting the virtue of U.S. rule over unruly nations that also happen to be resource rich or in the path of a planned pipeline. A small sampling of such articles includes:

- "The Answer to Terrorism? Colonialism," in which the *Wall Street Journal's* Paul Johnson (2001) argues for a return to the "'respectable' form of colonialism" that once held Iraq, Syria, Sudan, Iran, and Libya under "special regimes."

- "How to Keep Afghanistan from Falling Apart: The Case for a Committed American Imperialism," featured in the *New York Times Magazine*, in which Michael Ignatieff (2002) lauds the war on terrorism as "an exercise in imperialism" (28). He then chastises the administration of George W. Bush for not pouring *enough* money into the imperialist project: "[E]mpires don't come lite. They come heavy, or they do not last" (26). (Ignatieff, it must be noted, is a writer with liberal, not neoconservative credentials.)

- "The Future of War and the American Military," in which, for readers of Harvard's alumni magazine, Stephen Peter Rosen (2002) details with unabashed frankness how contemporary "imperial wars" must be waged: through the use of "unconventional weapons" and a "maximum amount of force . . . for psychological impact to demonstrate the empire cannot be challenged with impunity" (31).

Here and elsewhere, if there is mention of Vietnam, it is as a "syndrome" that the United States has, thankfully, recovered from.

While U.S. imperialism enjoyed such a renaissance, some of the Left's most influential voices initially dismissed the word as the shabby remnant of a bygone era. "Imperialism is over," argued Michael Hardt and Antonio Negri in *Empire* (2000, ix), an academic best seller that mostly set aside the superconcentration of wealth and power that has been the true hallmark of the post-1989 new world order so as to celebrate global capitalism's much mythologized potential to erase borders, hybridize identities, and diminish state power. The unabashed exercise of U.S. military power starting in October 2001 (prepared for by multiple military trial runs under Reagan, G. H. Bush, and Clinton) wasn't fully sufficient to change the academic mind. Even as the United States moved toward "regime change" in Iraq, psychoanalytic theorist Slavoj Žižek (2002) told some 200 students on my campus to *forget* the slogan of the May 1968 general strikes in France: *Be Realistic! Demand the Impossible!* All hopes for oppositional politics, he argued, crumbled with the Berlin Wall (a wall that he argued was itself the consequence of people having demanded freedom and equality in the first place). The most radical place for the would-be critic, Žižek advised students, is the "hole," where, refusing to take a position in any conflict, one can presumably spot and critique the flaws all around. What Žižek did not pause to consider is that most of his young audience had not heard the news of the student-worker alliance that took over and virtually governed France for two months in 1968. (How to forget an event they'd never heard of?) Indeed, most were too young even to recall the heady hopes of 1989 as the Berlin Wall was coming down, before anyone imagined that Stalinist despotism would be replaced by free-market tyranny and U.S. military and economic triumphalism. Most of the students addressed by Žižek knew very little at all of the history and politics of major social movements against tyranny and oppression; and in place of a history, politics, and problems of such movements, what he offered was abstention: *Demand nothing. Missions are stupid.*

In this same period, prominent feminists similarly disdained "recycled" 1960s radicalism, but they did so while urging a politics of opportunity. ATTAC's Susan George (2001a), for instance, wrote of the post–September 11, 2001, climate as one that might bring a restored belief in the U.S. state, creating the chance for a "new, updated global Keynesian strategy" (2), while Ellen Willis (2001) approved of the use of Western troops to "defeat patriarchal culture" in Central Asia. Even the anarchist activist and poet Starhawk (2001) initially called on George W. Bush to employ "the carrot as well as a stick" (7)—never mind that forms of the carrot, such as IMF policies aimed at privatizing public services and resources while lining the pockets of a few, are what she, Susan George, and others had until that moment admirably dedicated themselves to protesting. My point in offering this catalog of the U.S. Left's initial responses to resurging and expanding U.S. militarism isn't to lay blame on activists such as Starhawk for making the wrong argument. (At least, contrary to Žižek's advice for the period, she was arguing!) My point is that when phrases such as *imperialist war* and *oil pipeline* are evacuated, the resulting vacuum is refilled with—what else can we call the notion that the anti-choice, anti-affirmative action, anti-welfare George W. Bush could be the liberator of women?—confusion.

Confusion is what I too felt, deeply, as a student described to me what happened when she spoke up in a political science class against the U.S. bombing of Afghanistan. When the professor challenged her to say why, she fell mute while a classmate hissed, "Fucking stupid peacenik." This is a student who, in two writing classes plus an independent study with me, had reveled in inquiry, using her writing to pry open ruling arguments and probe the corners of experience. But when called on to defend a largely inchoate belief in a potentially hostile setting, she could not: Her rhetorical education had not prepared her to imagine arguing in the face of such staunch opposition.

I don't want to paint too grim a picture, because in this same difficult period, I also encountered voices of passionate opposition and incisive critique: Colleen Kelly of September 11 Families for Peaceful Tomorrows, who spoke against the use of her brother's death in the World Trade Center as a pretext for more killing; the University of North Carolina at Chapel Hill's Progressive Faculty Network, whose forum on Christian and Zionist, as well as Islamic, fundamentalisms challenged the ability of a Bush and an Ashcroft to defend women anywhere. Then there were Arundhati Roy and Barbara Kingsolver, whose email-circulated essays laid out in clear, accessible terms the corporate oil interests driving U.S. policy and also insisted on globalizing feelings of grief and fear; plus the nearly 100,000 people—many of them Arab and Muslim—who, despite real threats of detainment and deportation under the USA PATRIOT Act, turned out in April 2002 for the largest Palestinian rights rally ever held in the United States. These examples of arguments advanced in the most difficult, painful of circumstances are ones I still urge my students to seek out, as their lessons are rhetorically rich.

Yet—as North Carolina's Progressive Faculty Network found when its antiwar teach-ins were denounced by right-wing pundits Rush Limbaugh and David Horowitz, and as members of Berkeley's Students for Justice in Palestine also discovered when they were met with academic sanctions and criminal charges for a nonviolent protest in the birthplace of the campus free speech movement—those who engaged in protest in the United States in this post–September 11, 2001, period also risked reprisals. Moreover, those facing reprisal have received, at most, equivocal support from the traditional defenders of academic freedom. The American Association of University Professors, for instance, sent out a flier that for many weeks sat on my desk next to my copy of *Tropico*. "It's unfortunate," the flier warns, "but highly respected professors and researchers, who have a right to academic freedom, face legal action each time they stand before a class, present research or publish work" (AAUP Professional Liability 2002). The flyer continues not with a call to collective action or even to a conference; instead, it offers academics a chance to purchase professional liability insurance.

In this period we are afraid of much more than appearing ridiculous; we are afraid of appearing, of standing out, at all.

Feminist Rhetorics: Between the Failed Revolution and the Shabby Deal

Because feminist rhetorical theories and practices nurtured the early years of my teaching and research, I wish I could say they offered me in 2002 genuine alternatives to diffidence, opportunism, or embattled silence. Instead, what I found is much of the same wariness that marked Žižek's anti-activism speech, the AAUP's insurance pitch, and the cultural studies professor's warning that "No one will take us seriously." I've also found something else—let's call it a shared problem with history—that has helped me to see how we can claim what's been invaluable in feminist rhetorical practices *plus* intervene in this pervasive reluctance to have anything to do with (knee-jerk, unsophisticated, sloganeering) rhetoric at all.

To get at the longer history of this rhetorical reluctance, I want to take us next to April 2002 and the national antiwar demonstration in Washington, DC, where the demand *Free Palestine* was visibly, audibly, and repeatedly raised. At this rally, held just days after the Israeli Defense Forces (IDF) bulldozed Jenin and other West Bank refugee camps, a woman with a long commitment to joining peace activism with feminism said to me, "Why do all the signs have to be so negative?" The signs she pointed to were carried overwhelmingly by Arab women and men, many accompanied by young children and pushing strollers. *End the Occupation,* the signs insisted. *Stop the Genocide* and *Boycott Caterpillar* (the U.S. manufacturer of bulldozers used to demolish Palestinian homes). I tried to explain why I saw these messages as positive. Just imagine the worldwide sigh of relief if the IDF pulled out, if the spread of settlements stopped, if the United States halted its funding of and profiteering from this occupation. Or imagine how different a place northern Vermont would be for many women if people publicly proclaimed "Don't" and "Stop"—emphatic, resolute—to rape, to domestic abuse, or to the punishing dictates and denials of welfare reform. The woman shook her head.

"There's too much arguing here," she replied.

For many of the women I work with, political activism is defined by both pacifism and a strand of feminism associated with maternalism—the equation of women with mothering and what's understood as the related task of peacemaking. Sabina Lovibond (1994), in a critical assessment, cites developmental psychologist Carol Gilligan as a foundational figure in a politics rooted in maternalism. Intervening in the decidedly male-centered models of cognitive and moral development put forth by Jean Piaget, Lawrence Kohlberg, and William G. Perry, Gilligan urged a "[feminine] *sensitivity to morally significant detail*" to counter "[masculine] legalistic reliance on abstract principle" (780, Lovibond's emphasis). From Gilligan's intervention comes the work of Sara Ruddick, who argues in *Maternal Thinking* against allowing "rule-dominated 'fairness'" to "override care and sympathy" (1989, 96) and who highlights "maternal practice" as a "'natural resource' for peace politics" (154), because caretaking trains one to value above all the preservation of human life.

Of course, the equation of women with peacemaking predates its codification in contemporary feminist theory by Ruddick, Gilligan, and others within the maternalist tendency. Participants in the Women's Strike for Peace in the United States in the early 1960s, for instance, highlighted their identities as mothers and defenders of the family in arguing against nuclear proliferation (Tickner 2001, 58). Local activists I've spoken with point to the Women's Peace Camp at England's Greenham Common in the early 1980s and similar peace camps that popped up to promote antinuclear campaigns in Vermont as exemplary of political action nurtured by women's capacity to create life. It was also at this time, according to local activist lore, that consensus-based affinity groups became the prime means for organizing in Vermont. Abhorring argument as both masculinist and militaristic, individuals were to assemble according to affinity for one another. Predisposed to agree, affinity group members would have no need for debate.

The histories and legacies of these affinity groups can do much to instruct and inspire new activists today. (One of my favorite stories is of a northern Vermont radical feminist group that—when local police ordered a 9 P.M. curfew for all women in Burlington, to "protect" them from a serial rapist—plastered the town with the order that all *men* stay off the streets after dark.) However, the idealization of community and consensus around which these small groups formed *and* around which these small groups were unable to grow can also have—as numerous compositionists have explored within and beyond the classroom—

profoundly conservative effects. The idealization of community through sameness, not solidarity, and through consensus, rather than democratic voting that records and respects differences and disagreements, winds up deflecting debate and ultimately dividing people according to strict identity markers, obscuring shared interests and diluting collective power. Additionally, political conservatives such as Francis Fukuyama (champion of the view that 1989 marked the "end of history" as Cold War economic and military détente gave way to seemingly unchallengeable U.S. dominance) have readily latched on to the equation of women with peace. In this latest manifestation of separate-spheres rhetoric, these conservatives assert that in an aggressive and dangerous world, women must be protected from the political arena (Tickner 2001, 60).

In rhetorical studies, too, the advancement of a tie between men and aggression and women and receptivity—elaborated in the late 1980s and early 1990s by Jane Tompkins (1987), Elizabeth Flynn (1988), Olivia Frey (1990), and Catherine Lamb (1991)—had the unintended effect of making women scholars vulnerable to a conservative backlash. For example, Robert Connors, in response to Gesa Kirsch's excruciatingly controlled critique of his "Teaching and Learning as a Man" (1996b), set up Kirsch as a "discipline and punish" dominatrix (1996a, 971). Similarly, G. Douglas Atkins dismissed Cynthia Selfe's sharp (and smart) response to his wistfully retrograde "On Writing Well" (2000b) as nothing more than "personal anger" (2000a, 418) arising from "envy" for her lack of "a good pen" (2000a, 421–22). It was not only Fukuyama who has used the equation of women with the soft strokes of nurture to ban them from or ridicule them for public voice and participation.

There's one further difficulty I've encountered with maternalist rhetoric, and especially its founding disavowal of abstract principles and conceptual unities, that I can best illustrate with an anecdote. Recently, participants at a gathering of women union activists swapped stories of their families' experiences with labor struggles. Looking around the table, dropping her voice, one woman said, "Well, maybe I can tell this story in this group, though I don't think I could tell it anywhere else in this state." She then launched into a tale that involved a grandmother, a shotgun, and a (soon-to-be-dead) scab. In this tale, with all its (to recall Gilligan) morally significant detail, we find a direct challenge to the myths that women are predisposed to peace and that mediation is always preferable to confrontation. The catch is that adherents to maternalist feminism would have difficulty hearing this challenge and being open to examining this story within its specific material, historical conditions.

This story is too much at odds with the foundational belief about women's peacefulness. Moreover, by urging a confrontation with that foundational belief, such a story can expose as faulty the maternalist claim that women do not operate from any abstract principles at all. As this woman told the story, the other women around the table gasped, cheered, and launched into their own family stories of women fighting back. They were careful, however, to preface each tale with "I wouldn't tell this story anywhere else but. . . ." Not incidentally, half of these women were union staffers, employed not to organize militant picket lines and winning strikes but instead to negotiate individual settlements for laid-off workers and help negotiating teams decide whether to concede on benefits, wages, or both. No wonder, then, that they told these stories without pause to note the confrontation each story urged—potential confrontations not only with "scabs" and "bosses" but also with our unions themselves.

Here it would seem that another prominent strand in contemporary feminist rhetoric—postmodern or "third-sophistic" feminist rhetoric— could offer a needed antidote. In contrast to maternalism's containment of any conflict, practitioners of postmodern or third-sophistic feminist rhetoric would not treat the detail of the picket-line-defending grandmother as a bit of staticky noise that must be filtered out so that the clear message of women's pacifism can sound. "[T]hird sophistic ears," writes Diane Davis (who indebts her work to rhetorician Victor Vitanza, postmodern philosophers such as Jean-François Lyotard, and postmodern gender theorist Judith Butler), "are posthermeneutic *noise freaks*" (2001, 130, Davis' emphasis). Calling for a "rhetoric of exposition" that treats a thesis as a point of "naked vulnerability," these rhetoricians argue for discursive practices that expose foundational principles, even those that allow women to gather under the (shaky) sign of feminism, to "various encounters, interruptions, contradictions" (2001, 141). Here is the promise of a stance that would open up earlier claims about feminism, women, and peacemaking to debate, introducing, as Judith Butler puts it, a "moment of political hesitation" (1997, 5).

Too frequently, however, this moment of hesitation tends toward a *permanent* indecision with disinvolvement itself elevated to a virtue. Here third-sophistic rhetoricians join Gary Olson in calling for a rhetoric of nonassertion (e.g., Davis 2001, 141) and claiming a feminism that is a "way of being" unfettered by any oppositional agenda (Ballif, Davis, and Mountford 2000, 938). Echoing Žižek's (1993) appeal for "critical distance toward every reigning Master-Signifier" (2), for instance, Davis champions an "all-out attack on metanarratives" as "an attack on the politics of horror that has led us around by the nose since way before the Third Reich and has not let go of us since" (2000, 104). At times it appears as though third-sophistic rhetoricians, instead of urging disengagement, are actually placing their work at the very center of vanguard political activism. After all, if Enlightenment-era philosophy is responsible for every colonialist, imperialist, genocidal horror in modern history, and if as rhetoricians, we are devoted to an all-out attack on its deadly metanarratives, then our work (even if the majority in composition and rhetoric are contingently employed and consigned to Humanities' basement) becomes enormously, even singularly, important. It's the idealist alternative to a real paycheck.

In practice, third-sophistic rhetoric joins maternalist rhetoric in a proclaimed distrust of all platforms and principles *and also* in a failure to recognize its own excision of potentially challenging historical detail. For example, although much of the story of the twentieth century can be written under the heading of "the politics of horror," we also need to account for the persistent politics of hope: the 1917 International Women's Day revolt against Russian tsarism; the Warsaw ghetto uprising against the Nazis; the opposition at home and within army ranks that turned the tide against the U.S. war in Vietnam. Just as maternalist rhetoric might turn us away from such moments with the judgment "too much arguing here," third-sophistic rhetoric would dismiss such disruptions through its foundational story that "missions are stupid."

For both strands of feminist rhetoric, this distrust of programs and assertions arises not so much from the work of academics such as Gilligan as from the disintegration of 1960s-era social movements coupled with the disillusioning experience shared by many women involved in the New Left. Here we have the triple impact of (1) the political rebuff that, following the defeat of the May–June 1968 revolution in France, produced the deep pessimism of much continental postmodern thinking; (2) powerfully deployed right-wing reaction, including, in the United States, COINTELPRO's official program of infiltrating and disrupting New Left groups; and (3) the very real problems of sexism and heterosexism within the New Left, which was the impetus for the women's liberation movement in the United States and England but which also left a generation of activists convinced that personal politics, separatist politics, or the scattered interventions of autonomous culture workers were their only means to act.[2] Sheila Rowbotham (1973), for example, describes in that period the internecine warfare among small, sectarian Marxist-Leninist (that is, Stalinist) groups in London: "They prefaced every statement with 'The correct Marxist position is . . . '"

which one was to learn "by rote from pamphlets and articles" (18, 19). In the problems, particularly with sexist chauvinism, that women experienced within such groups (see also Eschle 2001, especially 94–95), we can locate both the move toward feminist separatism that marks maternalist rhetoric *and* the disillusionment with organization and activism that marks the third sophistics.

This historical hangover has been hard to shake: Disillusionment continues to be expressed in postmodern denouncements of "oppositional logic and rude calculation" (Ronell 1994, 297). But more than a nightmare that continues to weigh on the brain of the living (to borrow Marx's phrase), this disillusionment has also colluded in creating premature celebrations of our release from Cold War binaries with scant attention to the simultaneous rollbacks of people's actual living conditions and crackdowns on most people's actual ability to cross national borders in search of safety and sustenance. In an exuberant reading of Žižek's poetic account of the fall of Romanian communism, for example, Davis writes, "We are interested here in that postmodern moment, after the deterritorialization (no 'community') but before reterritorialization (new 'community'), when, in the flux of exploded identities, in the excess before re-distinction, the multiplicitous, splintered subject attempts to respond to her/his non- or rather poly-foundational multiverse" (2000, 46).

Unexpected openings and multiplications of possibility are indeed worth theorizing, pursuing, and celebrating, but a period of radical flux *does not at all* describe this post–Cold War moment. The opening created by the welcome collapse of "actually existing socialism"—that is, highly bureaucratized and repressive state *capitalism*—across eastern Europe was quickly filled by the United States as the lone economic and political superpower. By the end of the 1990s what we had witnessed was a rapid consolidation, not diffusion, of global capital, this wealth largely concentrated in the United States—a country well on the road to recovering from its "Vietnam syndrome" and poised to escalate its use of military force (particularly where oil reserves and pipeline routes are at stake) and to safeguard its dominance (especially against rising regional economic stars such as Iran, India, Venezuela, and a potential global contender in China). Recall Stephen Peter Rosen writing calmly and unabashedly about the need for the United States to be ready to deploy "unconventional weapons" and "maximum amount of force" to trounce all challenges to its global "empire" (2002, 31)—and this not in a top-secret communiqué but in a glossy magazine to be read by Harvard's alumni and potential donors. While former activists lamented (as Arundhati Roy sums it up) that we have no choice except to fall into place between "the failed revolution and the shabby deal" (2001, 32) and while some postmodernists tried to salvage reason to rejoice in theoretical absence and linguistic instability, the Right was reveling in its narrative of real resurgence.

Or much more accurately, and much less despairingly, what we should say is that with the apparent triumph of free-market capitalism backed by U.S. military supremacy (news of the death of the state proving to be premature), two sides have emerged in—there is no way around this—binary opposition and struggle. On the one side, there are the champions of neoliberal globalization who claim that "transnational companies"—aided, as needed, by U.S.-led military interventions from Port au Prince to Baghdad—"are bringing the promise of a better life with increased security and prosperity" (summarized in Tickner 2001, 70). On the other side are neoliberalism's persistent discontents, from the Teamsters and "turtles" (environmentalists and students) who joined for the historic battle in Seattle at the end of the 1990s; to the masses of unemployed and underemployed Argentine workers who rose up against IMF austerity measures and toppled a rapid succession of neoliberal governments in 2001–2002; to the 10 million people who participated in the February 15, 2003, global protest against a U.S. invasion of Iraq; to the refusal of Iraqis themselves to knuckle under to occupation. Such struggles mark the persistence of emancipatory projects that did not die with the fall of the Paris Commune, the rise of the Third Reich, or the reversals of the tremendous victories—those precious fragments of democracy and solidarity—earlier won by labor, civil rights, and women's rights activists. Far from being dismissed as alarmingly aggressive or hopelessly naïve, such struggles should claim the attention of rhetoricians, especially once we understand that we do not have, and should not desire, the luxury of distance from this world.

Lessons from Activism School

Both contemporary maternalist and postmodern rhetorics were born of the falling expectations and waning struggles at the end of what had been a contentious and consequential era, and both rhetorics urge, I believe, a profound disengagement from the world we're faced with now. But from both strands of feminist rhetoric there is still something of use for those making their way through "activism school." From maternalist rhetoric, *if* we can undo the gendered assignments of argument and receptivity, we can learn how to make arguments within a coalition, both with a commitment to continuing relationship and with the sense of mutuality necessary to sustain diverse groups amid difficult debates. From third-sophistic rhetoric, *if* we can push past its fears of involvement with contextual demands for "rude calculation," we find the means for resisting too quick of a settlement upon problematic arguments. Imagine, for instance, if enough activists in 1991 had taken the slogan "Sanctions, Not Bombs" as a "naked point of vulnerability"; imagine if we had claimed a "moment of political hesitation" so that we could inquire into the future consequences of such an assertion. *If* third-sophistic rhetoric can be relocated within a dialectic between the twin responsibilities of assertion and exposition, it offers a useful vantage point.

But to put our rhetorical commitments and training to work in useful ways, we must also redirect both strands of feminist rhetoric away from what in academic feminism has been a near-exclusive focus on identity construction, performance, and representation and toward a fundamental, pressing, not at all old-fashioned question: How do we fight women's oppression? What full range of rhetorical practices and analytic insights are demanded? A full analysis—and inquiry beyond mass media visual representation—is what Susan George (2001b), like many prominent feminists, fell short of when she remarked that media images of burkaless Afghan women had led her to "rethink" her position against the U.S. war. A full range of rhetorical practices is what I failed to offer the student who, despite three semesters of work with me, could not create under pressure a sentence to support her feeling that this war was not liberating anybody. When we remove that tension between exposition *and* assertion, inquiry *and* argument, unsettling *and* concluding, we fall short of teaching all that's needed both to analyze and go up against systems of oppression, to assess a situation and, when needed, take a side.

This isn't to say, however, that I agree with Andrea Greenbaum, who argues for introducing our women students to the "robust character of what has traditionally been considered masculine discourse" in order to "fortify a woman's ability to succeed in the academy . . ." (2001, 164). Traditional lessons in "strategies of rhetorical combat" (154) focus on the individual rhetor who—in keeping with traditional social/academic structures and rewards—seeks to rise, lead, and succeed *alone*. Such lessons benefit only the small minority of students going on to jobs defined by autonomy and control. In fact—as I realized the other day when the majority of students in my upper-division Literacy Politics class said they expect to go on to service-sector jobs in education, health care, and social work—most of our students' futures will depend on what they learn now about collective, not individual, rhetorical strategies. How do we work in relationship with others and build democratic organizations through a valuing of agitation as much as affinity? On what basis can we question top-down expertise and assert the authority of our on-the-ground positions and knowledge? How do we unpack euphemism, get the facts, dissent from a (corporate media–produced) status quo while being mindful of, and strategic about, our own and others' vulnerabilities?

For possible answers to these questions, I bring into the classroom rhetors such as Arundhati Roy (2001), who lays out in the opening essays of *Power Politics* the tenets of a "rhetoric from below," and June Jordan (1989), whose "Civil Wars" highlights the fundamental debates—about democratic participation and leadership, spontaneity and planning—faced in any mass social movement or local committee. I also turn to examples of fighting slogans generated by women and men who speak through strike campaigns. For instance:

- *Cram Your Spam!* from UFCW Local P-9, which struck Hormel in Austin, Minnesota, in a heroic attempt to ward off the meatpacking industry's return to the scandalous conditions of *The Jungle*;

- *Part-Time America Doesn't Work!* from the Teamsters who, under the brief term of reform president Ron Carey, won their strike against UPS with part-time and full-time workers joining together to demand full employment and pay equity;

- *Nurses Care. Does Fletcher Allen?*, which sprang up on yard signs across my town, spelling doom for a major hospital's plan to roll back nurses' wages, increase patient loads and mandatory overtime, and even cut nurses' health care benefits.

Here we find what I mean by "rhetoric from below"—not from official policy makers but from and to those who feel the daily effects of official policy. It's a rhetoric my students are largely unfamiliar with or have learned, as Roy puts it in her critique of academic abstentionism, to disdain as "crude," "simple-minded," and "one-sided" (2001, 23). There *are* problems with activist rhetorics to unpack: the problem of the slogan "Sanctions, Not Bombs" sanctioning warfare in another guise; the problem of a *Hey-hey, ho-ho* chant becoming so familiar, it's no longer heard. There is also an art to finding the right words for the moment, as a colleague of mine discovered when—shortly after the collapse of Enron and amid growing local concern about administrative spending and faculty cuts at the University of Vermont—she coined what became our faculty union's rallying cry: "Money for the classroom/Not the boardroom." This is the art of practical discourse; this is the search for the available means to move a recalcitrant boss, to deter a bellicose presidential administration. On the ground with this search is where we, as rhetoricians, could place ourselves. We've got quite a lot to say, and a lot we could learn, about these issues of language.

We have a lot at stake, too, in engaging with, rather than accepting, the seeming distance between activism school and the academy. That apparent distance, as Roy points out, leads to a double denunciation of activist discourse as "crude" and "simple-minded" and academic discourse as lacking the "passion, the grit, the audacity, and, if necessary, the vulgarity to publicly take a political position" (2001, 23–24). Meanwhile, the academic and the activist, the realm of theory and the realm of practical struggle, live in closer quarters than our usual ivory tower/trenches formulation would have it. Consider, for instance, the issue of *College Composition and Communication* in which Diane Davis' (2001) explication of third-sophistic rhetoric, "Finitude's Clamor," appeared. In that same issue, though segregated in the special section for non-tenure-track faculty, is an article by Mike Evces (2001) called "Public Rhetoric for Academic Workers: Tips from the Front Lines." Here Evces offers "rhetorical strategies from the academic labor movement" (A3), including advice for building coalitions with student and labor groups and creating public events with "catchy chants" and presentations such as a "grade-in" to evaluate a university administration's performance in such areas as health benefits and child care (A3–A5). In this issue of *College Composition and Communication*, we have, on the one hand, a call for a "rhetoric of exposition" that leads to an "*unsettling* of certitude" (141, Davis' emphasis) and, on the other hand, examples of concrete provocations by the growing ranks of contingent faculty asserting their rights to *more* certainty and control when it comes to working conditions and terms of employment. If we can push against the segregationist divisions, there is a potentially tense and productive discussion that can take place here: a tense and productive discussion from which most of us in this field, regardless of the (increasingly dubious) privileges of rank, would benefit as we consider the daily antagonisms—including bosses, bills, layoffs—from which a life in school is no escape. What might reengagement with rhetoric as a practical art—the tactical questions of mediation and confrontation—teach us? Maybe that activism school is where we need to be.

Notes

1. See also Susan Jarrett's (1991b) "Feminism and Composition: The Case for Conflict," which appeared just as the post-Soviet, U.S.-dominated "new world order," with its initial emphasis on low-intensity resource wars fought under the guise of humanitarian intervention, was taking shape.

2. See Terry Eagleton (1997) for a more extended reading about the conditions of political defeat and pessimism that gave rise to postmodernism in the European academies; Nancy Chang (2002) for an outline of COINTELPRO that also places this program within the longer history of U.S. programs for political repression; and Sara Evans (1980) for a history of civil rights and radical New Left organizations that simultaneously radicalized and sidelined women activists.

INTERLUDE

The Hard Line

In 1972 a General Motors vice president and labor relations director offered this depiction of the American autoworker to *Washington Post* reporters Haynes Johnson and Nick Kotz in their classic exposé, *The Unions*:

> [H]e's got a hell of a nice home, two-car garage. He has two cars. He's got a trailer that he hooks on the back of one of those cars and he hauls his boat up north and he's got a hell of a big outboard motor on the back of that and does that on the weekend in summer. And he probably has a summer place up north too, on one of the fine lakes in northern Michigan.... This is a fellow who has aspired to material things and has them. (122; also qtd. in Georgakas and Surkin 1998, 106)

Academics, I would venture, have two primary ways of reading such a passage. One reading would have us accept the vice president's representation more or less at face value. Such images of the American working class—white, male, socially conservative, intellectually disengaged, defined by habits of consumption rather than by relationships of production, amply rewarded for "aspir[ing] to material things"—pervade academic and popular culture. The second way of reading, less influenced by Adorno and Archie Bunker and more by *Roger and Me*, would be more skeptical. In this reading, we would note the year: Social critics typically point to the oil crisis and subsequent recession of 1972–1973 as a visible marker of the end of the long post–World War II economic expansion, ushering in the "twilight" decade of the American

74

dream (Smith 1992). From this reading, we might conclude that if there had indeed been a "golden age" for the American autoworker, his (and her) fortunes were about to change.

But if we further investigated how the auto executive's rhetoric squares with reality, we would find, even at this moment on the eve of massive economic reordering, very evident and startling discrepancies including the following

- Production speedups. Between 1946 and 1970, as the U.S. auto workforce increased 36 percent, the number of cars these workers produced shot up 170 percent;

- Escalating death rates. With an average of sixty-five on-the-job deaths each day (half from heart attacks), data from the National Institute for Occupational Safety and Health show that in the late 1960s and early 1970s more autoworkers were killed or maimed each year in U.S. factories than U.S. soldiers were killed or wounded even in the worst years of Vietnam;

- Joint management and union indifference to deteriorating conditions especially for unskilled workers. These primarily Black, Arab, and Appalachian men and women were often segregated into the oldest plants and most dangerous and physically wearing jobs with pay rates well below $4 an hour.[1]

While auto executives lauded "automation" as driving the stunning gains in productivity, Black workers in General Motors (GM), Ford, and Chrysler's most segregated and dangerous plants pointed to what they called "niggermation"—assembly-line speedups combined with involuntary overtime and shortened preparation, cleanup, and rest times—as the hidden and human source of ramped-up production (Georgakas and Surkin, 85–86). "Death on the factory floor," is how former *Nation* senior editor and labor writer JoAnn Wypijewski (1999) sums it up: "16,000 dead, 63,000 sick and sidelined, 1.7 million deafened or hearing damaged—*every year*" (142, my emphasis). At Dodge Main, Chrysler's primary assembly plant and also among its oldest and most dangerous, Black workers labored in the most hazardous jobs up to twelve hours a day, seven days a week (Wypijewski 143). No wonder so much of Detroit's urban cultural production in this period voiced the misery of the *employed* as well as the *unemployed*. To paraphrase Ford line worker Joe L. Carter's 1965 blues lyric, workers did not mind working but they did mind dying. The popular portrait of the contented American autoworker is also a cultural production—one that papers over Carter's lyrics and the escalating assault on workers that presaged the coming neoliberal economic order.

But the GM executive's assertions try to paper over something else, too: Between 1968 and 1974, Detroit's top automakers were on the defensive, faced with mounting opposition from workers, particularly Black autoworkers who, far from contented and having received no redress through the United Auto Workers (UAW), organized for action on the shop floor. At a time when African American autoworkers made up 25 percent of UAW's 1.4 million members (Gannon 1968, 16), Black workers who first formed the Dodge Revolutionary Union Movement (DRUM) and later the League of Revolutionary Black Workers sought to join the rhetoric of Black Power, the anger of the Detroit Rebellion, and the inspiration of worldwide national liberation struggles with lessons from earlier generations of labor radicals. They did so, write movement biographers Dan Georgakas and Marvin Surkin (1998), in a bid for what they saw as real power: not only the power of language, images, and ideas but also the power of their positions as workers able to halt factory production, strike hospitals and schools, bring city services and transportation to a standstill. These were their most effective, collective means to oppose racism and remedy the ghastly dehumanizing conditions in Detroit's factories, schools, hospitals, and neighborhoods (4, 36).

League members thus viewed the production line, not cultural production, as their prime site for exercising persuasion. Nevertheless, these workers drew on multiple rhetorical means—including leaflets, pickets, and strikes; also including film, music, book clubs, mural art, even a takeover of the Wayne State University student newspaper—to draw exploited and oppressed groups together in a series of remarkable confrontations with Detroit's powerful industrial and political elite. This largely forgotten moment is one we should look to for African American and working-class contributions to rhetorical history and powerful examples of public contestation. That's a point I'll return to, but first more about the development of this radical union movement that by 1972 had the U.S. auto industry on the defensive.

The heady aspirations and bold argumentative stance of League members are apparent in their earliest salvos against their employers. Consider, for instance, the letter to Chrysler by autoworker General (his first name, not a military rank) G. Baker Jr. Baker wrote and published this letter in early May 1968 following a wildcat strike—a strike organized at the shop-floor level, without union authorization—at Detroit's Dodge

Main plant. When 4,000 Black men and women and Polish American women walked out, resulting in a shutdown of Chrysler production lines nationwide, the company retaliated against Black workers, including singling out and firing militants such as Baker. Baker opens his letter by calling out Chrysler for its long history of divide-and-conquer racism. Then, in the letter's closing paragraphs, Baker makes what amounts to a declaration of war:

> Let it further be understood that by taking the course of disciplining the strikers you have opened that struggle to a new and higher level and for this I sincerely THANK YOU. You made the decision to do battle with me and therefore to do battle with the entire black community in this city, this state, this country, this world of which I am a part. . . . You have made the decision to do battle, and that is the only decision that you will make. WE shall decide the arena and the time. You will also be held completely responsible for all of the grave consequences arising from your racist actions.
>
> Thank you again.
>
> p.s. You have lit the unquenchable spark. (qtd. in Georgakas and Surkin 1998, 21–22)

Baker's assertions—"That is the only decision that you will make" and "WE shall decide the arena and the time"—weren't baseless swagger; his "WE" was not an imagined collectivity brought into being by rhetorical fiat. Instead, this letter was anchored to the collective aspirations and growing confidence of African American workers at Dodge Main. Just a few months before, inspired by the Great Rebellion, the massive uprising of July 1967, some of these workers launched the first issue of the newspaper *Inner City Voice*. *ICV*'s first editorial argued that while the July insurrection had "administered a beating to the behind of the white power structure . . . [t]hink about it brother, things ain't hardly getting any better. The Revolution must continue" (Georgakas and Surkin 1998, 14). There was real urgency about this matter since the blue-ribbon commission calling itself the New Detroit Committee— which included the heads of Ford, GM, and Chrysler, all of whom had seen their plants shut down by the uprising—had already put forward its plan to raze the central Detroit neighborhood that was home to the city's Black, Appalachian, and Arab working class. The "you" that Baker confronted with his "WE" was formidable, organized, with a great deal of money at stake, and with the city's political, major media, and police forces all on its side. On the other hand, by the late 1960s the number of African Americans employed in U.S. auto factories was approaching half a million. It was the goal of the League to show that the Black liberation movement had not died with the assassination of Martin Lurther King, Jr., and that as workers, African Americans had the means to carry on and escalate the struggle.

The need for emancipatory struggle was expressed in *ICV*'s incendiary headlines decrying auto factory exploitation ("MICHIGAN SLAVERY"), police violence ("COPS ON RAMPAGE—14 YEAR OLD SHOT"), and horrific poverty ("GIRL LOSES EYE RUNNING FROM RATS") (qtd. in Georgakas and Surkin 1998, 15). The League's program for change was also expressed in *ICV* editorials offering incisive, often beautifully poetic analyses of present conditions and practical arguments for a way forward:

> . . . the working class suffers from the conversion of the institution of the union itself into a part of the boss' apparatus. The sacred contract, once viewed as the register of the workers' gains, has become the written record of their subordination to the power of capital. . . . In this wasteland of labor's twisted hopes, where else could redemption come than from among those whose interests were at every turn sacrificed so that another, more favored group could make peace with the masters? Where else, indeed, but from among the black workers at the automobile manufacturing infernos of the city of Detroit? (qtd. in Georgakas and Surkin 1998, 37)

These were arguments that put African Americans as workers at the very center of change, not only as a group suffering mightily within the "infernos" of this system but also as the vanguard, the group with the drive and means to reverse the downslide of U.S. labor as a whole.

Through the summer of 1968, Black workers at the Dodge Main plant, now organized into the Dodge Revolutionary Union Movement (DRUM), would provide multiple demonstrations of their argument, shutting down production at Dodge Main four more times, the "Burn, baby, burn!" cry of the Detroit rebellion now re-presented as "DRUM, baby, DRUM" (*Finally Got the News* 1970). The first organizers at Dodge Main, write Georgakas and Surkin,

> had no intention of sharing the economic pie with Chrysler, and it had no intention of producing cars for profit. DRUM wanted workers to have all the pie and to produce goods only for social needs. (36)

DRUM's belief that 1968 Detroit was ripe for a revolutionary takeover of workplaces and neighborhoods ran ahead of actual conditions; however, its members proclaimed these goals while also advancing immediate demands for an end to racist and sexist discrimination, for more worker control, and for Black worker representation in the plants and in UAW (1998, 36).

The UAW (which League members claimed stood for "U Ain't White!!"), accustomed to ensuring smooth predictability in management–labor relations while securing small gains primarily for established generations of Polish American workers, was hardly pleased as from the spring of 1968 through the summer of 1973, pushing the stop button became a favored way for workers to deal with grievances on the line. When the DRUM members ran in a local union election in order to gain an even wider hearing for their arguments, the UAW sent police armed with hatchets and mace to drive them from the union hall. "Finally got the news/how your dues are being used!" raps Baker at a picket by Black workers outside a UAW convention. "Be bad, be bad, be bad/Can't do nothing if you ain't bad!" (*Finally Got the News* 1970). No matter the setback, DRUM members framed the argument to draw more people into bucking the UAW officialdom, standing up together against racist foremen, and joining, or organizing, a RUM. The idea of the revolutionary union movement and its use of the wildcat strike would spread to all three of the major automakers with the formation of DRUM II (Dodge Truck), FRUM (Ford Rouge), ELRUM (Chrysler Eldon Avenue), CADRUM (Cadillac Fleetwood), among others. Beyond the auto industry, there was also NEWRUM at the *Detroit News*, UPRUM at UPS, and HRUM for area health care workers (Wypijewski 1999, 144).

This movement of radical shop-floor organizations, which by 1969 had affiliated together into the League of Revolutionary Black Workers, did not rise spontaneously from the ashes of the Great Rebellion. The lead organizers had long been participants in events and study circles sponsored by small socialist groups that had survived the McCarthyist purges (Georgakas 2002). The League's members knew their labor and radical history. The echoes in Baker's postscript to Chrysler—"You have lit the unquenchable spark"—of Chicago anarchist August Spies—who, sentenced to death following the May Day 1886 mass strike, declared, "Here you will tread upon a spark, but here and there, and behind you, and in front of you, the flames will blaze up. It is a subterranean fire. You cannot put it out"—are not coincidental. In a dramatic example of literacy sponsorship (Brandt 2001b), League members had also met or corresponded with C. L. R. James, James Boggs, Amiri Baraka, Malcolm X, and Che Guevara. John Watson, who founded *Inner City Voice* and later won editorship of the Wayne State University daily newspaper, *The South End*, would travel to Italy to meet with radical autoworkers in Antonio Gramsci's former home of Turin. He would use V. I. Lenin's *Where to Begin* to argue that the League devote resources to producing a revolutionary newspaper as a key tool in fueling and coordinating activity. The League's newspaper would, as an early editorial promised, "take the hard line" (qtd. in Georgakas and Surkin 1998, 146). It would also constantly connect revolutionary activity and ideas with the conditions and questions of everyday people and everyday life.

In an early scene of the League's largely self-made documentary, we see John Watson in the editorial office of *Inner City Voice* framed by enormous images of Che Guevara, Mao Tse-tung, and Frantz Fanon, identifying the League with struggles for national liberation worldwide. Given Detroit's multivalent history of radical cultural production— poetry, blues, mural art—the bookstore founded by the League also stocked a great deal more than publications from Peking; and the documentary *Finally Got the News* (1970) opens with a rich visual montage to tell, through the rhetorical power of images and drumbeats, the interlinked story of African Americans' and labor's struggles. As that opening montage underscores, League members such as Baker and Watson were committed to expressing Black Power *as* workers' power. While expressing solidarity with the Maoist-influenced Black Panther Party—their first issue of the *South End* at Wayne State featured a black panther on either side of the masthead—they did not orient, as the Panthers did, on the unemployed but instead on plant workers with power at the point of production. Thus on the masthead of the *South End*, editor John Watson and coeditor Nick Medvecky (a white Appalachian student and League supporter) added to the Black Panther logo the assertion "One class-conscious worker is worth a hundred students." It was an assertion not meant to belittle Wayne State students, many of whom attended school part-time while working full-time, but instead to underscore workers' positions at the gears of the economy.

Today, when I introduce *Detroit: I Do Mind Dying* to students in my U.S. Literacy Politics class, it is the third chapter, "We Will Take the Hard Line," that holds their attention. There is the drama, of course, of a revolutionary group taking over and thoroughly politicizing a student newspaper, and particularly a student paper with a circulation rivaling the city's other top dailies. (Declaring that university resources belong to the wider public, League members also distributed the *South End* to factories, hospitals, and schools regionwide.) There's strong appeal in how the *South End* staff, many in their early to mid-twenties, stood up to against the Goliath of establishment Detroit: When critics charged the paper with editorial bias, staffer Mike Hamlin shot back, "There are two views, of course. The right and the wrong. You wouldn't want us to print the wrong one, would you?" (qtd. in Georgakas and Surkin 1998, 45).

But what students in my classes return to again and again is how the League went about its radical work in such a practical, down-to-earth way—not only taking that hard line but also winning broad support so that when other newspapers, politicians, the auto factory heads, and conservative university alumni clamored for Watson's dismissal, university administrators found their hands tied. As Georgakas and Surkin explain, Watson, Medvecky, and their staff were careful to meet each deadline, stay within budget, break no enforceable rules. Moreover, by encouraging all progressive groups to write for the *South End* and by dedicating special issues to women's liberation, Palestine, resistance to the Greek military coup, conditions at Detroit General Hospital, and so forth, the League created a radical united front. Granting ample space to sports and social events, it even won the support of the school's sports enthusiasts and fraternities ignored by previous editors.

In this way, the League drew the support of many layers of people in central Detroit who increasingly identified with the group's revolutionary aims. Watson and Medvecky, Wypijewski observes, "advanc[ed] DRUM's agenda without cutting threads to the common culture" (1999, 152). Indeed, League members, in all of their activities—from protest sit-downs in UAW's Solidarity House to each issue of the *South End*—wanted to make sure they offered concrete actions that ordinary workers could see themselves as participating in and leading. They didn't want, Georgakas and Surkin emphasize, to be seen as "movement heavies"—romantic, admirable, unemulatable (1998, 61). This wasn't a revolution to be carried out, Weatherman-style, by small militarized cells but instead to be won, fight by fight, by growing group of workers who were also part of and needed support from neighborhoods, churches, schools, community organizations. The impact of the such ongoing work on mass public opinion formation is especially apparent in the case of James Johnson. A Black autoworker at the Eldon Avenue plant, Johnson was not affiliated with the League but was defended by the League—in court, press conferences, rallies, and in the pages of *Inner City Voice*—when, facing suspension for refusing a production speedup, he shot and killed two foremen and one white worker (Georgakas and Surkin 1998, 4). Under the banner "Chrysler pulled the trigger," the League took the jury to the Eldon Avenue plant to see for themselves conditions there. Not only was the jury's verdict not guilty but also a subsequent jury ordered Chrysler to pay Johnson workers' compensation (Georgakas and Surkin 1998, 10–11).

Where the League's united front stopped was at the shop floor. Though League members were not Black nationalists—Watson explaining in a 1968 issue of *Radical America* that the League stood "against a separate state in which a black capitalist class exploits a black proletariat" (qtd. in Georgakas and Surkin 1998, 59)—and though their publications stressed the imperative of multiracial working-class solidarity, they made the tactical decision to organize the RUMs for and by African American workers alone. Why the League decided, at least for the short term, on a separatist strategy, becomes clear in the documentary *Finally Got the News* (1970). In a sympathetic segment focusing on Appalachian workers, an elderly white worker speaks of the hardships and grievances that Black and Appalachian workers share. Then he concludes, "Everyone else is getting their share. Certain groups are doing good—the colored and the mothers on welfare." As the camera pulls back, we hear John Watson: "We are for uplifting the working class as a whole," but "Many white workers end up being counterrevolutionaries in the face of a daily oppression." It is notable here that Watson says "in the face of a daily oppression" and not "in the face of a daily *privilege*." The idea of privileged white workers, even the Polish American male workers in skilled jobs who were the ostensible beneficiaries of the UAW's trade-offs, shows up nowhere in the League's handful of biographies and its documentary. Instead, the makers of *Finally Got the News* assess the apparatus—the promotion of racist resentment by the vitriolic George Wallace, the mass consumerist enticements to a life of debt, interviews with white and Black workers about how segregation operates in the factories and with working-class white and Black students about how segregation operates in the city's learning-to-labor schools—that divides and domesticates.

When I bring accounts of and documents from the League of Revolutionary Black Workers to my classes, it is in large part because League participants were remarkably accomplished rhetors as well as theorists of communication, Marxist strategy, and social change. (I say "remarkably" because their wide-ranging activity took place not only within the rousing conditions of the Great Rebellion and the Black Power movement but also despite the bone- and soul-crushing conditions of their workplaces and neighborhoods.) They practiced rhetoric not as "full-time" activists or professional policy makers but as workers, veterans, and students. In making their arguments, League members also used multiple voice registers and multiple means for delivery; they understood the power of the visual, the aural, the poetic. Their rhetoric wasn't moderate, and for anyone who wanted to compromise with Henry Ford II or Walter Reuther's idea of the UAW, what they had to say wasn't comfortable. The League was also not without significant problems that are worth working through in an advanced class concerned with grassroots public argument. For instance, while members included a considerable number of women workers and *Finally Got the News* devotes a segment to women's oppression (awkwardly tacked on at the end), women were not promoted to leadership roles. And, of course, evident to anyone who has visited Detroit in recent years, the League did not win its bid for the city's future. What the League did accomplish, however, was a resuscitation of the radical labor movement's persuasive tactics that had, with the McCarthy purges, been all but lost. League members also forced the UAW to confront the issue of racism, and their analysis of how corporate America and political elites roll back conditions for all—at work, at school, in public services and neighborhoods—by playing ethnic and racial groups against each other could be clarifying for antiracist activists today.

But how useful is such a history for us today? What about the common view that we live in a postindustrial society too radically different for past labor struggles and persuasive strategies to be of more than historical interest? These are questions I'll take up in the chapters to come, but for the moment, consider: when we learn that plans to rebuild New Orleans leave out most of who its actual residents were; when we read that globally prosperous corporations such as GM and Delphi are using the cover of bankruptcy to dump union jobs and pension plans; as my city school board announces dramatic budget cuts that hit only the town's working-class and new refugee elementary schools; or as the new president of my university lays out a vision that includes twenty-one vice presidents, a 25-percent increase in the student body, and pink slips for more than a dozen long-time Education and Extension faculty—when we consider all this and more, it seems apparent that there is much at stake for us in learning about this chapter in labor, urban, and African American history.

Notes

1. Production, injury, death, and wage rates are all quoted in Georgakas and Surkin 1998, 85–89.

2. Carter's lyrics are quoted in *Detroit: I Do Mind Dying* (Georgakas and Surkin 1998, 107–108), as well as featured in the documentary about Black autoworkers' struggles against exploitation and oppression in *Finally Got the News* (1970). Publisher unknown, "Please Mr. Foreman" was originally released as an independent label 45 rpm in 1968 and later appeared on *Work's Many Voices*, Volume II (released in 1984 by the John Edwards Memorial Forum and distributed by Down Home Music/ Arhoolie Records).

4

Making Space

You can't drink the water
of the lake
you must drive somewhere else to buy
bottles of water to drink

—JUNE JORDAN (1985)

Arresting Moments

Before the end of my Spring 2003 women's studies seminar, I asked
students how they would create audiences for their final projects. Having
spent our semester studying contemporary women rhetors such as Amira
Hass and Arundhati Roy as well as attending campus forums on the
pending assault against Iraq, we knew that exercising our public voices
could be heady, daunting, and consequential. One student reported that
when she'd raised questions at home about the U.S. government's aims
in Iraq, her mother had angrily replied, "If that's how you feel, you're
not welcome in this house." Another student wondered how she could
counter sexist posters that had popped up in the campus library. A third
student, working on a comic book for teen AIDS/HIV activists, wrestled
with how to represent the "face" of AIDS without racial, sexual, and class
stereotyping. I brought out several T-shirts my husband and I had spent
the weekend making. One showed a map of Iraq, its major cities replaced
by corporations (Figure 4–1). Across the map in large bold print was
the word (NEO)LIBERATED. Students in the seminar evaluated this
example of "visual communication" (George 2002), debating whether

"neoliberated" clarified or—too much an academic insider's term—obscured the shirt's antiwar argument.

It was about this time that Katie came through the door, breathless, apologetic, and holding a stack of what she described as June Jordan–styled "found" poems about her semester's major concerns—the buildup to the invasion of Iraq; the bulldozing death of Palestinian solidarity activist Rachel Corrie; the challenge of forming a position on such controversies amid conflicting reports and limited information—and her first attempts at asserting and arguing a stance, at informing and persuading an audience beyond herself and a handful of friends. One poem, titled "Action Alert: Bush Agenda" (Figure 4–2), was composed as a ransom note with jagged, multicolored words cut from magazines and pasted crazily across the page. Katie explained that she might perform these poems in a city poetry slam or put them on posters designed to look like meeting announcements. She looked at my T-shirts with interest.

"Something like that," she said. "I want these poems to be *out there*, not just in a chapbook where my friends will read them and say, 'Oh, Katie wrote a poem. Isn't that nice.'"

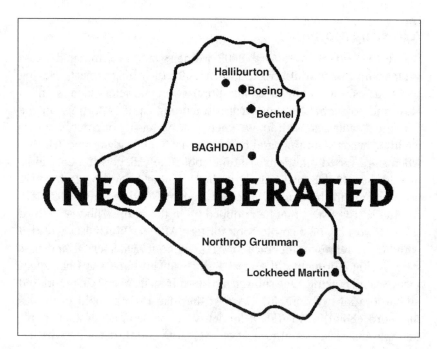

Figure 4–1

Figure 4–2.

The next morning when I checked my email, I found this message from Katie, sent late the night before:

I finished my ransom poem, made color copies, and then posted them around downtown tonight. However, I was stupid enough to post blatantly on a metal utility box on the corner of Main St. and S. Winooski, and a cop drove by and saw my friend (my not-so-trusty accomplice) and me walking away. I started to pick up my pace, since I knew he would quickly pull us over. . . . Yep, he got us.

Katie described sitting in the cruiser's backseat while the cop demanded her school and permanent addresses,

Content can land one in jail if it's deemed to have "the effect of force" (Schenck 1919, 51). "The most stringent protection of free speech," wrote Oliver Wendell Holmes in the Supreme Court's unanimous decision to uphold the espionage conviction of Socialist Party official Charles Schenck, "would not protect a man in falsely shouting fire in a theater" (52). Schenck, of course, had not actually shouted "Fire!," but had distributed leaflets urging resistance to the World War I draft.

then warned that next time she would receive a $50 ticket for each poster hung in a "nondesignated area." Both thrilling and alarming to Katie, he also read the poem, or a portion of it because its opening and closing lines were left behind when he tore it from the utility box. "Why did you write this?" Katie reported he wanted to know. "What do you mean by putting this up?"

Though in the end Katie was released and though her email to me concluded with a breezy, "I plan to do more tomorrow . . . I'll keep you posted (pun intended)," my heart continued to pound. This run-in with the local police was the unanticipated result of an assignment I had given. Did I know Katie's rights in such a situation? Could she, for instance, have refused to get into the cruiser? Was she required to give this cop her permanent address? Although postmodernism might train us to look askance at "rights discourse" as a sign of vestigial liberal humanism, the question of whether we have First and Fourth Amendment protections, especially in our increasingly privatized, "quality-of-life"-zoned downtowns, is far from passé. And what if this cop had seen the left-behind opening and closing lines to Katie's poem? These lines specifically addressed the president of the United States and ended with the warning—or was it a threat?: "We will contact you/Your time is up." Weeks before, a local rap artist had been visited by FBI agents who interpreted lyrics on his locally produced CD as threatening the president's life. What constitutes a threat? Had Katie's poem crossed a line? If yes, what would it mean for her to revise it, to post only in designated areas? Or, conversely, what would it mean for her to make a calculated decision to challenge the designations? Given that my class had not prepared her to make a calculated decision, what would such preparation look like?

This chapter chronicles my efforts, albeit not always successful and complete, to learn the history and name the tools that students in a public writing classroom need not only to imagine and build rhetorical space but also to anticipate and think through the discursive *and* extra-discursive obstacles they'll face in attempting to do so. By focusing on the

The first federal court rulings on speech and assembly held that the argumentative forms working-class and oppressed groups have developed and relied on—leafleting, soapboxing, pickets—inevitably lead to violence. Initially courts refused to grant these forms and forums any protections. One judge ruled that there can be "no such thing as peaceful picketing any more than there can be chaste vulgarity" (Atchison 1905, 584). Later courts sought a "workable language of control" (Mitchell 2003, 70), making a distinction between (protected) speech and (unprotected) conduct.

"extracurricular" rhetoric that takes shape around kitchen tables and in rented rooms (Gere 1994)—also in city streets and public parks, on picket lines and graffitied walls—I want to add to the growing body of work that could reorient us from regarding rhetoric as a specialized *techne*, to understanding and teaching rhetoric as a *mass, popular art*. Here rhetoric is redefined from the property of a small economic and political elite to the public practice of ordinary people, who make up the country's multi-ethnic, working-class majority in their press for relief, reform, and radical change.

I also want to address two interrelated silences in our current literature on public writing and public-sphere theory. First is the silence regarding the steady conversion of public spaces and resources into private, for-profit property. Such privatization has been the chief legacy of well over twenty years of neoliberal economic policy—"capitalism with the gloves off" (McLaren and Farahmandpur 2002, 37)—that has only intensified under the guise of reinforcing "national security." Under the thrall of postmodernists who would teach us to see horizontal and scattered pockets of domination and resistance, academics are in danger of missing (or through our silence colluding with) the all-too-real consolidation and application of state-backed corporate power that has been the chief legacy of our new world order. That's why I find it hopeful and heartening that so many compositionists are directing their attention toward working with students on public writing out of a belief that such writing can *matter* in tangible ways. But at a moment when—from the malling of suburbia to the vertical integration of radio, television, cable, film, music, and print outlets into a few media monopolies—we face dramatically shrinking material and virtual space, we must also examine the twentieth-century's contradictory legacy: On one side, the free-speech battles and subsequent Supreme Court decisions that have *liberalized* our speech and assembly rights; on the other, the economic and social policies known as *neoliberalism* that have greatly reduced the locations in which we are able to exercise these rights. It's neoliberalism's dramatic encroachments upon

Virtual reality is not a sufficient counter to or substitute for increasingly privatized and regulated geographic space. Although information technologies and the virtual communities they create played organizing roles in such historic events as the student takeover of Tiananmen Square in 1989 and the global demonstrations against a U.S. assault on Iraq in 2003, it was the physical taking of Tiananmen Square that made possible its transformation into a space representing democracy (Mitchell 2003, 148). And it was to prevent such a transformation that New York City cops herded thousands of frustrated antiwar protestors into pens on February 15, 2003, far from the rally they'd traveled many hundreds of miles to attend.

voice, visibility, and movement that lead me to sum up our current moment, in the United States particularly, as "privatized," (though this is a term we must also join much of the rest of the world in disputing, understanding that publicity rights have never been a given and have only been won through struggle).

Here, intervening in a second silence becomes crucial: the silence surrounding the rich history of in-the-street working-class rhetorical action against both the interests of capital and the state forces in place to protect capitalist interests. Neoliberalism—intent not only on privatizing public space (such as downtowns), services (such as education), and resources (such as electricity) but also on reprivatizing (as an individual boss's prerogative) hard-won environmental protections and labor rights—can appear to us as a backlash against the Keynesian welfare state. But we can also see it as a return to pre–New Deal arrangements between bosses and workers, as the return of the (limited) welfare state to its former status of watchtower state, charged with preserving and protecting the interests of a propertied minority. It's here that we most need to recover working-class rhetorical memory: Because if we can resist the common academic assertion that we live today in a radically distinct postmodern, postindustrial society, we can return to capitalism's long history for examples not only of brutal assaults on the rights and needs of workers but also of the creative and persistent ways in which ordinary people have organized to claim living room. As we face heavily regulated, restricted-access publics, we need this history to give us clues about working with others to create rhetorical space while anticipating the resistance that comes—as Katie found—from even the slightest challenge.

Class Actions

"Involving students in 'public writing' is fraught with headaches of all sorts," acknowledges Christian Weisser (2002) at the start of *Moving*

Today's celebrated urban planners eschew the reformism of a Frederick Law Olmstead, who designed New York's Central Park to teach "courtesy, self-control, and temperance" to the urban working class (Davis 1992, 156). Instead, they restrict and discourage public use through postmodern architecture, electronic surveillance, and physical as well as zoned barriers. In the neoliberalized American city, quasi-free market economic policies join with an architect's ingenuity and the firm hand of the state to keep immiserated populations in order and (when not on the job as low-wage service workers) out of sight.

Beyond Academic Discourse: Composition Studies and the Public Sphere (xi). Even the initial task of helping students identify forums beyond the ubiquitous "letter to the editor" assignment is greatly complicated by the fact that forums don't simply exist; they must be created. As Susan Wells (1996) explains, "Our public sphere is attenuated, fragmented, and colonized; so is everyone else's. All speakers and writers who aspire to intervene in society face the task of constructing a responsive public" (328–9). Later in this chapter I'll return to the formulation that *all* speakers face a similar task in constructing a public because the difficulties and stakes of public-sphere building are very much a matter of one's gender, sexuality, income, race, and immigration status, and also because one's potential means, strategies, and power in public-sphere building can be even more particularly a matter of one's class location.

What's important here, however, is Wells' crucial emphasis on the need for teachers who want to imagine public forums for their students to "*build, or take part in building,* such a public sphere" (1996, 326, my emphasis).

This is headachy, heart-pounding work, to be sure, especially because this building takes place under the conditions of neoliberal privatization, supported by a rhetoric of protective restriction and surveillance. The rhetoric—and reality—of restriction and surveillance (not only of the general population but also of university classrooms where students are presumed to require "protection" from professors' "liberal bias") has indeed been stepped up since September 11, 2001. However, urban historian Mike Davis (1992, 1998) and cultural geographer Don Mitchell

Strolling through a festive outdoor mall, such as the privately managed Church Street Marketplace in Burlington, Vermont, may give us the sense of being in public, experiencing the variety of people and perspectives that is the hallmark of city life (Young 1990, 119). But notice who is absent (or banned) from such a space. Next, try this: Drive (or test the public transportation) to the outlying "Bantustans" (Davis 1998, 393) from which an upscale market draws its low-wage labor force.

(2003) point out that it's over the past thirty years that our parks, plazas, shopping malls, and downtown sidewalks have been locked down against the homeless, drug dealers, peddlers, and a student such as Katie seeking, without a permit, to exercise her political voice. The renewed interest among compositionists in public writing thus comes at a moment when the promotion of public rhetoric is most urgent and also most difficult (or at least more difficult than at any point since the McCarthy period). Yet it's also because of the difficulty of going public that public writing advocates underscore remarkable rewards: the reward of "animated, engaged, and at times feverishly pitched discussions about the ways that students use their discursive talents to make voices heard" (Weisser 2002, xi); the reward of student projects leading to substantive action beyond the classroom, action that in turn reinvigorates a teacher's belief that one really can "teach for change" (Pough 2002, 484).

There's also rewarding learning that takes place when we and our students consider the myriad ways in which our attempts to make voices heard are *foiled*. Such discussions can lead students and teachers to reflect on ingrained lessons about who is and isn't authorized to speak on a topic. For instance, one of Katie's classmates, Jayme, explained to the class that she is pursuing a biology degree to gain the scientific credentials her parents had lacked when they tried to defend their small farm against the development of a neighboring slate quarry. Discussion can also highlight the pitfalls of arguing with intimate audiences. Another classmate, Cassie, described feeling demoralized when her boyfriend and his roommates laughed off her objections to *The Man Show*. Class discussion also needs to focus—as my women's studies seminar failed to do—on the policed boundary between permitted and prohibited acts of speech and protest. A third classmate faced possible academic sanctions for her decision to go public by hoisting an antiwar flag on the campus green without first applying for a permit and also without seeking permission to remove the American flag that had been flying there. I'm not recommending that we encourage students to risk penalties for their words. Rather, as I reflect on these stories from that semester, I'm disturbed by how frequently students felt (in a class drawing out no specific lessons to the contrary) that going public means going it alone. It's much easier, after all, for a university

> *Creating a public sphere often involves getting not only physical but also disorderly, acting against physical barricades and enforceable laws designed to limit how many gather and what is said. Yet it's only speech, not embodied action, that is protected by the First Amendment (Mitchell 2003, 54).*

At "The World Says No to War" rally, I stand at a barricade reinforced by 25 armed policemen. Hundreds of these barricades have been set up to prevent some 500,000 peaceful demonstrators from reaching the rally site. I don't stand alone but with an organized group, 500 strong. First we chant: "The whole world is watching and they're on our side!" Then we chant and push: "Whose streets? Our streets!" The cops know they've lost. The barricade topples, they stand aside, and we march unobstructed to the rally.

administration to sanction one student for her speech than to sanction one hundred.

What these moments from that semester also tell me is that *rhetorical space*—that is, public space with the potential to operate as a persuasive public sphere—is created not through good-intentioned civic planning or through the application of a few sound and reasonable rhetorical rules of conduct. Ordinary people *make* rhetorical space through a concerted, often protracted struggle for visibility, voice, and impact against powerful interests that seek to render them invisible. People *take* and *make* space in acts that are simultaneously verbal and physical. But, notes Don Mitchell (2003), giving a new application to Marx's aphorism, we rarely do so under conditions of our own choosing (35). Hence images of antiwar protestors facing down lines of cops in riot gear. Hence a twenty-one-year-old female college student facing four recalcitrant young men as she argues that *The Man Show* brings into their private living room the public problems of sexism and misogyny.

At the end of her influential essay on teaching public writing, Wells (1996) speculates about the texts that might be composed in classes where students not only study public rhetoric but also practice it in ways useful to their lives. "Some of our students' most useful writing might remind us of a 'zine; some might sound like a church bulletin. My guess, though, is that it won't sound much like E. B. White" (340). In addition to the form and tone such writings might take, Katie and her classmates prompt me to speculate with Wells about what the *delivery* of such writing needs to look like. A discussion with students about delivery might include naming the varying goals of a public

When contract negotiations stalled and our faculty union voted to launch a public campaign, several members counseled us to stick to "what we do best"—making reasoned arguments supported by solid, speaks-for-itself evidence. So we created careful charts, called press conferences. When the press didn't show, some of us got the okay to hold an educational "bake sale" featuring such goodies as Rice Krispies Temps ("cheaper by the dozen") and Vice Provost Cupcakes ("Now 40 percent more!").

argument, including the potential goal of deepening one's commitment to a position *even if* an immediate audience (such as Cassie's boyfriend and his friends) isn't likely, in that moment, to be swayed. A discussion about delivery might also include a definition of "culture jamming" and other anarchist-individualist practices of direct action that shaped Katie's after-dark, dressed-in-black forays downtown. Here we should consider the recent history behind this figure of the lone artistic revolutionary: the post–May 1968 disillusionment that led the "situationists" (and academics such as Michel Foucault and Theodore Adorno) to focus on autonomous culture workers—not a united working class with the potential to halt, and transform, a society's production, transportation, and services—as the locus of change. Important too are seemingly procedural topics such as whether to seek a permit for a public-space performance. As students and teachers ponder in the fullest way possible the rhetorical canon of delivery, there might even be (as one student suggested at the end of the women's studies seminar) training in civil disobedience or at the very least a guest lecturer from the ACLU.

In imagining such a classroom, I find myself very far not only from "On a Florida Key"—where E. B. White (1982/1941) gently rejected arguments for intervening in Jim Crow because desegregation would, in his mellow middle-class vacationer's view, come about in its own good time—but also from the academic conference or debate, our usual stand-ins for the idea of public rhetoric. Instead, when I bring to class a newspaper put out by migrant workers organizing for labor and civil rights or when a student asks about a bumper-sticker slogan—the battle, for instance, between the anti–civil unions *Take Back Vermont* and the pro–civil unions *Take Vermont Forward*—I find myself much

The "Balance the Budget" Bake Sale brought favorable top-story coverage on the 6 o'clock news and endorsements from student groups. It also brought expressions of concern from colleagues who worried about this "stooping to theatrics" and "mentioning money."

closer to the *actual* rhetorical struggles surrounding me and my students. However, by extending the common understanding of public rhetoric to include examples of "rhetoric from below,"[1] I'm not simply creating a more inclusive sense of what constitutes rhetorical action. We don't just add such argumentative forms to the usual examples of "rhetoric from above" such as a presidential address or newspaper editorials. What we do instead is create palpable tension between *individual* and *mass*, *legislative* and *extra-legislative*, *ruling-class* and *working-class* argumentative forums and forms.

Labor economist Michael Zweig (2001) estimates that 62 percent of the U.S. adult population are in the working class, with limited control over the nature and pace of their work. Although Zweig excludes (as I would not) nurses, social workers, and teachers from his definition of working class, considering these as middle-class professions defined by "autonomy and independence," he stresses that many of these jobholders have "experienced the progressive deskilling of their once-professional occupations in recent decades, with their work process increasingly dictated by authority from above" (xii).

To be sure, *ruling class* (to describe the group controlling the means of production plus the social apparatus needed to legitimize and reproduce control) and *working class* (to describe the group that must sell its mental or physical, skilled or unskilled labor power in exchange for a wage or salary on which to live) aren't words we're accustomed to uttering these days in academic and political circles. Even my state's "socialist" congressional representative speaks of "middle-class and working families"—never "the working class." When scholars in composition and rhetoric use the phrase "working class," it's typically to describe what is assumed to be a *minority* cultural identity, defined not by one's relationship to production and on-the-job control over the nature and pace of one's work but defined instead (in a selective appropriation of the work of Pierre Bourdieu) by a supposed set of habits and tastes. Then comes the argument for or against a mission of "embourgeoisement" (O'Dair 2003)—for or against assimilation into the *presumed* middle-class social majority that writing instruction and its instructors are assumed together to represent.

Left out of formulations of composition as an inherently "middle-class enterprise" (Bloom 1996) is an acknowledgment of the actual material conditions of most composition instructors: Most—including, increasingly, those of us on the tenure track—are vulnerable to top-down increases in workload and reduction in benefits. A similar future of production speedups, compensation cutbacks, and job/social insecurity await the majority of our students. This is a point I try to dramatize throughout this book—the difference it can make for us and for our students when we approach class as determined not by income or lifestyle but by one's *available means* for safeguarding terms and conditions of work, one's *available means* for influencing public policy and for fighting exploitation and oppression. Here, however, my point is primarily historical: When class is dropped out of public-sphere theories and histories, what also gets dropped out is the past century's major battles for public space and public speech. Even more, we miss that what was

Radical labor and women's histories don't proceed along separate tracks: Angered at being barred from the 1937 Flint, Mich., sit-downs, women organized speakers' bureaus, carried bullhorns, and, forming a 350-strong Women's Auxiliary Brigade to battle the police, also carried baseball bats (Brecher 1997, 216–17). Brigade cofounder Genora (Johnson) Dollinger later reflected, "The woman that had participated actively became a different type of woman . . . They carried themselves with a different walk, their heads were high, and they had confidence in themselves" (Zinn and Arnove 2004, 349). Thus women's (bullhorn- and bat-wielding) rhetorical practices were central to the strike, and the strike was central to creating new spaces and attitudes for women's rhetoric.

at stake in these battles—from Seattle in 1919 to Seattle in 1999—was the ability of a whole class of people to stand up as public selves at all.

Prior to World War I, in fact, the Supreme Court declined to hear any First Amendment cases. These cases, as Don Mitchell (2003, Chapter 2 *passim*) explains, were left to lower court judges who routinely ruled that workers are the property of their employers, property whose behavior employers have the right to control, including with police force. Additionally, Mitchell explains, lower courts ruled that—perhaps especially because the majority of urban workers were first-generation immigrants, bringing with them not only the languages and customs but also the radical traditions of their former homes—workers are by definition irrational and thus outside civil society. Subsequent Supreme Court minority and majority opinions—such as Oliver Wendell Holmes' oft-cited assertion that "the ultimate good desired is better reached by free trade in ideas" (*Abrams* 1919, 630) or William S. Brennan's defense of a "marketplace" for ideas (*CBS v. DNC* 1973, 193)—have had important liberalizing effects. They've also set, as Mitchell (2003) points out, the decidedly conservative and commercial cornerstones of our dominant assumptions about the proper (or improper) exercise of free speech and the appropriate (or inappropriate) use of public space. Moreover, these rulings have sought to define those times of "clear and present danger" (*Schenck* 1919, 52) that make permissible a government's intervention in the content of speech. Indeed, the Supreme Court's first three free-speech decisions, all handed down in 1919, upheld rather than overturned the espionage convictions of antiwar socialists—including, most famously, Eugene Debs (1918), who was accused of "obstructing the war" for suggesting in a speech that draft resistance is a right rather than a crime. Subsequent First Amendment decisions, argues Mitchell (2003), need to be read for the ways in which they not only liberalize interpretations

On summer Saturdays Burlington's City Hall Park welcomes licensed vendors to its farmers' market but bars the "marketing of ideas" by any individuals and groups looking for public exchange and debate. Even the park's perimeter is off-limits, as members of a migrant workers' rights group found when police halted them from gathering petition signatures just outside the park. Market organizers, police explained, have paid for not only the park but the atmosphere that surrounds it.

of speech and assembly but also remain concerned with controls and limits. This is especially the case wherever the free exchange and exercise of ideas by one class of people—from an antiwar soapbox speech to a factory sit-down—interferes with the freedom of another class to obtain and safeguard raw materials, labor, markets, or even (in the case of a festival marketplace or touristy farmers' market) *atmosphere.*

Or to put it another way, the twentieth century's major First Amendment findings have liberalized speech in *both* meanings of the word. They have, in the tradition of democratic liberalism, codified an expansion, a liberalization, of a sphere of personal liberty for thought, association, assembly, and expression. They have also, in the tradition of economic liberalism, reinforced the role of the state in securing and enforcing the rights of capital. The past one hundred years' street battles for speech and assembly rights were thus battles not only *against* capitalist property rights and privileges but also *against* the prior decisions made by court justices and other super-empowered officials who aimed to uphold those rights or at least dampen challenges. For instance, it was in defiance of state-sanctioned and state-enforced Jim Crow segregation that Black and white port workers united for the New Orleans general strikes of 1892 and 1907. It was in defiance of the anti-picketing ordinances sanctioned by the Taft Court (*American Steel Foundries* 1921) and also in defiance of the mass deportations of immigrant radicals (in a vicious decade-long pogrom culminating in the executions of Italian anarchists Sacco and Vanzetti) that New York City garment workers and Colorado coal miners struck in 1927. The tactic of the sit-down (first used in the United States in 1906 by 3,000

This story from a UVM alum illustrates the contest between liberalism as a sphere of personal liberty to speak and act as one sees right and fit and liberalism as private economic rights off-limits from public interference. During a grocery store staff meeting, when the former student asked why a disabled coworker was being paid less than others doing similar work, his manager formally sanctioned him for violating the store's policy against discussing individuals' wages.

There's a punch line to the UVM student's story of being reprimanded for raising publicly the issue of wages. Following that meeting, the store's workers met on their own and soon after voted to unionize—voted, that is, to make wages not an individual, private matter but one that must be publicly discussed and collectively negotiated.

IWW workers at a Schenectady, New York, General Electric plant) itself developed in defiance of—not to mention self-defense against—city police, state militias, and federal troops who over the previous 20 years nationwide had killed some 200 striking workers and injured 2,000 more (Lens 1973, 111; Smith 2006, 4, 82). The sit-down strikers correctly reasoned that employers would be wary about sending troops into plants where equipment might be harmed. This is the unruly and defiant history, a rhetorical history from those presumed to lack social and linguistic power, that can tell us how ordinary people are able to assert their own unified power against the alliance of capital and state. It's a history that can tell us too how in doing so, significant numbers of U.S. workers have historically defied not only bosses, governors, and National Guards but also the racism, sexism, homophobia, xenophobia, and able-ism that otherwise divide workers, block collective action, and thus benefit by far and away not the (usually posited as white and male) working class but the (primarily but not exclusively white and male) U.S. ruling class.

There is much to draw on for writing classes from the archives of U.S. labor and civil rights struggles: the well-known and lesser-known speeches, op-eds, and letters gathered in anthologies such as Zinn and Arnove's *Voices of a People's History of the United States* (2004); the frequently anonymous handbills, posters, comics, song lyrics, and graffiti that Cary Nelson gathers in the opening chapter of *Revolutionary Memory* (2003); and the visual arguments of agitprop muralists such as Mike Alewitz (Buhle and Alewitz 2002) and worker-artist-filmmakers such as the members of the League of Revolutionary Black Workers (*Finally Got*

President Bill Clinton's 1993 national address on health care reform is an excellent example of rhetoric from above that needs to be examined with its class location—and behind-the-scenes interests—in mind. While Susan Wells (1996) reads that address as an example of how even a powerfully sanctioned rhetor can fail in his search for a responsive public, health policy critics argue the opposite: Clinton's address was calculated to hide from public view the private interests, including the insurance industry, that had already set the "managed care"/ "managed competition" agenda for the 1990s (see Marmor 1994; Navarro 1994; and Himmelstein and Woolhandler 2001).

the News 1970). These archives offer lessons in "rhetoric from below" to be read side by side and, importantly, in tension and contrast with the many examples of "rhetoric from above" that are a writing class's standard fare. For example, Minneapolis coal truck drivers, in their fight to unionize during the cold Depression winter of 1934, had to fight against not only the police and National Guard but also the owner-controlled city newspaper. To keep their scattered ranks organized against both bullets and antistriker news headlines, the truckers started the nation's first daily strike newspaper (Dobbs 1972, 112). What a reading of the *Minneapolis Tribune* side by side and in tension with *The Organizer* can reveal is how much the available means for "constructing a responsive public" (Wells 329) are a matter of class and also how much the question of appropriate tone is a matter of context and high-stakes debate.

A useful pedagogical strategy can be to pair a text already familiar to students with the other text or texts it was originally in conversation or debate with. For instance, we might pair the now canonized "I Have a Dream" speech delivered by Martin Luther King, Jr., at the August 18, 1963, march on Washington with *New York Times* editorials and front-section news stories warning that the planned march "could cost rights votes" ("Negro Rally Seen as Threat to Rights Bill" 1963) and counseling against the "wrong method" of any civil rights action that could "block access and physically interfere with the passage of others" ("Right Goal; Wrong Method" 1963). To add a further layer of rhetorical complexity, we might include the original speech that SNCC activist John Lewis (1963) was to have read at the Lincoln Memorial that day, before being persuaded by the more conservative King to temper his call for Blacks to "burn Jim Crow to the ground—nonviolently." We might also consider not only the differences between the rhetorical approaches and methods of King and Lewis in 1963 but also their similarities by 1967, the year King delivered *his* incendiary "Beyond Vietnam." Or, to tease out what the *New*

> *From-below arguments can also shake up abstract pieties about "bridge-building" and "mediation," helping rhetoricians to consider instead the varied "between/against/for" moves necessitated by particular struggles. Bridge-building between* labor and civil rights *activists carried the sit-down from Flint to Montgomery, where it was used to fight* against Jim Crow *and* for Black civil rights *(Horton 1997). Similarly, the League of Revolutionary Black Workers was a bridge between* the radicalizing ideas of the Black Power Movement *and the tradition of the radical labor, enabling workers to defend themselves against* the concessionary bridge that UAW officials had formed with auto industry heads *(Georgakas and Surkin 1998).*

When members of the migrant workers' rights group and I met with the deputy police chief about the apparent ban on petitioning at the farmers' market, he observed that his own family's dairy farm could not operate without (primarily undocumented and with few public rights) Mexican workers. Then he explained that while our petition didn't violate the city's ordinance against "aggressive solicitation" we should consider that raising such a controversial issue in public can provoke an aggressive response. Hence the interference of market organizers and police. They were only concerned, the deputy chief claimed, about our safety.

York Times chose to overlook when it editorialized against a group of African Americans for blocking access to a racist employment office, a class might consider Anne Moody's (1968) painfully vivid depiction of a Woolworth's lunch-counter sit-in and the physical interference faced by Black students when they sought access to "whites only" counter service.

When we introduce class location and the challenges of rhetorical situation to our discussions of public-sphere creation and a rhetor's performance, we make it possible for our students to consider not only the need for striking workers and civil rights–era activists to engage in such tactics as takeovers and sit-ins. We also facilitate critical assessment of the view—from store owners, newspaper publishers, politicians, and judges—that such strategies are disorderly and uncivil: as the Taft Court put it, "inconsistent with peaceable persuasion" (*American Steel Foundries* 1921, 205) or, as the *New York Times* opined, "the wrong way to achieve equal employment opportunity" ("Right Goal; Wrong Method" 1963). If today's students readily agree that civil rights protestors had employed necessary means, we might also ask them to examine more recent tests of speech and civility. For instance, when James Watts—Ronald Reagan's secretary of the interior, reviled for overseeing the mass transfer of federal lands to private development—attempted to give an address at the University of Vermont, an audience member fired up a chain saw. Similarly, at a 1998 televised "town meeting" in Columbus, Ohio, the audience heckled and jeered as Secretary of State Madeleine Albright made the Clinton case for an invasion of Iraq ("U.S. Policy" 1998).

By chanting "One-two-three-four, we don't want your racist war," that audience was indeed uncivil and disorderly, keeping Albright from delivering a clear argument for regime change. Watts was likewise prevented—as chain saw and audience roared—from making his case for a fully privatized and developed West. One can imagine a somber newspaper editorial admonishing both audiences, "Wrong method!" for their illiberal reaction against both speakers. Yet, if we consider that

Watts answered the charge he was robbing future generations of their public heritage by declaring, "I don't know how many future generations we can count on until the Lord returns" (Balmer 2004, 723). Such affinity between the neoliberal and Christian Right agendas can lead to the faulty conclusion that the Christian Right drives U.S. economic and military policy. However, George W. Bush's warrants for invading Iraq included not only a crusader's belief in God's plan (Kaplan 2004, 9) but also the regime-change authorization promoted and signed into law by President Bill Clinton.

liberalizing speech and assembly rights means *expanding* whose voices and views can be heard, it was *through* the chainsaw that the audience member brought into full public view the Reagan administration's behind-the-scenes deal making; and it was *through* the chainsaw that he created, for a few minutes, a space for an outraged public response. The unruly Albright audience achieved even more than a slender moment in which to speak truth to power: The Clinton administration's failure to secure the expected heartland seal of approval for its planned ground invasion, a failure widely broadcast by the CNN cameras for which the town meeting had been created, effectively scuttled that administration's regime-change plans ("U.S. Policy" 1998).

If we set aside judgments of "civil" and "uncivil" or "liberal" and "illiberal," we can see that such events actually exemplify the chance encounters with new perspectives and conflicting views that Iris Young (1990) identifies as the hallmarks of the Greek agora and that are remarkably rare in today's scripted town meetings and policed farmers' markets. These moments of stepping out of bounds, in order to push wider the boundaries of public speech and debate, come to us from and can reconnect us with (if we can shake off the postmodern *ennui* regarding the simulacre of contemporary public life) a *contentious* history of rhetoric. And in this contentious history, the question of available means—banner-draped podium on the stage or chain saw from the floor? national newspaper op-ed page or embodied blockade of an employment office?—is also very much a question of class.

Arrested Development

Of course composition's histories of the public sphere have always been about class and class conflict. These include the ancient conflicts between aristocratic and emerging merchant classes that set the stage for ideological contest between Plato and the Sophists or Cicero's patrician construction of the ideal (oligarchic) orator at the height of power struggle between Rome's *optimates* and *populares*. The fabled Enlightenment

Most students of rhetoric learn of Plato's disdain for the Sophists. Some may learn the materialism/idealism philosophical divide between, say, Anaxagoras (who held the materialist position that man developed intelligence because he had hands) and Aristotle (who countered with the idealist stance that man developed hands thanks to the intelligence granted him by the gods). Yet few students are ever introduced to the stakes for Athens' aristocracy in sidelining both materialist philosophy and its disoi logoi *method, which threatened to strip this commercial slave society's antidemocratic customs, institutions, and hierarchies of their "universality and necessity" (Novack 1965, 186, 188; see also Berlin 1994; Meiksins Wood and Wood 1978; and Ste. Croix 1981, 412–16).*

salons and coffeehouses associated with the Habermasian conception of a middle-class public sphere must likewise be situated in their contradictory historical context of a new capitalist class reining in the revolutionary "rights of man" against the aspirations and demands of women, African Americans, colonial subjects, and the newly emerging industrial working class. Though most often our textbooks, graduate seminars, and public-sphere theories jettison the social and material picture almost altogether, leaving us with only the *ideas* or *philosophical debates* at these crucial junctures, traces of these historical conflicts are carried in the rhetorical principles and ideals we wittingly or unwittingly promote. When we speak of preparing rhetorical *leaders* or when we endorse the *gymnasium*'s refined intellectualism, agonistic gamesmanship, and enlightened authority over and against the marketplace's crass and unruly fracas (Arendt 1958; Halloran 1996/1982), we speak in the tradition of Plato and Aristotle that is inseparable from their deep belief in the rule of the many by the few and opposition to encroaching democratization that would further undermine the position and privileges of Athens' aristocracy. Or when we suggest to students that the ideal rhetor is a *disinterested individual* guided by the rules of *rational discourse*, we carry forward the interests and fears of eighteenth-century revolutionaries turned now toward establishing their position as the new ruling class. In contemporary rhetorical studies, when we emphasize with Kenneth Burke and John Dewey the problems of communicative understanding among (socially conscious but not class-defined) individuals, we carry forward their fears that—as Dewey summed it up in his debate with Leon Trotsky in a 1938 issue of *The New International* (Trotsky, Dewey, and Novack 1969)—class struggle must inevitably end in Stalinism.

I don't mean to imply that we should not present to our students aristocratic, republican, and liberal conceptions of rhetorical practice—

and further examine with students the historically specific fears with which the "unruly mob" is regarded by Western rhetorical history's leading figures from Cicero in 70 B.C.E. to Dewey in 1938. Patrician and middle-brow rhetorical values are deeply embedded in our profession, in academic and political culture, and, crucially, in students' own ideas of what it means to compose and deliver an argument. But our teaching should not overlook that these values are shaped within particular struggles and asserted against other values suggestive of a competing political and economic order. As James Berlin (1994), paraphrasing Marx, points out, "[I]t is within rhetorics that humans become aware of ideological battles and fight them out. . . . This is why there are always at a given moment a plurality of rhetorics, even during the most repressive times" (117). When rhetorical textbooks and public writing classrooms drop or downplay those ideological battles—including the plurality of rhetorics they engendered and, especially, the stakes all around—we wind up with a rhetorical history that is hagiographic (*Aristotle wrote* The Book *on rhetoric*), impressionistic (*Rhetoric—high art or just a knack? You decide!*), or strictly academic and taxonomic, our own disciplinary spin on philosophy's and critical theory's dematerialized genealogy of ideas (*Sophists: the first postmodernists*). We wind up too with a field whose own development is arrested, with aristocratic, bourgeois, and middle-class notions of public forums but little or no mention of soapboxing, flying pickets, the vernacular rhetorical arts that have historically and necessarily been deployed by those with no access to the sanctioned forums.

It's not simply a matter of oversight, this dropping of working-class rhetoric from our histories and readers. Our one-sided histories of rhetoric both arise from and persist through a central conundrum: How do we recognize the decidedly unquiet history of working-class contestation when its very unruliness appears to exclude it from our field of men (and occasionally women) standing at podiums or poised over paper? How do we learn from mass rhetorical arts when—if we've studied Cicero's rhetorical principles but not the historical context and political stakes shaping his political

We must also learn to recognize the particular strategies working-class and oppressed groups employ if we're to appreciate more fully much of today's work in composition and literacy. Our field's studies of working-class colleges (Greer 1999), small-town Wisconsin families (Brandt 2001b), hip-hop communities (Richardson and Lewis 1999); and urban, low-income African American families (Cushman 1998) can't be placed within—and shouldn't be defined as on the margins of—public spheres defined as competition among elite peers or as private individuals meeting in a disinterested discussion of public affairs.

conservatism—we view the crowd as ruled by frightening "impulses" that must necessarily be checked by the "the eloquence of one man" (Cicero 2001, 293)?

It is further not surprising that our textbooks and anthologies would most often present us with such a dematerialized, disembodied, and just-about-argument-free picture of rhetoric through the ages if we consider that our histories are also expressions of the contemporary society in which we write. And in contemporary U.S. society, actual rhetorical practice is constrained not only by neoliberal economic privatization, which eliminates the material spaces in which people without much economic means and political clout might meet and argue, but also by the ruling norms of the liberal public sphere, which prefer that people without much means and clout not meet and argue at all. The liberal public sphere has long preferred "thin" versions of political life with most citizens serving as "spectators" to a professional governing class (Barber 1988, 18) or a "procedural democracy" where participation for most people means voting every two to four years while "a small number of private (corporate and military) interests, in the pursuit of maximum profit, make decisions of sweeping impact" (Giroux 2002, 75). Upholding civility and order as its god terms, the liberal public sphere resembles almost not at all the publics most often discussed and celebrated in our professional journals (Arendt's *agora* of agonistic display, Young's city of difference and chance). It shudders even at limited, middle-class Habermasian contestation.

Liberalism's ideals of civility and order, nevertheless, can seem like needed common sense, a humane approach to the potential chaos of public (and academic) life, and a needed counter to the sparring of today's cable news pundits and radio shock jocks. In such an atmosphere, what we find in our rhetoric textbooks can seem like wise counsel: "People who know about rhetoric know how to persuade others to consider their point of view without resorting to coercion or violence" and "[U]nfair social and economic realities only underscore the need for principled public discussion among concerned citizens" (Crowley and Hawhee 1999, 4). Promoted as moral imperative, however, such counsel erases the history of the many who have needed to be uncivil (consider the muckraking exposés of Upton Sinclair) and disorderly (consider Harlem's Depression-era rent strikes) in order to challenge both an unjust civic order and the exclusion of whole groups of people from the category of citizenship altogether. As the basic rights won and extended by those earlier generations are now rolled back, such counsel also may impede

When abortion rights activists called for "bubble laws"—such as the Florida law, upheld in Madsen et al. v. Women's Health Center (1994), proscribing anti-abortion pickets within Thirty-six feet of clinics—they aimed to safeguard clinic access. Bubble laws also had another effect: Physical pro-abortion clinic defense lines were largely abandoned and with them vanished a public, visible, and mass argument for abortion rights.

our ability to take on—and to grasp what historically has been necessary to take on—our society's most pressing issues and glaring inequities (Benhabib 1998, 77–8). When we additionally sidestep the question of where civil discussion might take place, we further veil collusion between the liberal public sphere's low level of tolerance for (might-turn-unruly) public argument and neoliberalism's elimination of material spaces for public life and contestation altogether.

Indeed the very language of liberalism has historically operated in periods of proclaimed "clear and present danger" to reinforce the imperatives of order, stability, and security over *any* guarantees of public rights. Consider just this partial list of state-ordered repression carried out in the name of the greater public good: the roundup of 10,000 resident aliens, by order of President Woodrow Wilson, in the infamous 1919 Palmer Raids; the internment of 110,000 Japanese and Japanese Americans between 1942 and 1946 ordered by President Franklin D. Roosevelt; the McCarthy-era execution of the Rosenbergs and the Supreme Court's upholding of the conviction of college professor Lloyd Barenblatt for refusing to answer questions posed by the House Un-American Activities Committee; and COINTELPRO's vicious harassment of civil rights, Black Nationalist, and other New Left activists through the 1960s and into the early 1970s.

This is the history that set the stage for the Bush White House to proceed with its own aggressive, but not at all unprecedented, suppression of civil and labor rights (Chang 2002)—a suppression that marks a *continuation* of *one side* of a long history of struggle over power and rights. For instance, when Homeland Security Secretary Tom Ridge warned

Another unanticipated consequence of bubble laws is their use to prohibit union leafleting at workplace entrances or petitioning near stores, bus stops, bank tellers—just about anywhere where one might find an audience (Mitchell 2003, 44–45). A bubble law's "argument-free" ethos is also readily universalized. Hence the manager who tells the migrant workers' activists that the farmers' market must be kept a "neutral space" for people to "enjoy the farmers' market experience." Operating here is the anti-rhetorical virtue of neutrality, freedom from difference and debate.

On a cold February morning I pick up Mohammed and his family from the home where they were placed by local refugee services. They are among fifty families in Burlington awaiting appointments with Canadian immigration, which considers them all asylum seekers from the United States and its new requirement (issued in late 2002 and, several months and several hundred deportations later, rescinded) that all noncitizen adult men from twenty-six predominantly Muslim countries report for fingerprinting, photographing, and questioning. Mohammed, a ten-year resident, from Pakistan, has four children, all U.S. citizens. But he's heard about the Iranian men detained in L.A., and his oldest son, he explains, is tired of harassment. We drive to the mall. His son needs a winter coat and his wife some warm sweaters. They also need hats, boots, new jobs, new home, a place where they can live.

West Coast dockworkers that their planned strike posed a "threat to national security" and would necessitate a military response (Sustar 2002; Cockburn and St. Claire 2002), he was authorized not only by USA PATRIOT Act's new category of "domestic terrorism" but also by the 1947 Taft-Hartley Act, allowing military intervention to break strikes that threaten the "national interest." Jimmy Carter's earlier invocation of Taft-Hartley to force striking miners back to work and Ronald Reagan's use of the same law to fire *en masse* the nation's air traffic controllers serve as further reinforcement. Similarly, as the Bush White House oversees just in one sweep the deportation of some 13,000 Muslim men on mostly minor visa violations (Mann 2003), we should recall not only the mass deportations of Italian and German immigrants in 1919 (under the guise of fighting Bolshevism) but also the Clinton-era anti-immigration legislation, which used the cover of fighting terrorism to militarize the nation's borders and purge much of what we'd recognize as due process from deportation proceedings. These and other seeming *departures from* the tenets of liberal democracy are actually logical *expressions of* its founding dichotomy between order and disorder, civilization and barbarism, deliberative citizen and threatening mob.

Historically, too, the "mob" most feared and against whom presidential executive orders are issued and secret programs are launched are large groups and movements of people attempting to redress economic and social injustices. In the late 1910s, for instance—when all immigrants were required to register with the government (precursor of the Ashcroft-era registration requirement for men born in predominantly Muslim countries) and some 6,000 immigrants were detained under suspicion of pro-Bolshevik sympathies (a foreshadow of the McCarthy-

Following the worldwide demonstrations that brought more than 10 million people, including at least half a million in New York City, out against a second Iraq war, the New York Times *admitted, "[T]here may still be two superpowers on the planet: the United States and world public opinion" (Tyler 2003). At a moment when the* New York Times *itself had failed to distinguish not only between U.S. and world opinion but deep divisions within U.S. opinion, the sizable share of the population saying "No war in Iraq" managed to deliver that message.*

era witch hunts)—the "mob" threatening the Wilson administration and the U.S. ruling class was, in fact, an increasingly organized and militant labor movement led by immigrants armed with socialist, anarchist, and other radical traditions (Brecher 1997, 104–14; Smith 2006, 89–91). It was particularly against an exploding labor movement and the threat of workers' arguments—expressed through mass strikes, the launching of labor parties, and, in the case of the United Mine Workers and the Industrial Workers of the World, or "Wobblies," a commitment to desegregated unions—that the 1917 Espionage Act, the 1919 Palmer Raids, and the murderous white supremacist rampages of 1919's "Red Summer" were launched. At pressured moments (Seattle's General Strike of 1919, the mid-1960s turn of the civil rights movement toward Black Power and antiwar militancy), U.S. liberalism reveals its limited tolerance for arguments that might actually alter, and indeed have substantially altered, social and economic arrangements. The deportations of immigrant radicals that proceeded through the 1920s *could not* prevent labor's astounding resurgence in the 1930s. Even a program as powerfully malevolent as COINTELPRO *did not* stem the rising tide of the Black Power, gay and lesbian liberation, women's rights, and antiwar movements.

By acknowledging this history and by including it in our study of rhetorical history and its lessons for today, we are then in a position to talk with a student like Katie about the long history of public space surveillance and public voice restrictions that her encounter with the cop gave her an inkling of. Moreover, we can consider the long and varied history of seemingly powerless individuals and groups resisting,

Even within neoliberalism's shrinking space for public argument, surprising openings sometimes appear. Take France's 1994 law requiring that francophone songs comprise 40 percent of radio station play lists. Passed as a bulwark against American pop music and on a tide of French chauvinism against North African and Arab cultural influence, the law in fact boosted the airwave viability of radical hip hop by disenfranchised Arab and African youth in the impovished banlieues of Paris, Strasburgh, and Lyon.

confronting, and subverting restriction through creative means that have included (but have also included a great deal more than) Katie's anonymous poetic interventions. Yet if we are to acknowledge and learn from the legacy of working-class rhetorical action, we must contend with an additional contemporary academic tendency—to dismiss the working class as a relevant force for progressive change.

Who's Afraid of the Working Class?

Here we need to return to the construction of critical theory (and rhetorical theory) as an autonomous history of ideas and debates— "conversations"—divorced both from the larger social history that shapes and urges a set of ideas and from historical and contemporary contexts in which such ideas might actually be tested. Today's most radical theories, observes Susan Searls Giroux (2002), "theorize *the political*" but don't extend toward securing the *physical* spaces needed in which to act politically (81). A strict separation of even the most radical-seeming theory from the complications of context—part of theory's inward turn, which Jenny Bourne (2002) sums up as a turn away from politics as "something done 'out there' in meetings and parties" to politics as something done "here in the person" (199)—isn't simply more of the same age-old ivory tower isolation. The *ennui* (or sometimes outright disdain) with which actual involvement is regarded has a specific history both in the limitations of New Left radicalism of the 1960s and, profoundly impacting the theoretical schools still in sway today, in the defeat of the May–June 1968 revolution in France. For such influential or soon-to-become influential thinkers as Foucault, Lyotard, Deleuze, and Guattari, that defeat appeared as confirmation that Marx had erred in positing the working class as capitalism's gravediggers—as, that is, not only the victims of history but also potentially its agents. Far from being imagined as vanguard *or* as abject, the working class in post-McCarthy theorizing is figured instead—in a blend of Daniel Bell's (1976) claims of widespread abundance enjoyed by the American working class and Herbert Marcuse's (1964) laments of endemic working-class apathy—as well heeled and bought off. Titles by Bell, Marcuse, and Andre Gorz remain academic bestsellers even though their obituaries for the U.S. and European working classes proved immature. Poland's Solidarity Movement was shaking the foundations of the Stalinist regime in Poland at the very moment Gorz (1982) was penning *Farewell to the Working Class*. Daniel Bell's declaration that U.S. autoworkers had become too complacent for

In Living Room *(1985), poet June Jordan did not join postmodern political thinkers such as Ernesto Laclau and Chantal Mouffe (1985), who promoted, under the banner of radicalism, a denial of any "unified discourse of the Left." Instead, in this collection that chronicles and laments the loss of living room for people struggling from the American Midwest ("Des Moines Iowa Rap") to the Middle East ("Apologies to All the People in Lebanon"), Jordan insists on the necessity of radical rhetorical solidarity, exemplified in the collection's closing poem: "I was born a Black woman/and now/I am become a Palestinian" ("Moving Towards Home").*

militancy hardly squares with the doubling of wildcat (unauthorized) strikes by U.S. manufacturing workers between 1960 and 1969 (Smith 2006, 220–22).

By imagining and advancing the notion of a *complacent* U.S. and European working class, academics of the 1960s and 1970s did more than fail to stay in touch with these pitched labor battles that in the early 1970s also grew out of and fed back into the political battles of the Black Power, women's, and antiwar movements. (As Georgakas and Surkin [1998] point out, the autoworkers who organized the League of Revolutionary Black Workers were inspired by and sought to carry into the factories Detroit's Great Rebellion of 1967.) In imagining and advancing the notion of a *complicit* working class, academics also missed the decline in working-class fortunes that had become evident in both the United States and Britain by the late 1970s. Moreover, those theorists, profoundly disillusioned by the struggles of the late 1960s, contributed to the virtual vacuum in Left political thought that aided what became by the 1980s a hard pull to the right.

Today, this theoretical torpor, minus its historical basis, is further codified in critical theories that replace mass action from below with (if any alternative is posited) classless "culture workers" as the instigators of, at most, *local* and *contingent* change. Hence enthusiasts of neo-Marxists Oskar Negt and Alexander Kluge (1993), who broadly theorize a "proletarian public sphere," turn to indy media and the Internet as potential sites of democratization—without considering how to support or even recognize those groups attempting, against the consolidated forces of capital and state, to claim not only airwaves and cyberspace but also streets and workplaces. Nancy Fraser (1992) looks to local, alternative, and largely middle-class arrangements such as child care collectives and feminist publication initiatives as offering strengthened decision-making voice—without considering that most people don't have the autonomy to choose an alternative over capitalist arrangements and further that the decisions most profoundly impacting our lives and communities are

Activists in the AIDS Coalition to Unleash Power (ACT UP) made full, artistic, and effective use of from-below and do-it-yourself argumentative forms. These ranged from plastering price-gouging drug companies and pharmacies with "AIDS Profiteer" posters to, dressed as Grim Reapers, taking over the meeting of a local government board that had just cut HIV/AIDS funding. Importantly, ACT UP activists staged these interventions not for a situationist's love of avant-garde artistic disruption but to make—and win—the life-or-death argument that HIV/AIDS drug protocols be speeded up with treatments made available and affordable.

not locally made. Similarly, when I ask my students for examples of ordinary people taking rhetorical action, they typically speak of "edgeworkers" and "culture jammers" (e.g., the solitary student who transformed campus stop signs into STOP BUSH signs or Katie with her anonymous poem posters). Anarchist-informed political agitations do indeed offer an attractive "just-do-it" *ethos* and a needed hands-on practice in public-sphere intervention. But edgeworking and culture jamming also share with democratic liberalism a "tyranny-of-the-majority" distrust of mass democratic participation as well as the Marcusian academic view of the larger public as (at best) complacent and unaware.

When my students' individual and small-group exercises in public agency—including their participation in spoken-word poetry forums, shareware collectives, and Taco Bell boycotts—bring them confidence and lead them to the additional tools they'll need to challenge increasingly concentrated power and genuinely have a voice, I'm all for it. I'm all for insistence that *there is an alternative.* Yet I'm concerned that when, as Susan Searls Giroux (2002) puts it, "agency gets reduced to making lifestyle decisions [and] wise consumer choices" (75), such attempts at public participation will quickly appear to these students as sadly inconsequential. Fear that her work might be without consequence was what Katie expressed when she first brought her poems to class and wondered what impact they could have beyond publication in a chapbook to be read by friends. The textual manipulations in her poem "Action Alert" were inspired by Ana Castillo's (1994) theorizing of a Chicana poetics, born in part from Castillo's disenchantment with the disintegrating Chicano movement in the early 1970s. But when Katie sought to shift from exploring the linguistic dimensions of (r)evolutionary change to creating rhetorical space where public discussion and debate of the poem's issues could actually take place, she hit the limits of a poetics/politics fixated on solitary acts of writing. Likewise, when we go no further than considering with our students the

A refreshing example of collective rhetoric uniting large and diverse groups of people against neoliberalism's global assaults is the slogan taken up at the 2002 protest of the World Economic Forum in New York and at the World Social Forum in Porto Alegre: "They are all Enron and we are all Argentina!"

alternative publics of independent media, food coops, or do-it-yourself zines, we hit the limits of these rhetorical means, alone, to take on what seem likely to be the biggest issues ahead: health care, abortion, Social Security, entrenched and increasing racial and economic segregation, immigrant and Arab scapegoating, and ongoing, escalating war. As was true in 1935 and in 1968, the majority of this society—including most of our students and also most of their teachers—will need more than the individual and largely middle-class rhetorical solutions of the electronic town meeting, blog punditry, or (equally individualistic and suited primarily to the *ethos* and autonomy of the middle class) scattered, spontaneous cultural interventions. That is, if we want to have real decision-making influence.

It's here that we need to offer students at least an inkling of the mass rhetorical arts needed to build a Camp Solidarity, prepare for a street-taking demonstration, deal with the challenge of sustaining a democratic movement. It's here too that we need to introduce the history—and the very concept—of working-class power, not as a theoretical construct (as it largely appears in the work of Negt and Kluge) and not as a musty anachronism (as in automatic academic dismissals of the term) but as something with here-and-now significance for us and for our students. Katie, for instance, now teaches in a community-based literacy program for migrant workers. Monthly she witnesses her students' struggles for living room in a post-NAFTA world; monthly she also faces the question of how to make her bare-minimum salary cover the cost of her rent, transportation, and health care. Though she is not subjected to the superexploitation of the migrant workers who receive pennies for the tomatoes they pick and fear any publicity that will attract the notice of

Seeking health care coverage, a small ironworkers' local has picketed the entrance to a hospital-wing construction site. In response, the builders bring in replacement workers from Mexico via South Carolina. As the strikers debate their options, an organizer from another union chimes in, "I'll bet they're illegal. I could have the INS here in a minute." The president of the ironworkers' local shakes his head. Instead, they select someone on the picket line who speaks Spanish to talk with the workers about the picket and their shared need for jobs with health care, safe working conditions, and the right to organize without fear of being fired or deported.

border patrol or their vigilante supporters, Katie's own "privileges" seem pretty slim. When I add to my syllabi such texts as Jeremy Brecher's *Strike!* and Sharon Smith's *Subterranean Fire*, I'm not just trying to give working-class history its due. A majority of my students are going on to jobs—as teachers, social workers, health care providers, engineers, service workers, and technicians—that are, or are increasingly subjected to the disciplining and contingency of, working-class jobs. In the workplace and in social, political spheres beyond, what power they have will be collective, not individual. The worth of their labor, the safety of their working conditions, access and equality in their schools and other civic institutions, the health of the environment in which they live—all this and more will depend on their knowing at least something of this history.

Lessons Learned

Students in my Spring 2003 women's studies seminar did not, of course, go out and build a Camp Solidarity, nor did I shape this seminar to provide the history and tools we need even just to hang a poster downtown. Still, I'm astonished at what the students were able to do—though much too much on their own. Cassie—the student frustrated by her attempt to convince her boyfriend and his roommates to turn off *The Man Show*—organized a panel on the destructive impact of welfare reform in Vermont. More than seventy people attended the panel including a reporter and photographer from the state's largest daily newspaper, despite the fact that—as Cassie repeatedly and worriedly pointed out—she was "just" a college student with no "official" sponsors. In a conversation at the semester's end, Cassie emphasized the importance of learning the basics of how to organize and build an audience for such a forum, not only for her education in public-sphere creation but also for the encouragement of other women lacking official sponsorship as well: "[W]e don't live in a place where standing up and getting on your soapbox is valued, especially as women. And I think that's what needs to change."

Consider this potent combination of art, embodied struggle, and rapid communications: An email arrives from the Labor art Mural Project (LaMP) announcing that Israeli bulldozers had rolled in to plow under agitprop artist Mike Alewitz's latest project, a mural in East Jerusalem at the newly built Rachel Corrie Peace Center, painted with U.S., Palestinian, and Israeli labor activists. The next day, following a flurry of emailed and faxed protests from around the world, the bulldozers retreat. This collaboration of workers and artists has been—for the moment—saved.

The public visibility of a soapbox is what Katie, with her anonymous postering, may have been avoiding—initially, that is. But as it turned out, Katie didn't hang up any more poster versions of "Action Alert." Instead she went to the Church Street Marketplace during the noon hour and passed out copies of the poem in person. She also engaged in conversation with those who stopped to puzzle over the poem or talk about its ideas. Out of those conversations, Katie told me in a postsemester meeting, she was now rethinking the "air of intellectualism" in the poem, which, she'd decided, should show more of her own frustrated search for the facts of the bombing of a Baghdad market or explain the story of Bakhat Hassan whose eleven family members were gunned down by U.S. soldiers at a checkpoint south of Karbala. At the conversation's end, Katie said she was reconsidering the poem's in-the-margins command to "Empower yourself," explaining that she might add to it a specific invitation to an antiwar meeting or teach-in.

"I definitely talk about collective revolution," she said, "but how do things evolve and how do we forge any sort of revolution if people don't come together?"

And there it is: why we need to make rhetorical space—at a grocery store to talk about wages, in a panel to hear from women about the felt impact of workfare, in a festival marketplace to talk about U.S. soldiers ordered to shoot—and why in doing so we are regarded as dangerous indeed.

Note

1. "Rhetoric from below" owes its phrasing—and its implied argument about the collective actions of ordinary people as the force that drives progressive change—to independent socialist Hal Draper. Against the autocratic Maoist and Stalinist politics that dominated the New Left of the 1960s, Draper (2004) offered a clear and appealing vision of "socialism from below."

INTERLUDE

"This Is Not a Rally"

A month and a half before the U.S. assault on Iraq, students in my senior women's studies seminar and I attended a faculty panel titled "Is Iraq the Problem? Is War the Solution?" The panelists, from the Political Science, History, Economics, and Religion departments, sat high on the stage in the nearly 200-year-old Ira Allen Chapel. Well over 1,000 students, faculty, and staff packed the pews and balcony. Describing her role as facilitating an "open and free dialogue," the panel's moderator introduced the speakers as "faculty experts." She pointed to the microphone set up among the pews and explained that, following prefatory remarks, students could line up at the microphone to pose questions to "our experts." She admonished students to keep their questions "brief" and to avoid making arguments or what she termed "diatribes."

The first student at the microphone, following the opening remarks and another reminder from the moderator about brevity, identified himself as a political science major. His question, he said, was for the panelist from the Religion department, an Islamic studies scholar and the panel's only woman. "What qualifies you," the student asked, "as an expert in international or foreign policy?"

The moderator leaned over and spoke into the religion professor's microphone: "Are you asking where she earned her credentials?"

"No, not really," the student replied. "I'm asking what qualifies a member of the Department of Religion and various other departments to discuss policy issues. What gives you the authority to actually participate on this panel?"

114

Here the moderator cut the student off: "The people who organized this event brought people with *expertise* and *that's* why they're here. Next question."

Soon after, my students and I returned to our classroom to discuss the panel, which had been for us particularly fascinating and vexing because our seminar, in contemporary women's rhetorics, focused on the politics of *ethos*, the authority to speak even when—especially when—we are not credentialed as experts. The week before, we had considered Arundhati Roy's (2001) send-up of (privatized) expertise, which removes from public debate such profoundly important decisions as whether to build a dam that would displace a million of India's poorest citizens. We had talked too about the scholars from the University of Nebraska–Omaha's Center for Afghan Studies who had appeared regularly on network and cable news programs in the buildup to the bombing of Afghanistan—and the question of what difference it makes that the Center's major funder, UNOCAL, had been seeking for more than a decade to run a pipeline through Afghanistan. The point of these discussions wasn't to throw over the idea of expertise altogether. As one student noted, she wouldn't want a librarian to take out her appendix. But why, we wanted to know, is it so often extraordinarily difficult for ordinary people to ask and learn, "What *are* the experts up to?" What gendered division of intellectual labor—and in whose interests—worked to cordon off those concerned with cultural production from those examining and weighing in on economic and military policy?

During that early discussion, I'd asked students, too, about their own relationship to authority. Why was it, for instance, that the topics these students had said were of chief concern to them at the moment—war, the economy, Israel and Palestine, abortion rights—did not show up on any of the students' lists of what they felt they could write about? One woman explained that she'd sometimes tried to argue with her stepfather against free trade agreements but always wound up "tongue-tied" and "mixing up the facts" until her stepfather dismissed her as "too emotional." Most students said they associated trade agreements as the very opposite of anything that would arouse the emotions. They associated all things economic with obscure figures such as Federal Reserve Board chairs who periodically raise or lower interest rates to the inexplicable delight or dismay of Wall Street traders. Or they associated economics with what they viewed as a particularly mystifying set of classes at UVM that most had avoided taking. These were smart, inquisitive students who had paired their women's studies major with second majors or multiple minors because they feared a women's studies degree alone lacked legitimacy.

But they had also learned very well the academic divisions constructing economics or Middle East policy not as a relation between people and also not as a set of rationalizations that serves the interests of one class over another but rather as a set of intricate and absolute laws to be properly applied by a specially trained few. At the end of that class I wrote on the board, "Why I take globalization personally" and "Neoliberalism: It's a women's issue." I asked students how they would feel if I assigned this for the next week's paper. "But we're not economists," one student pointed out. Then she paused, forehead wrinkling. "Though neither is Arundhati Roy—is she?"

These students are not alone in feeling ill-equipped to write about globalization, a word they often hear but for which they have no clear definition. Nor are they alone in feeling unauthorized to write against or even question, as one student put it, the barrage of "Pentagon says" reports and press conferences they watch daily (in this buildup to war) on CNN. "[A] great many people with PhDs in English," writes Harriet Malinowitz, "know little or nothing about the actual workings of the World Trade Organization or the history of the immensely powerful international organizations [such as the International Monetary Fund] . . . or about contemporary trade treaties or about the specifics of U.S. foreign policy" (2003, 250). These subjects, Malinowitz argues, should not be regarded as the exclusive property of the social sciences, particularly because, shaped by rhetoric, they need to be approached through a rhetorical lens (250). I'd further argue that even though our disciplinary training teaches us *not* to regard a religion professor as an authority on foreign policy, a composition professor as a Social Security expert, or a women's studies student as needing lessons in the debates surrounding fast-track trade legislation or the gaps in a "Pentagon says" televised report, we all desperately need space and encouragement for practice in public argumentation on all of these topics. We need such space, practice, and authorization because these policies and their effects are not only worked up in language; they also play out—are very much felt—in our daily lives.

For instance, here's how one economist (in what became a *New York Times* "Quote of the Day") summed up neoliberal economic policies as they are felt in the daily lives of most workers (including in today's corporatized universities):

> To the extent that companies can squeeze another drop of blood out of their existing work force, they're doing it. Eventually you reach the point where there's no more blood to be given, but we haven't reached it. (Leonhardt 2004, A1)

Squeezing blood from a workforce until there's not one drop left: This sounds to me like a topic that should be everyone's business to talk about. A war that has proceeded on patently false warrants and that by its fourth year had killed more than 3,000 U.S. soldiers, had killed a half million Iraqis while making refugees of 2 million more (Burnham et al., 2006): This too should be everyone's business. But then on the other side is the question, "What gives you the authority?" We must be able to answer this question. We need to understand too how such a discussion-stopping, participation-denying question has come to be framed.

The difficulty, of course, is that our academic training *doesn't* prepare us to take on such a question with much confidence. We don't learn to study the world in which we live as an interconnected and entirely felt totality. Instead we study curricula divided into discrete and highly specialized disciplines: rhetoric, economics, political science, history. The division of labor that marks the Fordist method of production hasn't disappeared with the common academic claim that we're living in a "post-Fordist" economy. Far from it, Fordist regimentation penetrates deeply into just about all aspects and relationships within society. This is the *globalized Fordism* that Hungarian Marxist Georg Lukács (1997) foresaw, with atomized production processes and logics no longer bound to the physical proximity of departments within single factories or factories within the same hemisphere:

> The fetishistic character of economic forms, the reification of all human relations, the constant expansion and extension of the division of labour which subjects the process of production to an abstract, rational analysis without regard to the human potentialities and abilities of the immediate producers, *all of these things transform the phenomena of society and with them the way in which they are perceived.* In this way arise the "isolated" facts, "isolated" complex of facts, separate, specialist disciplines (economics, law, etc.). (6, my emphasis)

At the very least, Lukács can tell us, the bureaucracies and disciplinary turf wars we struggle against in our universities are a direct expression of capitalist logic and of the benefits that flow to capitalism when social relations are abstracted into isolated, reified categories, each with its own distinct history, methods, laws, and experts who understand (or are certainly bound and beholdened to) these histories, methods, laws. What is so astonishing, then, about the economist quoted in the *New York Times* (Leonhardt 2004) is that for a moment, the reifying and obfuscating veil was dropped: The story of rising productivity and record profit runs and the story of falling wages and disappearing benefits, usually presented as strictly separate and unrelated, are joined—and moreover they are connected, viscerally, to the human body from which blood/productivity/ profit is being squeezed. A "Quote of the Day" indeed! Within the usual atomized order of things, that economist has gotten quite out of line.

For his open challenge of a member of the faculty, the political science student was also regarded as out of line. Yet there is also a way in which this student was not out of line, not according to the academy's training. By challenging the religion professor's right to speak to the question of war, this student was speaking from the logic that the university, especially the neoliberal university, instills: Political science is a discipline devoted to and singularly authorized to opine on the topic of war; religion (or any discipline in the irrelevant humanities) is not. And so too from this logic spoke the panel's moderator as she trumped the student's political science expert with the more general category of faculty experts who, nevertheless, assume the same "phantom objectivity," an "autonomy" that is "strictly rational and all-embracing," in need of no (and indeed hostile to) public explanation (Lukács 1997, 83).

The nature of authority and the construction of expertise were, of course, the hot topics when my seminar students and I returned to the classroom after the "Is Iraq the Problem? Is War the Solution?" panel. Students immediately pointed out the event's evident contradictions: the moderator promising an "open and free dialogue" but then advising students to keep questions brief; the speakers stressing the urgency of the moment but the audience discouraged from debate or even answering with applause. Interestingly, however, they disagreed with one another about the exchange between the political science student and moderator. Some students heard the young man's question as arising from a democratizing impulse to question professorial authority; they objected to the moderator's refusal of the question as paternalistic and belittling, the equivalent of a parent rebuking an impertinent child and packing him off to bed without dinner. Other students noted that the young man had singled out the panel's only woman and one of two panelists of color; they argued that the student's question was racist and sexist, the equivalent of telling the religion professor to "just shut up." These students maintained that the moderator was right to use her authority to silence him; silencing the religion professor, after all, was what this student had aimed to do.

With our time running out, I asked why only one of them had joined the line to pose a question—and then only in the final few minutes:

the event wrapped up before her turn ever came. The students who had reached the microphone first, the only students whose questions were voiced, were all men and all political science majors. They had clearly felt prepared and entitled to stand and speak. Why not the seniors in women's studies? "Maybe it's the size of the audience," one student ventured. "Or no. It's how the whole thing is introduced. They're experts. I'm not. I don't know enough. That's what's intimidating."

Then I remembered the student who'd joined the queue too late to pose her question. "So what were you going to say?" I asked.

"I was going to ask if the religion professor *could* tell us what gave her the authority, what made her feel empowered to speak," she replied. "I thought it would be *helpful* for us to know."

Her question—and what happens to the very idea of *ethos* under neoliberalism's specializing, privatizing logic—is central to the next chapter. Here I'll flag one additional problem to bear in mind. A Marxist such as Lukács would argue for resisting atomization and for taking on totality if we want to reconnect with a reality and even with our very selves from which we are successively estranged. This does not mean that we collapse all distinctions and erase particularity and specificity. Rather, as Marx put it, it means that we understand all "relations of production in society form a whole" (qtd. in Lukács 1997, 9); and that disciplinary knowledge, while appearing to be about *things*, is very much expressive of—and also obscures—relations among people (83). (When the economist described companies squeezing the very last drops of blood from workers, he named a fundamental and exploitive relationship between people in capitalism.) In fact, the effort to apprehend the totality of economic, social, and political arrangements makes it possible to glimpse and appreciate the "human qualities and idiosyncrasies" that "abstract special laws functioning according to rational predictions" write off as "*mere sources of error*" (89, Lukács' emphasis). Hence a women's studies senior seminar in contemporary women's rhetorical practices taking on at least some study of neoliberal economics, human and physical geography, the history of imperialism, contemporary debates over "peak oil." Hence a women's studies seminar aiming to do so from the understanding that we need to take it all very personally, taking lived experience as our "point d'appui" (Smith 1987, 159)—yet without forgetting that no one is an isolated individual, that this is a project of considering what generalizations, from what standpoints, we can form or confront as we try to explain "[H]ow does it happen to us as it does? How is this world in which we act and suffer put together?" (Smith 1987, 154).

But here is the problem: Our most common conception of academic freedom doesn't articulate the value and necessity of seeing and understanding a subject in relation to others. "Teachers are entitled to freedom in the classroom in discussing *their* subject," reads the American Association of University Professors' (AAUP) classic statement on academic freedom, "but they should be careful not to introduce into their teaching controversial matter *which has no relation* to *their* subject" (2001, 3, my emphasis). Further, while effective rhetorical action for public space, voice, and decision-making power by a segment of the population wider than a professional governing class has frequently been denounced (in its historical moment at least) as disorderly, the AAUP's academic freedom statement also prescribes limits on faculty action outside as well as inside the academy: "When they speak or write as citizens, [faculty] should be free from institutional censorship or discipline, but their *special position in the community imposes special obligations*" including the need "*at all times*" to "exercise *appropriate restraint*" (3–4, my emphasis).

What, then, is appropriate restraint? Consider 1,200 University of Vermont students, staff, and faculty sitting in the pews of the Ira Allen Chapel, facing forward, listening attentively, for more than an hour to arguments for and against a war that, regardless of this "dialogue" and "exchange," would very soon be getting underway. At one point the economics professor, a native of Iraq who had just detailed the deadly impact of sanctions on Iraqi citizens, asked the audience to join him that night for an antiwar event. The room burst into loud applause, foot stomping, even cheers. The moderator tapped her microphone. "Please," she said as the temporarily unruly room came back to order. "Remember: *This* is *not* a rally."

5

So What Gives You the Authority?

> [I]nstead of an argument, or an explanation, or a disputing of facts, one gets insults, invective, legal threats, and the Expert's Anthem: "You're too emotional. You don't understand, and it's too complicated to explain." The subtext, of course, is: Don't worry your little head about it. Go and play with your toys. Leave the real world to us.
>
> —ARUNDHATI ROY 2001, 25

Slim Expectations

Just before the 2002 midterm election, a reporter asked if it worried me that so many college students don't care about politics. His question surprised me. For the past half hour we had talked about the work of students in a community-based literacy politics class. We'd looked at Web and print zines students had put together with high schoolers at a downtown youth center. I'd shown him the online poll (*Why do you think George Bush really wants to go to war with Iraq?*) a student had helped one teen set up. I had just explained to the reporter about voice, visibility, and why it matters that the teens have public forums in which they can represent themselves differently than they are typically portrayed by teachers, social workers, and the youth center's fund-raising brochures. Along the way, the reporter had offered his own observations, including that such community-based teaching can't move beyond a handful of courses without a university-wide commitment to small classes and manageable workloads. Our conversation was about politics through and

121

through. Why, then, was he saying that students—the students who made this class work—don't care about politics?

Then he explained: His real concern had to do with why so many eighteen- to twenty-year-olds were expected to sit out the upcoming elections—as many as 88 percent, he noted, with a worried frown. I couldn't dispute this. I doubted that those of my students who were registered voters had requested absentee ballots or planned a Tuesday drive to their polling place. I imagined walking into the next class and saying, "Those of you from Vermont, whom do you prefer—Jim Douglas or Doug Racine?" I imagined students looking at me and blinking. Of course, these students could, if prodded, note a few differences between the Republican and Democratic candidates for governor. One appeared to be for something called the Circumferential Highway whereas the other appeared to be against it. One candidate called for repealing the statewide school-funding law, which requires well-funded school districts to share property tax revenues with those that are cash strapped, whereas the other candidate spoke of reform to provide "relief" for wealthy towns. I'm sure that most students could have said, given these shades of difference, which candidate they preferred. But no, I couldn't say that when it came to choosing between Douglas and Racine, the students in this class particularly cared. The issues they did care about—the question of a war against Iraq, another 1,200 laid off from the local IBM plant, tuition hikes and financial aid cuts—were, naturally, not on the ballot at all.

My response to the reporter at the time was brief and terse: Don't reduce politics to its very least and most passive form; look at everything these students are doing that constitutes political action; before we moralize about the sanctity of the vote, maybe we should reflect on Florida in 2000. More recently, however, I've had to rethink my anarchist-inflected dismissal of the reporter's concern about widespread disengagement from electoral politics. Today, I have two ways of looking at the question that might appear to contradict and cancel out each other, but both of which I think we need to hold in dialogue and debate when we consider the available means most people believe they have to exercise public decision-making power.

For starters, I would say to the reporter that if students, and most of the rest of us, don't care about politics, it's because we've *learned* it is not our *place* to care. Moreover, many of us, particularly as teachers of composition and rhetoric, are positioned to *teach* that it is not for most people to expect more by way of political participation than voting for the available candidates once every two years. Though this may seem like a surprising claim to make in a chapter that starts with a community-based class—surely such classes demonstrate our field's commitment to teaching rhetoric as a fully participatory democratic art—I'll echo Susan Wells (1996) in venturing that especially in service-learning classes, we can be positioned to teach the slimmest expectations for public voice and public decision-making power. Consider how busy we and our students become in such classes, how involved—and involved most often with government and private-agency advocacy *on behalf of* a group of people, much more so than activism *with and by* a group of people making public demands. With all of this busyness, we can miss that at the pedagogical heart of such a course is *acceptance* of policies enacted from above, not consideration of what it would take to mount a substantive *challenge* from below.

Take my Fall 2002 U.S. Literacy Politics class as one example. In that class, students and I studied national issues—tax cuts, budget deficits, No Child Left Behind—but we did so primarily to understand their local effects, especially on the youth center and its neighborhood and schools. We also discussed the impact of this national agenda on our own educations and restricted opportunities: the loans students were carrying, the second mortgages their parents were shouldering, the credit cards they were using to pay their tuition bills; their anxieties over how majors in English, philosophy, and sociology could be translated into post–graduation jobs with health care benefits. Such conversations helped put us more on a solidarity footing with the youth center's teens. Never, however, did students and I consider how we, with members of the youth center and anyone else suffering the devastations of the past thirty years' wage and social program cuts, might argue back. We did not ask what it would take to launch an effective opposition (something much bigger than an individual op-ed) to the massively debilitating social and economic agenda before us. We did not look to history to see where and how such opposition had been effectively mounted in the past, with what gains, and also suffering what reactions, setbacks, splits, and pacifications. Although I can defend these omissions—one can do only so much in fifteen weeks; social movements are not made in classrooms—the fact that I've been teaching this class in this way since 1999 gives me pause. *You can't fight city hall; you can only ameliorate some of the suffering it creates.* This is one way of summing up the lesson that such a class, taught again and again, imparts.

Such a class can wind up making what Susan Wells calls "a convincing argument for the impossibility of social change" (1996, 399). Students are not only positioned, as Ellen Cushman points out, as missionaries who believe they are "imparting to the poor and undereducated their greater knowledge and skills" (1999, 332); they and their teachers are prey to the historical amnesia that keeps us from recognizing that every reform and every program now under attack came into being through the analysis, organization, and action of the very people worked up in voluntarist discourse as poor, uneducated, and, especially, helplessly passive. Moreover, by keeping under wraps the history of the mass public agitation required to win the entitlement programs now being fast dismantled, such a class suggests that these problems of housing, jobs, health care, and education have *always* been properly dealt with in the private sphere of volunteerism or in a bureaucratic maze of government and quasi-governmental relief agencies. Thus a course starting with the Marxian aim of examining the totality of only seemingly individual and local problems winds up reifying atomistic piecemeal solutions: Maybe poverty isn't an effect of individual will but that's about as far as our response to it can go. (Here I recall how often the former dean of my college would lament, "But we live in *capitalism.* . . ." In the sigh that completed her sentence, we were to understand that there could be no parity for lecturers, no reduction of the twenty-six-seat course cap for first-year composition, no search to replace a retired tenure-line professor—the totality of the system producing all these local manifestations impervious to intervention and even to fuller discussion. We live in capitalism: end of story.)

No wonder, then, that when one of the youth center teens said, as another election approached, "Why can't we vote for universal health care?", his partner from my class was dumbfounded. *Vote? For health care?* A junior majoring in political science, she'd never thought of such a thing. Or, more to the point, she'd *learned* not to think of such a thing. She's not alone, of course. Health policy critic Vicente Navarro (1993) points out that since Gallup first posed the question in 1952, at least a plurality and often a majority of Americans have consistently said they would like to see a government-administered universal health care program. Neither Cold War nor neoliberal rhetoric—neither the bogey of Communism nor of Big Government—has diminished these aspirations. Yet the pedagogy of slim expectations has proven effective indeed in teaching most of us not to expect that just because most of us want public health care, we should have the right to vote and make it so.

So goes my first response to the question of why such widespread apathy, why such low electoral participation. Most recently, with another— very different—midterm election, I think we have also witnessed the almost complete failure of the pedagogy of slim expectations as people from "red" states as well as "blue" voted to end one-party rule. In multiple blows to religious conservative and neoconservative agendas, people also turned out to vote against bans on gay marriage and abortion rights in Arizona and South Dakota, to vote for stem cell research in Missouri, and in nonbinding referenda in Illinois and Massachusetts to call for troops out of Iraq *now*. That this marked an overwhelming repudiation of the Bush agenda and the Iraq war can't be denied. My state's public radio station broadcast exit interviews with voters who spelled out what they were using their votes to voice concern about: war and health care, war and the economy, war and the environment. As the *Chicago Tribune* put it, even though the Democrats demurred from offering even a "memorable bumper sticker" (Tackett 2006, A1), people acted on the slogan that was available: *Your Vote Is Your Voice*.

The day following this election, however, an odd dispiritedness prevailed among students in my U.S. Literacy Politics class. We didn't talk about the election. Instead, to flesh out the concept (from nineteenth-century radical education, reclaimed by twentieth-century cultural studies) of "really useful knowledge," we looked at news clips and stories from the University of Vermont's 1985 mass student-led campaign to push for divestment from apartheid South Africa. The class was intrigued by this chapter in campus history (which I'll return to in *Living Room*'s epilogue), and discussion was lively. Yet when one student raised the question of potential for student organizing and social change today, there was none of the postelection buoyancy I would have anticipated; in fact, it seems fair to say that pessimism took reign. In retrospect, I realize I shouldn't have expected otherwise. After all, the issue we'd been examining in recent weeks—particularly through Jonathan Kozol's *Shame of the Nation* (2006), the bipartisan "No Child Left Behind," the just-released recommendations of Education Secretary Margaret Spellings' Higher Education Commission, and the University of Vermont's own "strategic change" and "signatures of excellence" documents—wasn't "neoconservatism" or "the Bush agenda" but instead neoliberalism, or more specifically, the penetration of market logic into every facet of social and civic life including public K–12 and higher education. Words that would mark a repudiation of neoliberalism—words such as *access*, *equality*, or *free and universal*—or a slogan that would underscore opposition to contemporary capitalism's economic and military wings— *Money for Schools, Not for War*—weren't part of any major candidate's platform. Maybe, then, I should not have been surprised that the day after a Congress-altering election, the students in this usually boisterous class showed little by way of high spirits regarding the weeks and months ahead. These elections were disconnected from, or on their own insufficient to address, these students' concerns about access for the youth center's teens to our state's increasingly competitive and pricey university, about health care and livable wage jobs, about taking on the restoration of racial and economic apartheid that neoliberalism both drives and defends as the market's free hand or the exercise of private choice.

Of course, my hope in this book and in my teaching is that we can turn to twentieth-century mass social movements—movements that raised the demands of health care, housing, retirement pensions, and full civil rights; movements that have said no to lynch mobs, fearmongering, and false populist prophets—as historical examples of effective, from-below rhetorical action. These movements highlight not only the oppression and exploitation produced by capitalism but also the central, and in academe often omitted, Marxist tenet of workers' power. What better way, after all, to fight today's restrictions on public writing and public being than by returning to the strategies and tactics of those earlier struggles for public rights?

I don't want to suggest, however, that all we must do is recover, then apply the rhetorical lessons of radical from-below history. If such were the case, we—particularly compositionists who teach a working-class majority of students—would have recognized the legitimacy of working-class rhetorical models long ago. But standing between us and the lessons of such vibrant examples of rhetorical action is a problem of *ethos* and, more specifically, a neoliberalized and privatized *ethos* that aims to convince most people that it's just not their place, it's just not within their means, to take on the issues—health care, economy, war—that are also foremost on their minds. The popular election-year bumper sticker *Your Vote Is Your Voice* becomes under neoliberalism *Your Vote Is Your [Only] Voice*.

Who Am I to Argue ... ?

Let me give another illustration of this by returning to my Spring 2003 women's studies seminar. If that seminar concluded with the issue of delivery and the question of how to reach a wider audience with our voices and views, it didn't start anywhere close to there. Instead, we began with the most basic question of invention: Can we invent ourselves as people with voices and views at all, particularly on the issues pressing upon us the most? At first, the answer appeared to be a resolute and troubling "no." In our second meeting I asked students to make two lists: the first, a list of everything each writer felt she was an "authority" on or at least felt knowledgeable about enough to join a broader conversation; the second a list of the questions, events, and problems most on her mind just now. For virtually every student in the room, the first list included family, friends, jobs, hometowns while the second list held abortion rights, unemployment, women's safety, racism, the environment, and war. Though these were seniors and though a third of these students had combined their women's studies majors with second majors or minors in math, biology, English, economics, and environmental science, none of the eighteen students listed her academic field(s) on her authority list. In fact, none listed *any* of the topics from the second "concerned about" list in the first "knowledgeable-enough-to-discuss" list.

To display this divide, I drew up two overheads summarizing the two lists (Figure 5–1):

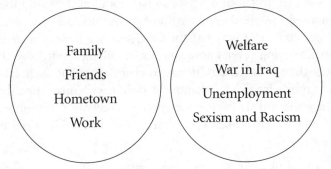

Figure 5–1

Then on the overhead projector I overlapped the two transparencies (Figure 5–2):

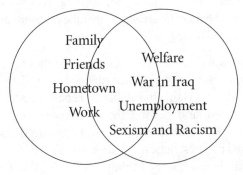

Figure 5–2

As women's studies majors, these students readily recognized this blurring of the "domestic" and "public" spheres whose gendered history they'd studied over the past four years. But for almost all of these students the idea of writing in *either* sphere, never mind in the overlap, appeared daunting. As one student, Danielle, explained, "These are two things [personal and political] I've never done before. I've really shied away from anything political and away from anything really with my own voice."

One class meeting later, as we discussed Arundhati Roy's (2001) *Power Politics*, students readily offered their own experiences with what Roy terms the "Expert's Anthem" of a neoliberal agenda intent on privatizing political decision-making power. Jayme, from rural Vermont, described town officials dismissing her mother when she'd tried to speak out at a public meeting against relaxed slate quarrying regulations; testimony, the officials claimed, could come only from those with expert credentials. For Ann, a student from Puerto Rico, dismissal had come from her stepfather. "Whenever I try to tell him what's so bad about NAFTA and the FTAA [the proposed Free Trade Agreement of the Americas]," Ann said, "I get tongue-tied and start mixing up the facts, and then he says, 'See. You're so emotional. You don't even know what you're talking about.'" For Danielle, from suburban Connecticut, it was in civics class that she learned not to expect much from her attempts at civic engagement. Recalling one class where she and classmates were urged to rely on "common sense" to understand *New York Times* reports on the Middle East, Danielle asked us to imagine:

> Thirty of us little Westport suburbanites sitting in a classroom discussing the Gulf War, the Gaza Strip. All I can remember thinking was, "Hmm. Where are these regions again in relation to the United States? Who occupies what territories and how are they divided?" From the seventh grade through high school I did not think I had the "common sense" to grasp politics—especially those of the Middle East. The most I learned was that the problems are ancient, complicated, and boring.

Danielle was far from alone in that assessment that not only the arguments of Israel/Palestine but most any international conflict zone we could put out on the floor—Haiti, the Balkans, Lebanon, Afghanistan—were ancient, complicated, and beyond their understanding. Not that these students felt any more emboldened when it came to domestic issues. As Congress debated new restrictions on abortion, the students said that they did not really know the history leading up *Roe v. Wade* (1973) nor how subsequent legislation and rulings, from the Hyde Amendment to *Webster* (1989), had already greatly restricted *Roe*'s reach.

None of these students spoke, it should be noted, with any kind of complacency about these admissions. They were women's studies majors because they saw themselves as socially attuned and concerned. Many of them already had their seats on buses and vans that would head for New York City on February 15, 2003, to protest war in Iraq. Others would attend the Code Pink peace rally in Washington, DC, later that spring or help plan the student strike that took place during the week of the Shock and Awe bombing of Baghdad. They were eager to discuss Roy's *Power Politics* (2001), Amira Hass' *Drinking the Sea at Gaza* (1999), and essays by June Jordan (1989). Where timidity set in was over the question of what they themselves would write. When at the end of this class period I wrote on the board, "Neoliberalism: It's a women's issue" and "Why I take globalization personally," and asked the class how they would respond if I assigned one of these topics for their next writing, Danielle responded with a whisper: "I'd have to drop the class."

With this account, I don't aim to point out the shortcomings in the University of Vermont's women's studies curriculum nor to fault these eighteen students for failing to cultivate at least one area of expertise in their four years at the university. I also don't aim to echo C. Michael Halloran's (1982) frequently cited lament about a decline in public discourse and lack of place for rhetorical education in the contemporary university curriculum. These were bright, inquisitive students who fully earned their 120 college credits (and, in Jayme's case, with combined sociology, biology, and women's studies majors, quite a few credits more). They had learned a great deal in their four years at the university, including, I would argue, the ideal of the orator that Halloran describes—"the civic leader who understood all the values of his culture and used artful speech to make those values effective in the arena of public affairs" (185)—*plus* their mismatch with this ideal. Here we could say that these students face the same struggle with a gendered construction of *ethos* that JoAnn Campbell describes among the nineteenth-century enrollees in Radcliffe's English A (1992): *How to imagine oneself as the ideal orator when that orator is so clearly inscribed as male?* Compounding this difficulty is the fact that most of the students in this seminar did not come from elite, or even upper middle-class, families: *How to imagine oneself as the patrician, as well as patriarchal, civic leader?*

Further, when I consider the following outtakes from a discussion with students about how they do and don't feel "authorized" when they sit down to write for an audience beyond themselves, I notice an additional problem they face in constructing rhetorical authority—authority circumscribed not only by gender and by class but also more specifically by an idea of *professionalism*:

Ann: When I think of papers I think of MLA format. It's hard because I want to make it sound professional: bam, bam, bam, matter of fact, it's all right there, it sounds good, no one can question your authority.

Jayme: You're made to feel you have *no right to speak* unless you have that degree that says you're allowed to speak. When you turn on the news . . . you see the same interviews on CBS and CNN, the same experts re-used and re-used and re-used. (Jayme's emphasis)

Ann: Also I was thinking about being a woman writer. . . . We're not supposed to write about our personal things so when you *do* do it, you have to do it well—and I'm always afraid of not doing it well.

Lauren: I still feel like there's no place for public speech or not no place but it's very hard to find a place. It's like what am I supposed to be, Walt Whitman? Am I supposed to shout it, you know, from the streets? Avenues that you think you could do good, you're also afraid of because you're going to labeled *eccentric*. (Lauren's emphasis)

Again and again in this discussion, students circled back to *credentials, authority, sounding professional, being accepted as professional, doing it right, not seeming eccentric, not sounding too emotional, doing it well,* and (what also came up again and again) *without challenge.* In these formulations, the wherewithal to enter Halloran's (1982) "arena of public affairs" isn't only a matter of having the right citizenship, gender, and street address, though that's there too. It's also a matter of having the right job, the right set of institutional credentials: *How to imagine oneself if not as a Whitmanesque oracle then as a professional, credentialed rhetor?*

We should also say that for these students, even the limited-participation civic arena Halloran (1982) harkened to mostly does not exist. Instead, if we survey the arenas for public speech and debate these students can most readily find, we find—of course—CNN's *Crossfire,* Fox News' *The O'Reilly Factor,* and ESPN radio's *Mike and Mike* (where guests are routinely told to "just shut up"). We also find academic and other liberal forums (forums such as the faculty panel on Iraq we would typically oppose to *The O'Reilly Factor* or *Crossfire*) where students likewise hear—and much more deeply learn—that it is very far from their place to speak. I've repeated this "knowledgeable about/concerned about" listing exercise in subsequent senior seminars made up of mostly English majors. The results are much the same except that some of the students also *defend* the divide by arguing, "You've *got* to be a student of theory or Shakespeare or fiction writing for years; you've got to go to graduate school or, like Arundhati Roy, win a big award before you're really *authorized*." Hence, while composition teachers often worry about first-year students who feel overly authorized to set forth unexamined, unsubstantiated claims, what I'm seeing in senior seminars is another, perhaps greater worry waiting to be flagged: students, men as well as women, who have learned in four years of university education that they cannot wield much rhetorical authority at all.

Privatizing Politics

These concerns run counter, I realize, to the belief held by many in our field that ours is a moment not of shrinking rhetorical space and authority, especially for ordinary people with no special credentials, but instead, thanks to weblogs, podcasts, and YouTube, a moment of expanding reach and authority. As Kathleen Blake Yancey argued in her celebrated 2004 Conference on College Composition and Communication address, members of the new writing public of bloggers and podcasters "have a rhetorical situation, a purpose, a potentially worldwide audience, a choice of technology and medium—and they write" (301–2). Here the biggest question facing the discipline becomes how to maintain our currency, and what appears as an attractive solution is the idea of hitching our wagon to the stars of new information technologies, transforming composition from a "gateway" or pre-disciplinary course into a new major—into our very own credential-granting arena of expertise in multimedia rhetoric and communication.

Plenty of evidence supports arguments that composition is in danger of making itself irrelevant by paying too little attention to evolving practices of and varied forums for communication. Literacy specialists (Heath 1983; Mahiri 1998; and Taylor and Dorsey-Gaines 1988, to name just a few) have long noted the impoverishing gap between official, school-sponsored and unofficial or "extra-curricular" (Gere 1994) literacies. That's a gap we ought to see as our business to bridge, first by recognizing with Yancey and others how much our students are already writing in high-tech and low-tech forums. In the past few years that I've become especially interested in how people outside official offices of power find and create audiences, I've learned that in any given class I teach, up to a quarter of students are do-it-yourself zinesters, slam poets, documentary videographers, and bloggers. Several years ahead of My Space, the Facebook, and other networking forums, one student "repurposed" an Internet dating bulletin board to advertise her band. Another, on the steering committee of the Campus Anti-War Network, was busy using email and cell phone to coordinate a nationwide, multisite "Speaking Truth to Empire" tour. Many more of my students are active and appreciative audiences to spoken-word poets in downtown coffeehouses even if they don't put their own voices forward. Those in our field who are pursuing the promise of do-it-yourself communication technologies are right that the forums being created give us refreshed perspectives on the rhetorical canons of invention, arrangement, style, memory, and delivery. Indeed, it was only when I started recognizing these myriad extracurricular rhetorical forums that I was moved to pull the canons off the shelf, dust them off, and start talking with students about their potential relevance for evaluating our going-public efforts.

Nevertheless, I can't say with much certainty that these students, including those who participate in poetry slams or update a daily blog, believe they have a rhetorical situation, purpose, and audience that extends much farther than an affinity group of, at most, six to ten other people. Even at the conclusion of my Spring 2003 women's studies seminar, students still worried over how and whether to extend their voices beyond intimate groups. Danielle, for instance, who had spent much of the semester researching the twentieth-century history of Israel and Palestine, was wary of a classmate's suggestion that she write a letter to the editor critiquing this particular newspaper's coverage of the Middle East: "Maybe I still don't know enough." Similarly, Jayme explained her reasons for pursuing what was amounting to a triple major—in biology, sociology, and women's studies—even though it threatened to add another year to her schooling and at least another $10,000 to her already substantial debt: "I know I can't get a PhD in everything and I need to be able to speak and feel empowered, but I'm so used to being told to shut up unless you have the information, unless you have that expertise, unless you have that degree that says you're allowed to speak." I think we need to take the words of Danielle and Jayme as a sign of another shift well underway in the realm of contemporary communication. This shift, which is profoundly and powerfully antidemocratic, is one we can start to glimpse by examining the mass media consolidation that's occurring in tandem with the seeming proliferation of new-technology options for delivery.

In fact, media critic Robert McChesney (2004) argues that antidemocratic tendencies in the U.S. media are greater today than they were thirty years ago—perhaps greater than they've been since the Gilded Age (48–49). Along with the proliferation of new information technologies has also come an incredible consolidation and integration of virtually every means of media production and delivery—print, film, radio, television—under the control of just five mega-media-conglomerates. Through not only the broad horizontal reach of their market share but also the vertical integration of the means for making and delivering news and entertainment, these "congloms" saturate viewing, listening, and reading audiences with the same repeated headlines—"Paris Hilton!", "Weapons of Mass Destruction!", "We Can't Cut and Run!"—delivered through multiple channels.

This isn't to say that independent media do not exist in the United States or that many people don't turn to the Internet to access international newspapers that may provide a wider range of perspectives. A friend sends me a feature story from a San Antonio paper about readers seeking the relief of Leftist independent publishers from what is otherwise a monotonous corporate reading diet (Sorg 2005). Veteran White House correspondent Helen Thomas (2006) turns to a book published by the indy New Press, Anthony Arnove's *Iraq: The Logic of Withdrawal* (2006), for the means to argue that the U.S. military can and must leave Iraq. (In an illustration of rhetorical memory's ethical appeal, Arnove chose his title to recall Howard Zinn's [1968] history-making *Vietnam: The Logic of Withdrawal*.) The story of Gretna, Louisiana, sheriffs firing guns over the heads of 200 desperate people, foiling their attempt to flee Katrina-battered New Orleans, breaks first in the Chicago-based *Socialist Worker* and from there spreads across the Internet until finally the mainstream press, including the *New York Times*, has no choice but to pick up the story (Bradshaw and Slonsky 2005). Yet although these examples suggest the reach and efficacy of independent media in the United States, we shouldn't overlook that small press and media outlets do not by and large set the terms for the national debate about Iraq, No Child Left Behind, or Social Security. Similarly, we shouldn't overstate the current potential of blogging and podcasting to expand and complicate debate. The majority of bloggers and podcasters take up cultural and lifestyle topics or, when they do discourse on war, abortion, or Society Security, tend to repeat the narrow terms, and *personas,* for debate available in the mainstream press. In fact, argues McChesney, the idea of the Internet as a wide-open world for independent expression may be a "blatant ideological ploy by powerful media firms" so that "they may be better poised to crush the competition generated by new technologies" (2004, 217). At the very least, any discussion about the exciting potentialities of the Internet should be accompanied by recognition that there's much pressure coming from advocates of the "free market" to replace open networks with closed ones, transforming the information highway into one long toll road (219).

The field for democratic discussion and debates narrows even more as deep cuts to newsroom budgets result in news organizations seeking the cheapest means possible to deliver the news: directing reporters and camerapersons to stick to White House pressrooms or embed with a military unit, or replacing expensive investigative reporting with relatively low-cost celebrity punditry (McChesney 2004, 79). In such conditions, the "news" becomes the argument of one party leader or pundit rebutted by another, journalists serving as "stenographers" for those in power (70). Periodic breaks in this pattern—for instance, briefly unembedded and utterly aghast correspondents outside the New Orleans Convention Center in the wake of Hurricane Katrina berating FEMA bureaucrats for their appalling neglect—only reinforce our awareness of how rare it is to hear today's press actually challenge official positions.

The playing field for various points of view on the political spectrum is also far from level. Right-wing think tanks such as the Heritage Foundation and the American Enterprise Institute—founded with endowments of over $1 billion in the 1970s for the express purpose of changing the "liberal media" that had "lost" the Vietnam War (McChesney 2004, 111–12)—feed the sound bites of their "scholarship" to Congress and the press. In the echo chamber that results, Senate Republicans, the White House, Fox News, the *Wall Street Journal,* and the Cato Institute all repeat the same claim: for instance, that Social Security is broken. Though Senate Democrats, Democratic presidential wishfuls, National Public Radio, the *New York Times,* and the Brookings Institute may respond—cut benefits, change the indexing—the founding claim, begging to be turned into a question—Is Social Security really broken?— goes unprobed. Overall, while claiming not to tell people *what* to think, the media do, as McChesney argues, tell people what to think *about* and set the narrow poles for *how* to think about it (70). To this I would add that the media's overwhelming reliance on official sources and think-tank-generated experts has a further impact: telling us that these are the select set of people who are credentialed and certified to hold views on the problems of the day, problems much too complex for most of the rest of us to grasp.

What we are presented with is a problem of *ethos*—how current media arrangements predispose us to define very narrowly what constitutes an authoritative appeal. Moreover, given that at least 40 percent of what passes as news on any given day is actually generated by the public relations industry for specific corporate and political interests (McChesney 2004, 71), we face the particular problem of a thoroughly neoliberalized *ethos* under which the very authority to speak, argue, and act in the public realm is repackaged as a private and exclusive commodity. What neoliberalism does is take the already limited *ethos* of liberal democracy—one whose boundaries have been subject to public contestation and transgression by working-class and oppressed groups through the nineteenth and twentieth centuries—and moves it deep into restricted-access, restricted-view regions of corporate boardrooms, quasi-governmental agencies, industry interest groups, and think tanks, task forces, and institutes all receiving a fecund mix of private and public funding. Out of this murky region issues the terms of debate, and over time, settled policies for an era: managed care, welfare reform, school choice, the war on terror.

From this perspective, I hope it becomes evident that if most people don't follow in fine detail congressional debates over Social Security or international trade, monetary, and, ultimately, military policy and if a great many people get tongue-tied about how and whether to make arguments regarding public schools, affirmative action, and trade, it's not because the majority of Americans are comfortable with the status quo and want to green-light the neoliberal agenda for further erosion of social entitlements and rights. Rather, it's because we are trained, daily, in the belief that these are properly the area of economists, bankers, foreign policy experts, and maybe the occasional agronomist or engineer. Or if we break with that training and seek a public explanation and accounting, we're met with what Arundhati Roy calls the "Expert's Anthem": "You're too emotional. You don't understand, and it's too complicated to explain" (2001, 25). Activism itself, Roy points out, becomes privatized (24)—the province of a Bono or an NGO. Under neoliberalism, a new wisdom is born: *Don't you even worry about city hall; it's in expert hands.*

We're the Experts—Just Leave the Thinking to Us!

That *ethos* itself is fast being privatized—neoliberal economic theory trouncing any claims of liberal democratic theory—is the argument at the heart of Roy's aptly named *Power Politics* (2001). In *Power Politics* Roy offers a series of essays that walks readers through neoliberalism's double—material and ideological—privatizing whammy. Taking water privatization in Bolivia and India as examples, Roy points out that before a Bechtel, Vivendi, Enron, or GE can transform a public resource such as water into a private, profit-producing commodity, it must make an effective argument for the transfer of this public resource to private ownership. In the case of India's Big Dam projects (plans to build monumental dams to convert water into an electrical power producer), the case must be made that such a transfer of power is worthwhile, or at least inevitable, even though these dams would submerge land occupied by more than a million of India's poorest citizens. How to win consent for such a massive displacement of the Indian population for a project with little or no promised public benefit? The international dam industry, Roy points out, could direct its countless PhD-certified consultants to study what Big Dams will, or won't, contribute to food production in India. The players promoting Big Dams could also win consent by ensuring that decision making is transparent and democratic (2001, 26–27).

Instead, with the full collusion of the U.S. and Indian governments, Roy argues, decision making is submerged within deeper and deeper layers of bureaucracy and obfuscation, and such submersion is justified in the name of—what else?—expertise. About the 2000 World Water Forum, which brought 5,500 bankers, government officials, engineers, economists, and corporate heads to the Hague to *collaborate* on water privatization, Roy writes:

> What they're lobbying for is not simply the privatization of natural resources and essential infrastructure, but the privatization of policy making itself. Dam builders want to control public water policies. Power utility companies want to draft power policies and financial institutions want to supervise government disinvestment. (2001, 43)

What a World Water Forum does, despite or even with the aid of the "activist" ring to its name, is naturalize the idea of putting public policy into the hands of private interests who all piously declare that they respect the universal right to water and will show that respect by selling water at its "true price" (Roy 2001, 41). Instead of making a public argument for how and why Big Dam projects and water privatization schemes are beneficial to more than a tiny percentage of a population (a tough task!), this assemblage of corporate, governmental, and bureaucratic interests argues that such issues are simply beyond the public's cognitive grasp.

Privatization thus operates on two planes: the material and the ideological. On the material plane, we find the transfer of public property, resources, services, and policy to private ownership and prerogatives. (We can also think here of Main Streets converted to "business improvement districts," public school districts placed under private management, shares of Medicare and Medicaid handed to for-profit insurers, and post-Katrina New Orleans streets turned over to Blackwater Security patrols.) Facilitating this material transfer is the transfer of decision-making authority regarding these resources, services, and policies to successively remote and specialized bodies. (We can think here of global institutions such as the World Bank and national bodies such as the Federal Communications Commission. We can also think of "old boys'" associations: the "Jackson Hole" group of insurance industry heads who advised President Bill Clinton to promote big-bucks-generating managed competition as health care reform; the oil industry heads consulted by Vice President Dick Cheney to set the terms for the nation's energy policy.) All are three or more degrees away from any sort of democratic scrutiny, debate, and intervention. And all justify their removal from public accountability in the name of a privatized, leave-it-to-the-experts *ethos*, the prime ideological means through which the material ends of neoliberalism are accomplished.

Of course resistance is still possible. I think of Massachusetts and Illinois voters saying, resoundingly, "Bring the troops home now." I think of Arizona bucking the national trend on gay marriage bans. I especially think of the surprisingly sizable number of Gallup Poll respondents who, from 1952 to 2002, have always responded "yes" to a government-administered public health insurance program. But the national discourse, its terms and its poles set by a very few, has an impact, including on the discourse of ostensibly independent bloggers. Recently, during a discussion of Kozol's *Shame of the Nation* (2006), I asked students in my Literacy Politics class how they would make an argument for universal, free public education. Nearly all of the students (who define themselves as "liberal," "progressive," or "Left") were stumped—and they were stumped not by the question of *how* to make an argument for public education but *whether*. The Reagan era mantra that President Bill Clinton took up and repeated when he too insisted, "The era of Big Government is over," appears to these students now as unarguable. Similarly, when we read an interview with U.S. Education Secretary Margaret Spellings (Norris 2006), even though these students immediately spotted (and decried) intimations that standardized testing might be extended to higher education, no one among these usually very close and careful readers noted Spellings' market terminology: Higher education is an *enterprise*; the federal government is a *one-third investor* in this enterprise—an increasingly wary investor because universities have failed to demonstrate the *value added* (a term Spellings uses twice in the very short interview) to students who complete their degrees.

The Expert's Anthem, then, does more than refute the notion that policy-making authority should be extended to any kind of mass public. It also trains a population in the belief that most people lack the means to comprehend, let alone weigh in on, the complexities of the issue at hand. It would train us to accept not only the idea that the singular purpose of higher education is to produce specialized experts but also to accept that the value of those experts and the value of their particular credential-granting institution is to be measured in the marketplace. In fact, if we go one step further with neoliberalism's drive to create new markets for profit making, we can see how expertise itself—divided and subdivided, then subdivided once more into increasingly obscure specialties and subspecialties—becomes a booming enterprise. Foreign policy, homeland security, energy policy, water policy, environmental economics, and—yes, most certainly—communications all become part of what Roy (2001) terms a "huge professional market for all kinds of 'expertise'" (26). Even punditry—with blogs serving as a proving ground for would-be professional editorialists—becomes a particular seat that a few can scramble to secure on the Expert Express.

Of course liberal democracy has long depended on a narrow set of ideas about who governs, who stands within the bounds of civil society, and what constitutes legitimate participation and credentials to hold forth on a topic. Restriction was necessary if the European and American revolutionaries of the eighteenth century were to protect their new ruling rights not only from the recently dethroned aristocracy but also from an increasingly concentrated and immiserated urban working class that was taking *The Rights of Man* and asking, "And why shouldn't these be rights for us?" The growing problem of a *thinking* working class was what Henry Ford gave voice to when he complained, "How come every time I want a pair of hands I get a human being?" (qtd. in Rees 1998, 221). Needed here was a capitalist pedagogy, manifest not only through public school curricula but also in the schooling of everyday life, to encourage people to accept as natural and enduring their more-than-a-feeling alienation from social and political power. This is the context in which we should place the problem of student—and mass—apathy, understanding that apathy isn't an aberration in our current economic and political system but precisely what the system has depended on through all its phases and transformations. Hence we *could* say that neoliberal constraints on authority are simply the continuation of what Roy calls "the old Brahminical instinct. Colonize knowledge, build four walls around it, and use it to your advantage" (2001, 26)—except that something more, in Roy's view, is happening in our current moment. Those four walls become eight and eight become sixteen, all in a mighty effort to shield from view just *how much* wealth is being transferred into private hands.

Take, as a prime example, the recent FCC giveaways of the information age's most valuable publicly held asset: the electromagnetic spectrum or, simply, "the airwaves." That commercial television and radio broadcasters have long occupied this virtual "commons" rent-free would not in itself be a problem in the following cases: *if* they were among independent producers who could also find a place on the spectrum; *if* commercial radio and television broadcasters adhered to the public oversight and public-interest programming requirements that they had promised in lieu of rent; and *if* overall it was widely understood that the airwaves *are* public property and that any new communications development—cellular phones, digital television, wi-fi—must be accompanied by public discussion of how best to allocate spectrum space in the public interest. But as McChesney (2004) points out, seven out of ten Americans (including me until I looked into neoliberalism's impact on the canon of delivery) aren't aware that the airwaves are public property, and nine out of ten don't know that commercial broadcasters use the airwaves at no charge (2004, 52). When the FCC makes a decision, then, to double the spectrum space for commercial broadcasters free of charge or convert broadcasting licenses to permanent private-ownership-like rights, the public can scarcely protect the massive resources being given away (2004, 213–14, 218). Moreover, the FCC itself—composed of past and future members of the National Association of Broadcasters; its Spectrum Policy Task Force made up largely of industry insiders plus bankers, attorneys, and engineers—is imbued with the neoliberal belief that business interests *are* the interests it is charged with representing (McChesney 2004, esp. 20, 44–45, and 51). Far from making aberrant or anomalous decisions, the FCC is right in line with the prime aims of neoliberalism: every aspect of life privatized and market-driven, government and its agencies ensuring that this market operates optimally for the biggest, most organized, and most powerful of business interests ("deregulation" actually a misnomer for regulating in the interest of monopoly or oligarchic capitalism). The FCC *has* no notion of a public, of any realm outside the market.

As would-be public writing teachers, we should be concerned by the selling of public resources intimately connected to people's means to deliver their arguments; we should be concerned by the construction of expertise that dramatically narrows the field of who is authorized to speak about this mass transfer of power and virtually all other pressing public questions. When it comes to *ethos*, after all, we do have some expertise ourselves, including access to the history of how answers to the questions of *Who speaks? Who rules? By what rights?* are justified or contested at key junctures. But before we conclude that more institutions offering undergraduate specializations in rhetoric and communications are needed, I want to return to the classroom and to what students are already learning about rhetorical expertise—lessons that put calls for further specialization in, I think, a troubling context.

Recruiting Apathy

Later in the Spring 2003 semester, students in my senior seminar examined an op-ed written by the state's former governor, Madeleine Kunin. Kunin (who came to the United States from Europe steps ahead of advancing Nazism) opens this op-ed, titled "Images and Sounds of War" (2003), with a description of how

> our lives roll out from sunrise to sunset as usual—go to work, run to the grocery store, pick up the mail, check for phone messages, scan the Internet, walk the dog, make dinner, do the dishes, and watch the evening news.

But the evening news, Kunin goes on to consider, brings "wrenching" images such as that of a U.S. Marine "cradling a wounded child whose mother has just been killed." Kunin ends with the argument that while "We feel helpless to change the course of events," the "best we can do, in our everyday world, is to keep these men and women in our thoughts" and "hope—there must be hope—that perhaps this time we will learn to work for peace."

The discussion that ensued among my students was guided by two questions I wrote on the board: How does Kunin construct her audience?

What does she suggest this audience has the power to do? In particular, the class puzzled over Kunin's "we": Did this "we" for whom war was a periodic disturbance include those listeners with ties to the Middle East or with family members deployed or awaiting deployment to Iraq? Did it describe and include the daily routines and worries of a third of Vermonters who struggle with sublivable wage jobs or of women, unlike Kunin, who work double and triple shifts (one or two jobs plus child care and housework)? Was the "we" at the commentary's end—the "we" that might be in a position to "learn to work for peace"—the same "we" running through a daily middle-class existence at the beginning? Is Kunin herself split into two voices and positions: that of the "average" citizen positioned to witness and worry over the events of the day while feeling "helpless to change the course of events," and that of the politician, a former governor and ambassador, who might be positioned and authorized to "learn to work for [or against] peace"? And even if she suggests in the end there is only a minority within the "we" with any power to act, why the overriding elegiac tone, the sense of helplessness even from someone so close to sanctioned offices of power?

At this point we contrasted Kunin's ambivalent call to action with the scene Arundhati Roy offers near the conclusion of the title essay in *Power Politics*: "We set out at three in the morning. We walked for three hours—farmers, fisherfolk, sand quarriers, writers, painters, filmmakers, lawyers, journalists. . . . We were not just fighting against a dam. We were fighting for a philosophy. For a worldview" (2001, 82). Where was our fight, in this moment, for a philosophy, for a worldview? Is it, as Kunin suggests, that "we" are just too busy with jobs, dogs, and dinner to care? What about the Vermont antiwar rally—with a record attendance of 5,000 people—at which Kunin had been an invited speaker? Why the omission of that rally and its attempt to speak and act from her commentary, from this "we"?

Such were the questions we puzzled over until finally, one student, Lauren, exploded: "The recruitment of apathy! I've been trying to think of what to call this, how to name it—it's everywhere! We hear it *all the time!*—and it just came to me. That's what this is, that's what she's doing: She's *recruiting apathy.*" Lauren continued:

> Here we are wondering what we can do, where we can go, what logical steps we can take. Instead of answering those questions or talking about people are already trying to do, she [Kunin] tells us, "You can't do anything. Well, you can hope. You can pray. But mostly, you can't *do* anything." This is where apathy *comes from.* We *learn* it.

The "recruitment of apathy" is an apt phrase, I think, for summing up not only the rhetorical effect (however unintended) of Madeleine Kunin's op-ed but also, especially, the rhetorical effect (again, however unintended) of the faculty panel on the buildup to war that I've earlier recounted. Consider again that scene: hundreds of students filling the pews, facing forward to regard the faculty panel high on the stage. Consider the instructions given by the panel's moderator—pose questions to the panelists; do not engage in argument or "diatribes"; do not applaud or cheer any statement with which you agree; *this is not a rally*—that further position the audience as passive auditors. And then there is the political science student who went to the microphone to say to the panel's only female participant, "What qualifies you as a an expert. . . . What gives you the authority to actually participate. . . .?" By countering the student's specific category of the political science expert with the more general but still exclusive category of "faculty experts," the moderator *affirmed* the logic that *war must be left to the experts*. With any response not framed as a question—clapping, whistling, stomping, booing, chanting, haranguing, or even simply stepping up to the microphone to state, challenge, testify, invite—placed under the heading of disrespectful and disruptive, the panel became a study in how we learn (and how we teach others) to sit still, face forward, hold our applause, and—on the eve of what was being touted as a Shock and Awe firestorm on a scale not seen since Dresden—hold our utter dismay.

I'm not trying to single out that panel's moderator for censure. I am a part of the university, schooled by the university; and, faced with 1,200 hooting, foot-stomping audience members, I might have rapped the microphone too. I also don't mean to single out as unusual Madeleine Kunin's commentary. In fact, her *wait, hope, and maybe next time* conclusion was entirely congruent with how most of us conducted our classes, our research, our lives that spring—not because we were too complacent to do otherwise but because overriding any sense of *must say and do something* was the much stronger question of *What?* Millions had turned out for demonstrations on February 15, 2003. The world had said no to this war, and this war was going to happen anyway. *Who are any of us to stop it?* An older anarchist friend of mine sent me a bagful of buttons with his wishful response to the question: *General Strike! When the Bombing Starts, We Stop!* I gave the buttons to teens at a central Vermont high school, who'd learned of the mass school walkouts or "blowouts" led by Chicano students in 1968 Los Angeles, and, on the first day of Shock and Awe, followed suit.

Most of us did not strike, stop, or even pause in our usual routine on March 20, 2003. Those who attended in the 2003 Conference on College Composition and Communication—the year before Kathleen Blake Yancey gave her keynote address on the agenda-setting rhetorical power of Internet composers—will recall trooping into meeting rooms, sitting down, facing forward. We listened. We clapped. We delivered papers, asked questions, and, I am sure, learned a lot. But a part of what we, with our students, are also learning at such moments—against every instinct, I think, to jump up, call out, *say* something, *do* something—is to mind our proper place. "Is Iraq the Problem? Is War the Solution?"— that's a question for a different conference, a different discipline, not our own. Or so the usual lesson goes.

So What Gives Us the Authority?

In the end, what made the faculty panel and the Kunin commentary stand out for students and me as unsettling and instructive (these were the two moments students repeatedly pointed to in final portfolio cover letters, course evaluations, and half a dozen postsemester interviews I conducted) had little to do with their actual content (which was far from unusual) but instead with the context: a seminar of students discussing the problems of privatized *ethos* against a backdrop that included not only impending war but also visible, vibrant mass public contestation. In such a context, we could see—and also oppose—the "recruitment of apathy." We could even talk about, if not repeat, the history of mass strikes against war. Such a context made momentarily visible—and arguable—what the alternative *could* be. Looking back at these final class periods of the semester, I find myself wanting to echo the refrain that Kathleen Blake Yancey wove through her 2004 CCCC chair's address: *Yes, we had a moment.*

But in these moments the argument for our field should not be to buttress our authority and assert our (value-adding) relevance through four-year degrees in multimedia rhetoric and communications. As a field, we need to stand against constructions of expertise that have already dramatically narrowed the plane of who is authorized to argue about pressing public questions. (A student like Jayme is already pursuing a triple major to shore up her *ethos*. What she needs are lessons in rhetoric across and between her fields of study, not another specialized degree she can't possibly pursue!) I do understand why in our increasingly neoliberalized universities, we feel great pressure to create a program, or product, with market appeal. I understand the pressure my university's top administrators feel to create a niche for UVM within the national higher ed market. Yet every progressive movement of the past 200 years has fought to free education from narrow, parochial, exclusive, and exploitive private interests. The fight for education as a full public right continues today. We can consider here the mass strikes by students, teachers, and workers in France over the past several years against education privatization schemes and our own Immigrant Rights movement of 2006 that included mass high school walkouts reminiscent of 1968 when Chicano students converged on the Los Angeles Board of Education bearing signs, "We demand schools that teach!" Most recently, in the walkout of 900,000 Chilean high school students (opposing the continuation and deepening of Pinochet-era school privatization measures in a country also generating a great deal of private wealth) under the banner "Copper on the ceiling and education on the floor," we can see rhetoric not as a specialized or bureaucratic *techne* but as a mass practical art.

Not everyone in the academy can or should teach a course with a title like "The History of Rhetoric in U.S. Social Movements." Not very many students will have a chance to take such a course either. And that's why—regardless of discipline and specialty, in two-year, comprehensive, and research institutions—we should be collectively concerned about the disturbing gap between actual demonstrations of mass public argumentation and what many of our students, in their classrooms and in the wider culture, learn about leaving arguments to the experts or until the next election. At the very least, we might start asking our seniors to tell us, "What do you now feel knowledgeable enough about and empowered about to speak or write or agitate on for an audience beyond a classroom?" What we hear might be unsettling. What we hear might also tell us something we need to know.

Epilogue
Education Goes Public

The City Is Open!

In April 2006, amid mass walk-outs and strikes nationwide for immigrant rights, half a dozen University of Vermont students attempted to enter the president's wing of the administration building. It was early morning, and although the students, members of a campus livable wage campaign, said they only sought a meeting, each sported a fat backpack. They were met at the door by the president's chief of staff, determined to halt what appeared to be the first attempt at an administration building takeover in fifteen years. With the door to the wing locked, the students retreated to discuss this unanticipated obstacle. A tent city on the campus green was their improvised solution: with access to the president's wing denied, the students decided to make their statement in the space available.

As it turned out, those two dozen tents and tarps—pitched in full view at the center of campus—provided a much better means for communicating the students' arguments than a president's office takeover ever could. In past takeovers—organized by students between 1985 and 1991, first to force the university to divest some $7 million in stocks from apartheid South Africa, next to push for the creation of a U.S. ethnic studies program and other antiracist initiatives—the aim had been to stop university business. *No University Business While the University's Business is Racism*, declared a placard at the entrance to the administration wing during a 1985 blockade. In April 2006, however, the members of the Student Labor Action Project did not so much aim to *stop* university business as to broadcast

> *More than half the university's service workers, with a starting salary of $9 an hour in 2006, fell below the state's livable wage standard of around $12 an hour for a one-person household, as did 279 of the campus's 632 clerical workers* (Nopper 2006). *Available data further suggested that most Sodexho-contracted food service workers, with an average wage nationally of $8 an hour, also fell well below the threshold* (Nopper 2006).

145

little known, behind-the-scenes facts *about* university business: the administration's recalcitrance about adhering to the state government's livable wage guidelines when it came to compensating service, clerical, and "part-time" teaching staff; the award of multi-million-dollar building contracts to companies employing nonunion labor with no assurance of health care coverage.

Previously dealt with in rounds of petition and denial, these issues of how top administrators distributed the university's resources were brought into the open and publicly broadcast through Tent City. The circle of tents and tarps soon included a camp kitchen, town meeting circle, and soapbox for announcements, speeches, and entertainment. Custodial and maintenance workers from the campus's UE local, clerical staff amid a union drive, along with students from a cooperative-living dorm helped keep Tent City stocked with food and drinks. Banners and plywood signs surrounded the camp: *Unite for Livable Wages, UVM Can Do Better.* Beyond livable wages, there seemed to be an additional argument asserting itself through Tent City: This student-made venue on the green—not the administration-produced posters proclaiming *Our Common Ground* and also not the $61-million student center under construction a stone's throw away from the campsite—expressed the actual values around which UVM's constituencies could unite. Faculty brought classes to Tent City. Student guides brought prospective students and parents. Joining in its town meetings were city and state officials, even the state's representative to the U.S. Congress. Participants distributing leaflets declaring *The City Is Open!* conversed with students who passed by on their way to classes. They offered tents to others who wanted to "camp for justice." Here was a group of students who were not only publicizing arguments to change the university's employment and contracting practices; they were representing what a public university and public education—visible, inviting, frequently contentious, always participatory—could look like.

Although UVM Can Do Better *may seem like a prosaic slogan, in this setting—a shantytown spreading in the shadow of a massive new student center that was rising up to challenge a mountain-lined horizon—it was dramatically effective.*

The City Is Open! appeared to be just the right slogan and Tent City just the right means for a movement aiming to open up for public discussion and participation an increasingly privatized, top-down, closed-door state university. When top administrators responded to the students' actions by keeping the door to the administration wing locked around the clock, an armed security guard clearing visitors for entry, the contrast enhanced Tent City's *ethos* and emphasized its call for transparent, accountable university governance. "The administration can't hide locked in their offices forever," wrote the students in their daily blog. "[T]hey *have* to notice us, and they *need* to recognize the importance of this issue" (UVM Student Labor Action Project 2006, authors' emphasis).

That Was Then and This Is Now?

Six months later, students in my U.S. Literacy Politics class are asking what Tent City—dismantled following a police raid on its fourth night, the university administration promising to convene a task force to study "basic needs" compensation—had really accomplished. In recent weeks we have read Laben Carrick Hill's collage-style history of the Harlem Renaissance, *Harlem Stomp!* (2003), followed by *Detroit: I Do Mind Dying* (1998) about the League of Revolutionary Black Workers. We have just taken a first glance through television news clips, campus and city newspapers, fliers, posters, press releases, and photographs telling the story of how University of Vermont students first forced the trustees to divest from apartheid South Africa, then launched what became an increasingly tumultuous and ultimately successful six-year push on university administrators to create and staff an ethnic studies program. We have been talking about the roles of writing and forms of rhetoric in these movements plus the bigger questions about the uses of education to broaden democracy and the importance of extracurricular literacy forums in historical expressions of Black power, workers' power, and student power. Such historical studies provide needed counterweights to literacy studies' usual stories of either personal struggle and achievement or foil and defeat; through this segment of the course, I'm hoping we'll find new directions for returning to our earlier discussion of Jonathan Kozol's *Shame of the Nation* (2006) and the distributing evidence of apartheid schooling here in Burlington. Those earlier discussions have provoked two persistent questions for which we need answers: "What can be done?" and "What is it *we* can do?"

By now students see that the youth center with which our class works, while providing needed space and support for more than one hundred children and teens from working-class and refugee families, isn't equipped to address sharp inequities in the city's school system and neighborhoods. And even if social services could be a vehicle for social change or substantive relief, several students point out that their own sizable student loan debt would make it hard for them to get along on a nonprofit's wages for longer than a year.

So I'm not surprised when early in our initial discussion of the 1985 student-led divestment campaign, a student in this class raises the question about prospects for campus organizing today. Another student answers with the example of Tent City. Around the table a dozen hands go up, nearly the entire class eager to get on the "stack" (the list of who's in line to speak). First one by one, then all at once, the students around the table pour out a litany of complaint and lament. *Tent City accomplished nothing. Maybe they meant well, but the Frisbee and the bongos were completely frivolous. Yeah, it looked liked they were just out to have fun.* Sniping erupts between one student who had been part of Tent City and another student across the table: *At least we were doing something. Yeah, well I don't see how it changed things for any janitors.* I bring us back to the stack. Next is a student who says she's hesitant to speak because she doesn't want to "kill" the discussion but perhaps the real question is whether the tools of the past can serve us at all. The problems appear to be very much the same, but what about the conditions? Are they enough the same or—with media congloms and free-speech zones, deindustrialization and offshored jobs—has too much changed? She hasn't killed discussion; a dozen hands go up. On this question, too, these students have much to say.

It's often asserted that Toyotist "teamwork" and "flexibility" have restored the link, severd by Fordist assembly-line production, between workers' brains and bodies. But before we conclude that Toyotism supplants Fordism, consider: In today's factory, office, hospital, and school—all workplaces in which Toyotist rhetoric reigns—teamwork is aimed at increasing production, not solving problems like position and benefits cuts. In fact, speculates Daniel Singer (165) what contemporary capitalsim attemps by assigning workers a few mental functions is not "the reversal of Fordism but its final fulfillment . . . : the thinking cog in the machine" (1965).

It's because I want students in a class such as U.S. Literacy Politics to grapple with such questions—What are the prospects for argument here where we stand? Of how much use can the tools of the past be? What has changed, and what has remained, or been rolled back to, the same?—that I bring into the classroom texts and artifacts from twentieth-century social movements, including student movements from Berkeley to Burlington. Through these texts I stress that the past century's most progressive and dramatic reforms were not initiated by elected officials or won by lone oratorical exemplars but were instead driven by the aspirations, agitation, and organization of ordinary people. At the center of my courses in literacy, rhetoric, and public writing, then, are varied examples of working-class and oppressed groups (people also busy with jobs, family care, rent to pay) who have improvised from the resources at

Today's antiwar veterans and war resistance counselors carry on the tradition of the GI coffeehouse but, with new homeland security measures, are barred from military bases where Vietnam-era activists had met the soldiers with whom they organized. Today's UVM students agitating for livable wages carry on the tradition of students pushing administrators to act in the interests of social justice but also face police (added to campus after a three-week occupation of the administration building in 1991) when they seek to organize a sit-in.

hand to challenge and change a repressive status quo. Through these classroom lessons, I aim to at least suggest a history of rhetoric that includes a *great many* men and a *great many* women speaking collectively and well. But my goals are not only historical; I do have a notion that these case studies offer useful ideas and orientations for today. And here we come to the questions—the key questions—students never fail raise: What real difference did these movements make? What are the obstacles to identifying with and drawing on these lessons here and now?

Concerns about changing conditions and contexts are ones with which participants in all social movements must grapple. In fact, what can be most instructive is examination of how rhetors have come to grips with the constraints of their particular situations. Such examination underscores that exercising rhetorical memory is never mechanical, case studies of from-below rhetorical action all the more valuable because they raise these questions of whether and how such actions are possible today. But maybe we especially need an examination of the past because evidence abounds that students— from the University of Vermont to UC-Berkeley, from Columbia and Kent State to Seattle Community College (just a handful of campuses where students, between 2002 and 2007, have stood up against sanction for speech and protest)—are *already* looking to the struggles and tactics of previous eras for guidance. The UVM Student Labor Action Project's president's wing takeover is just one example. That's a prime reason why I'll return here to the 1985 chapter in campus activism at the University of Vermont, in dialogue with my current students' hopes and concerns about our available means for acting on the problems we face today.

I have another reason, too, for wanting to demonstrate the pedagogical worth of

Context matters too when we evaluate demands. By 2004, for instance, the once-progressive demand for civil unions lagged behind agitation for full LGBT marriage rights. And while marriage equality is a substantive reform for many thousands of working- and middle-class people, "freedom to marry" is most progressive within a longer campaign to uncouple basic rights—such as universal health and disability coverage—from both a "breadwinner" and a "boss."

such an historical case study: to counter the academic commonplaces that more than 150 years of liberation struggles have produced little by way of substantive improvements in social institutions and people's lives or that between ourselves and past struggles is a postindustrial or postmodern divide. The university I joined in 1995 was a much different place *because* students over the previous decade did not declare a great divide between themselves and civil rights arguments and strategies from previous generations. This was a university that in 1995 had finally funded programs in U.S. ethnic and women's studies, had finally committed resources for recruiting women and minority faculty, had finally acknowledged its direct responsibility for low minority student enrollment, and had also—again, finally—pledged to address the racism on campus that had been flagged in a U.S. Civil Rights Commission investigation. In 1995, this was also a campus still buzzing with the memory of "Diversity University," the makeshift classroom buildings students and faculty had constructed on the campus green in 1991 to offer the multiethnic history and literature classes still largely unavailable in the faculty-senate-approved curriculum. All the more remarkable—and instructive—is that students persisted in pressing for these gains under difficult ideological conditions; in their major actions of 1985, 1988, and 1991, these students managed to hang on to the "fragments of democracy and solidarity" (Toussaint 2005, 249) that Reagan-era divide-and-conquer rhetoric had attempted to obliterate.

While UVM's anti-apartheid activists cited a handful of classes as influential, they didn't organize for action in classrooms but in extracurricular student "clubs." Faculty are present in video and print artifacts from the period; however beyond the three or four who demonstrated (and faced charges) with students, most faculty appear in the role of an increasingly involved audience. As student activity escalated, this faculty audience was persuaded to act too, through senate resolutions, arguments in public forums with administrators, and even confrontations with police.

What follows is pieced together from interviews with philosophy professor and activist Will Miller, conducted the summer before his death in 2005, as well as from the posters, fliers, news clippings, videos, press releases, letters, and notes that made up his personal archive. I won't attempt a full story of events between 1985 and 1991. I can't even describe fully the variety of educational and agitational forums created by students just in the fall of 1985. Through this sketch and accompanying glosses, however, I hope to manage what rhetoric as an art of inquiry ought to do: keep the questions—What's the use of history? What good could a Tent City do?—in play.

Crossroads at UVM

Late August: An Appropriate Addition to Convocation

This issue won't be decided by protest.

—UVM President Lattie Coor in advance of the September
1985 trustees' vote on divestment from South Africa[1]

When University of Vermont President Lattie Coor told reporters at the start of the 1985 fall semester that protest would not settle the divestment question, he may have believed his statement would hold true. Although students had previously presented petitions and verbal arguments for divestment to trustees, this campus had not seen the mass rallies and sit-ins that had spread elsewhere. In a closed-door meeting during the summer break, a subcommittee of trustees voted to recommend keeping at least $5 million of the university's endowment invested in companies doing business in South Africa, selling stock only for those companies that would not adhere to the "Sullivan Principles." Now, with the full board scheduled to vote, just as students and faculty returned for the new school year, university officials decide to move the trustees' meeting to the gymnasium, in the event of a larger-than-usual turnout. Throughout the first week of classes, students calling themselves the ANC—Apartheid Negation Congress—have leafleted outside the bookstore and library. In addition to calling on the campus to pack the bleachers at the Saturday meeting, the ANC also organizes a "funeral march" of more than one hundred students, joined by a handful of faculty and staff, into the university's convocation ceremony the Friday before. Newspaper photographs show the provost on the dais in the university chapel. Lined up beneath him are the protestors who, dressed in black and bearing coffins, address the audience with banners and signs: *Your Tuition Supports Apartheid.* Such a demonstration was far from usual. This "public ivy," relatively quiet even at the height of the Vietnam War, had been downright tranquil since the mid-1970s. It was now the mid-1980s—the

The Sullivan Principles purported to reform South Africa by securing pledges from multinationals that their South Africa operations would be desegregated and promote Blacks and other nonwhites to supervisory and management positions. UVM students, however, charged the board with "hypocrisy," pointing out to the press that only 15 percent of Sullivan-subscriber IBM's South African employees were black and that GM, whose board member Leon Sullivan formulated the principles, had refused recent calls to halt vehicle sales to the regime's military and police.

height of the Reagan revolution, a heyday for College Republicans. So it must have seemed improbable to President Coor that, despite convocation's signs of discontent, things would heat up now.

Recently, as members of UVM's faculty union debated whether to bring Fair Contract *placards into the academic year's opening convocation, I pulled out a photograph of the protesting students and faculty at the 1985 convocation—a reminder that we would be carrying on, not departing from, campus tradition.*

News coverage from that school year's start, however, anticipates a much different story about to unfold and situates the president's claim—"This issue won't be decided by protest"—within multiple counters. For example, one TV news station introduces its report on the upcoming trustees' meeting with a video clip depicting South African police bearing down, with tear gas and guns, on thousands of striking mine workers. The scene shifts to students and faculty gathered outside a UVM classroom building making signs and banners—*Embargo South Africa, Not Nicaragua*—to carry into convocation. President Coor appears briefly, just before crossing the green to convocation, and explains to a reporter that the trustees will properly decide issues on their merits and not in reaction to protest. That assertion is immediately followed by video footage of the anti-apartheid funeral march into convocation. The report closes with the convocation scene—the visual contest between the provost on the stage and the coffin- and sign-bearing students standing below—while philosophy professor Will Miller explains in a voice over, "One of the functions of convocation is to set a proper intellectual and moral note for the school year, and in that sense, I think this procession represents an appropriate addition to convocation."

Mid-September: *A Corps of Activists—Growing, Vocal, Committed*

It's like we've tried other things, and now we're trying this.

—STUDENT DURING AN ADMINISTRATION BUILDING SIT-IN

Following a 12–11 vote by trustees in their September meeting to maintain investments in South Africa, approximately 100 students, who have been holding signs and coffins behind the chairs of trustees, angrily exit the gym for a meeting outside. This impromptu meeting is soon followed by a widely publicized meeting attended by 250 students who weigh in with ideas for future actions. Those ideas include a picket outside the local IBM plant, which is both a prime divestment target and, students charge, an obstacle to democratic decision making:

Among the trustees who just voted to keep UVM investments in South Africa are three employed by or on retainer with IBM.

The press are on hand for this meeting, and one TV news report moves from footage of students discussing the proposed picket to striking Black South Africans under fire from police. Then, following a brief clip showing trustees voting against divestment while surrounded by coffin-bearing students, the report moves to a short interview with a representative from UVM's Union of Concerned Students, who spells out the connection between South African strikers and Vermont protestors. Students, this spokesperson explains, seek divestment both in "symbolic solidarity" with South African workers and to strike a "small material blow" against the apartheid regime. The report concludes with video footage showing clusters of students leafleting along a campus walkway. The walkway is lined with informational tables around which more clusters of students are gathered and talking; a group hoists an anti-apartheid banner next to the campus bookstore. "Corps of activists," the reporter tells us. "Growing, vocal, committed."

Assertions of solidarity between the striking South African workers and UVM divestment activists plus complicity between the South African government and UVM administration are further underscored in visits to campus by members of the African National Congress, who join students in teach-ins. Neo Mnumzana, chief representative to the UN for the African National Congress, also told trustees at their September meeting, "However palatable you can make slavery, it is still slavery."

In the coming weeks, anti-apartheid student activists—200 directly affiliated with the Apartheid Negation Congress and at least another 150 to 200 others participating in larger events—will file conflict-of-interest charges against three trustees with ties to companies targeted for divestment. (Because all trustees are required to file financial disclosure statements with the provost's office, members of the Union of Concerned Students routinely investigated—and reported each year in their broadly distributed *UVM Dis-Orientation Manual*—the financial ties of the university trustees, nine of whom are "self-perpetuating" with the power to name family members, friends, and business associates as their successors with no legislative, gubernatorial, or voter oversight.) Front-page newspaper stories chronicle the "Conflict of Interest Controversy" and the "UVM-IBM Conflict Scandal." A trustee responds with an op-ed for the city's daily newspaper dismissing the idea of scandal and defending South African investment as a socially responsible means for shareholders to pressure the South African government. Students bring to campus another African National Congress representative who refutes the shareholder pressure argument.

The Dis-Orientation Manual *and Union of Concerned Students particularly catch the attention of my students today: What was the relationship of the union to student government? How did these groups manage to work together? According to adviser Will Miller, the Union of Concerned Students united progressive campus groups so they could push on a recalcitrant administration and also pool student activity fees. Later, a new, conservatizing requirement that campus groups appeal separately for their funding would combine with identity politics to dissolve the union. Nevertheless, the union's primary organizational principle—groups send delegates for coordinated work on shared social justice and civil rights issues—remains a possibility for collective action today.*

Students also begin acting beyond legal and lobbying channels. Accompanied by the local press, who report that students have "shed tranquility," seventy-five activists link arms and, forcing their way into the president's wing, sit down, filling the hallway and blocking office entrances. TV news footage shows an administrator explaining that the president is away and unable to meet with students. Next we see students using the sit-in for an impromptu brainstorming session. Someone has taped large pieces of paper to the hallway walls. While participants call out ideas, one student stands with a marker and writes suggestions down. After word arrives that the president has agreed to a next-day meeting and the students file out, a reporter asks two women if the event was just a publicity stunt. They point to the pieces of paper affixed to the wall. "We've made a very concrete list of demands," one student explains, "and we're going to expect that those demands be fulfilled by the university."

October: *All the Means of Persuasion*

Can I ask you a question? Who is the university? I'm a faculty member. You're not speaking on my behalf. On whose behalf are you speaking? Who is the university?

—UVM PROFESSOR TO THE DEAN OF STUDENTS, DURING THE ARRESTS OF EIGHT STUDENTS AND THREE FACULTY MEMBERS BLOCKING THE ENTRANCE TO ADMINISTRATIVE OFFICES

Despite President Coor now urging compromise—an eighteen- to twenty-four-month "cooling off" period, followed by the start of divestment—trustees vote yet again in an October meeting against divestment and then move into executive session. Expelled from the room, students pound on and kick at the locked meeting doors. TV news crews, also expelled from the room, film the locked-out students as they move from shouting, "Let us in! Let us in!" to planning their next administrative office takeover.

At this next takeover, however, campus security guards are on the scene, announcing that they had been deputized to make arrests on behalf of the university. News footage shows guards handcuffing students and heaving them into waiting squad cars. (In total eight students and three faculty members are arrested—the first arrests for protest in the university's history.) This news report, like so many others from that fall, also features multiple counters to an administrator's on-camera claim that, as students around him are being dragged away, "appropriate order" is being restored. There is a professor, who, although not part of the blockade, challenges the arrests. His question to the administrator overseeing the guards—"On whose behalf are you speaking? Who is the university?"—is answered visually: A crowd of students, faculty, and staff swells protectively around those who'd initially formed the blockade; the administrator is visibly isolated; the security guards move awkwardly, and they even attempt jokes while maneuvering through layers of people, ferreting out individuals for arrest.

Amid this scene, the reporter observes that, as in the previous blockade, the president is reportedly away from campus and unavailable for comment. The story ends with a note from the anchor that one faculty member, Will Miller, now faces a felony charge of "impeding an officer." Footage then shows us the moment Miller committed his "crime": when he tells the security guard preparing to handcuff him, "This is a university. This isn't policing in the street. We're committed to a certain amount of dialogue." The report concludes with the day's events in South Africa, a video clip of police opening fire on a protesting crowd, killing three teens.

Newspaper and television reporters also give top-story coverage to another student initiative: Having learned from a faculty member about a shantytown built at the University of Kansas to represent and protest the oppressive conditions of South Africa's Bantustans, students gather with hammers and saws on the section of the campus green closest to busy Main Street. There, as news cameras record them singing South African and U.S. civil rights–era protest songs, they construct "Crossroads," a plywood and scrap-metal shantytown whose two main buildings they eventually outfit with woodstoves. Here two dozen members of the ANC and Union of

Throughout the fall, local news stations pair coverage of striking and protesting Black South Africans with leafleting and demonstrating UVM students. Juxtaposed video images not only bolster the ethos of the students but also, as UVM administrators begin responding with police and arrests, imply an unflattering parallel between the university administration and the repressive South African government.

Concerned Students will live and sleep, in rotating shifts, for the next six weeks. Signs and sculptures surrounding the shantytown provide verbal explanations and assertions of Crossroad's arguments. *Steve Bilko Died in Chains/UVM Trustees Polish Those Chains* announces a hand-lettered sign at the entrance of one shack. Propped up against the university's granite cornerstone, visible to Main Street's stream of cars are two black coffins. One is labeled *South African Blacks*, the other *UVM's Integrity*.

But what especially animates Crossroads is the students' commitment to remaining there, not returning to comfortable (and heated) dorms and apartments until the trustees grasp and act on their argument. Like the larger-than-life El Salvador solidarity mural that greets cars arriving in Burlington and to campus from the east, Crossroads is a vibrant and accessible visual argument. More, with dozens of students always present, holding ANC meetings, talking to visiting classes and city council members, and calling press conferences that bring reporters and cameras in droves, Crossroads is an ongoing and intensifying rhetorical event. As winter moves in, the city newspaper carries front-page photographs of snow drifting high against the shanties' outer walls. Inside students are shown bundled in sleeping bags, reading books and writing papers with mittened hands. One news station starts using a "Civil Rights" graphic for all reports on Crossroads and other student-led divestment actions. City officials explain to the press that because the students used less than $1,000 in building materials and have vented the wood stoves properly, Crossroads violates no ordinances, and because no students had previously camped on the green, university administrators have no policy they can enforce with an order to take Crossroads down.

> *Following Crossroads, administrators began limiting campus green access and activity, first by planting the green with dense clusters of trees, inhibiting large group gatherings and visibility. Additionally, administrators specified time, place, and manner restrictions: Students must belong to a recognized student organization and apply for a limited-time permit; the green's southern end, most visible to Main Street, is not among permitted locations; students may not sleep in "symbolic structures" and must show proof of insurance, with $1 million coverage for bodily injury and $50,000 for property damage, before erecting a structure.*

December: *Changing Hearts and Votes*

> *We may not have changed the hearts of some of the trustees, but we definitely changed their vote.*

—Student following the December 1985 trustees' vote to divest UVM stock from South Africa

News archives suggest that UVM administrators themselves were increasingly drawn to siding with, or at least not impeding the activities and arguments of, the students. An associate dean, also a Black South African, shifts from counseling patience and petition in September to suggesting to one TV news reporter that trustees should visit South Africa: "Only a hard core racist," he observes, ". . . would not be moved."

When December arrives, bringing another regularly scheduled trustees' meeting with divestment once again on the agenda, every sign indicates that this time, the students will prevail. Almost nightly during this last week of classes, local television news broadcasts feature live reports from Crossroads. Announcing that this is a "university problem" and not one for the courts, the state's attorney dismisses the disorderly conduct charges against students and faculty arrested in two office blockades; dropped too is the felony charge against Will Miller. Calling for "reconciliation" between administrators and students, President Coor (whose reprimand by a faculty senate angered by the handcuffing of students had been widely broadcast just a few weeks before) announces that he now supports full divestment, to be completed within eighteen months. Though the student activists had called for divestment within six months, they decide to claim this compromise as a victory. Anticipating a favorable vote from trustees, one TV news reporter announces, "Months of student demonstration at UVM had had the desired effect."

Nevertheless, the students continue to organize and demonstrate right up to the moment of the vote. Their actions include a march down Main Street to the only area bank dealing in South African Krugerrands. Its president also chairs the UVM board of trustees and has previously opposed divestment. Televised reports show students, explaining that this bank deals in "blood money," standing quietly in long lines. One by one they close their accounts. One report then cuts to footage from South Africa showing funeral marchers attacked by state police; the link between blood and money is visually affirmed.

As the weekend of the vote approaches, students also call a statewide conference, to be held next door to the trustees' meeting. Among the attendees are students from Middlebury and Dartmouth who have begun work on their own divestment shantytowns. Opponents of divestment who had previously appeared in press reports defending the South African regime and continued investment—as a bulwark against communism; as an appropriate means for exerting shareholder pressure—now switch gears. They decry trustees and the university president for "allow[ing] themselves to be coerced by any popular movement." Nevertheless, when the trustees vote, it is 12 to 7 in favor of full divestment, and the last

While reporters appear to be among the "hearts and minds" that were won—perhaps through the persuasiveness of divestment arguments combined with students' openness with the press, particularly when trustees locked their meeting doors—editorials are sharply critical. The city's newspaper awards a "brickbat" to President Coor for declining to discipline the students. A local TV station runs an editorial praising the divestment decision but castigating trustees for allowing a "fringe element" to win the question through "coercion."

report from Crossroads underscores the movement's profound appeal: A reporter stands knee-deep in snow outside the shanties, which students have begun to dismantle, erecting in their place a plywood billboard to tally the divestment progress. These students, the reporter says, gesturing at the snowy ground, slept here for sixty-three days.

Yesterday Once More?

Taken as a single snapshot, the fall of 1985 at the University of Vermont provides a view of effective, from-below rhetorical action. Working through multiple (legal and extralegal, linguistic and extralinguistic) channels and protest registers, the students used each event to build both in numbers and in intensity. Notable too is that while six to eight student leaders are visible from the opening convocation march to the closing of bank accounts at the downtown bank, each event featured multiple spokespersons prepared to address journalists, administrators, police, trustees, and each other, explaining and arguing their positions. Such a snapshot is instructive for students in my classrooms today, especially because it provides a counterpoint to more recent campus organizing trends, which have featured two or three dedicated (and primarily male) leaders making plans in small groups for maximum surprise. In contrast, the students organizing against apartheid publicly advertised all marches, pickets, and sit-ins, drawing hundreds of students and substantial press coverage. Women figured prominently as organizational leaders, spokespersons, and participants prepared on the spot to take the bullhorn or answer a reporter's question, and among students speaking to the press in the fall of 1985 were those in their very first semester, suggesting that organizers reached out right away to new activists. To aid transition from one school year to the next was also the Union of Concerned Students and a small number of faculty and staff.

Yet as instructive as this four-month period of intense activity and argumentation is, there's also something misleading about looking at this or any campaign only through the snapshot of a single season, especially if one is also looking at past grassroots organizing in order to draw lessons for the present. For instance, the students who formed the

Deborah Brandt's (2001b) concept of literacy sponsorship might further explain the overwhelmingly positive reception of both Crossroads and Tent City: the resistance of and repressive crackdowns against Black South African workers in 1985 and U.S. Latino workers in 2006 providing urgency, momentum, and sponsorship for local actions. The national demonstrations, strikes, and walkouts for immigrant rights in 2006 created a moment in which it was imaginable, within the bounds of acceptable rhetorical practice, for a group of people—even on this ostensibly "apathetic" college campus—to contest the social order.

Apartheid Negation Congress started the Fall 1985 semester prepared for escalating action *because* the previous years' petitions, student government resolutions, meetings with administrators, and appeals to trustees had yielded no results. Their campaign for divestment, which had begun in 1979, was already half a decade old. Moreover, the Union of Concerned Students decided to follow up on its divestment victory, according to their adviser Will Miller, by taking up the question of campus racism and multicultural diversity. What followed in 1986 and 1987 was not a continuing escalation of events but a return to petitioning, appeals, and task force recommendations that neither the trustees nor the faculty senate felt moved to act upon. Then came, in the spring of 1988, a one-week takeover of the administration wing by a dozen students of color with more than a hundred additional students camping out in the corridor. When President Coor, who negotiated an end to the takeover by signing an agreement to create an ethnic studies program, promptly resigned, a new president declared the agreement null. The question of campus diversity returned to committee, where it remained until 1991 when two dozen minority students, this time joined by two faculty, took over the administration building. This second occupation, three weeks in duration, made headlines in the *New York Times* and, when a popular band played a benefit concert outside the occupied building, in *Rolling Stone*. When local photographers caught the latest university president scaling a ladder late one night, aiming to appeal to students through his office window, he too submitted his resignation. All patience running out, students and faculty constructed Diversity University on the campus green to sponsor

Fast-forwarding from the early 1990s, we can consider that the next major event in UVM's history, the creation of a faculty union, owes much to the spirit of the previous fifteen years. By 2000—having witnessed the departures of five presidents on a campus that, despite the dimming memory of Crossroads and Diversity University, retained identification with social activism through the global economic justice movement—people were prepared to argue that faculty, tenure track and adjunct together, could govern themselves.

the classes that had not yet been approved. It wasn't until the mid-1990s (a decade that saw two more presidents come and go) that official steps were finally taken, including the creation of a program in U.S. ethnic studies.

It is thus over a ten-year period that we get a fuller picture of institutional change. That picture reveals how substantive progressive change was not brought about through the grace and vision of a high officeholder nor the steady steering of academe's middle management. Instead, change had to be pressed upon corporate trustees, reluctant administrators, and a faculty senate that, tellingly, moved only when students did. This isn't to say that the positions and actions of top- and mid-level officials make no difference at all in the dynamics of social argument and change. To the contrary, even though this period in campus history can't exactly be called revolutionary, what students both helped create and took rhetorical advantage of was a revolutionary state of affairs: The administrators and trustees could no longer rule as they had; neither were students, and increasingly faculty, willing to be ruled as they were.

Today the university's official publications promote a social justice *ethos* that has not always been part of UVM's history—a history that includes the promotion of eugenics research and a black-face minstrel show that was not finally disbanded until the early 1970s—but was created especially by students organizing from the mid-1980s into the 1990s. Tent City carried on that history of struggle over where campus arguments will take place: on the green with the widest possible audience and broadest possible participation or in limited-access committees and boardrooms, where pressing questions of justice and fairness have most often languished unaddressed. But did Tent City actually become part of a campaign that achieves a downward redistribution of campus wealth? Was it just a one-up event that, as some of my students worried, accomplished nothing at all? This is a story still in the making, but for now, consider:

"We have a very conservative student body," a colleague from a midwestern university told me. "It's not like UVM here." Yet in 1964—while UVM drew thousands to its annual "Kake Walk" minstrel show—this rural midwestern campus was launching the civil rights movement's historic Freedom Summer. Decades later, upsurges in global economic justice and antiracist organizing prompted a neighboring city newspaper to take note of students on this supposedly conservative campus with the headline "The Kids Are All Right." More recently, a student labor solidarity coalition and the student newspaper banded together to support striking university workers—and reportedly faced administrative reprisal for doing so.

On the final night of Tent City, following a potluck attended by more than 200 students, staff, faculty, and area union members, someone in administration got nervous. As the potluckers departed and a dozen students retired into their tents, nine cruisers and one paddy wagon pulled in, carrying armed police called by the provost's office to clear the camp and hand out trespassing citations. "Our night of Shock and Awe" was how a colleague in anthropology described and denounced this use of force, while the university president and provost argued that it was for "campus protection" and "students' own good" that armed police were sent in.

For my part, I think back to the potluck just hours before the raid. Here—and not inside the colossal new student center—was a real hub of campus life. Here was a large group of varied people gathering together without a permit, making plans without administrative sanction, dining at the same table without one group paying and the other serving. What a potential upset to the "natural order" of things! What if we'd started saying, "Whose green? *Our* green. Whose university? *Our* university." No wonder they called the cops—for their own protection, for their own good.

Note

1. All quotations are from news reports and editorials that aired on the region's ABC, CBS, and NBC news affiliates or appeared in the Burlington Free Press, the Vermont Cynic, and the (now defunct) Gadfly between August and December 1985 and are part of the late Will Miller's personal archive. That archive is presently being cataloged and preserved by the advisory board of the Will Miller Social Justice Lecture Series, established shortly before his death.

Works Cited

"AAUP Condemns Actions of University of South Florida Administration in Al-Arian Case.'" 2003. Press release. www.aaup.org/newsroom/press/2003/amSF.htm

AAUP Professional Liability/Marsh Affinity Group Services. 2002. "You Could Be Sued for Simply Doing Your Job." Mailing. Seabury and Smith: June.

American Association of University Professors. 2006. "Trends in Faculty Status 1975–2003." www.aaup.org/AAUP/pubsres/research/trends 1975–2003.htm

———. 2001. "1940 Statement of Principles on Academic Freedom and Tenure." *Policy Documents and Reports*, 9th ed. Washington, DC: American Association of University Professors.

Abrams v. United States. 1919. 250 US 616.

Alderman, Ellen, and Caroline Kennedy. 1995. *The Right to Privacy.* New York: Knopf.

Almeling, Rene, Laureen Tews, and Susan Dudley. 2000. "Abortion Training in U.S. Obstetrics and Gynecology Residency Programs, 1998." *Family Planning Perspectives* 32 (November–December). www.guttmacher.org/pubs/journals/3226800.html.

Arendt, Hannah. 1958. *The Human Condition.* Chicago: University of Chicago Press.

Arnove, Anthony. 2006. *Iraq: The Logic of Withdrawal.* New York: New Press.

Atchison, Topeka and Santa Fe Railway v. Gee. 1905. 139 F. 582 (CCSD, Iowa).

American Steel Foundries v. Tri-Cities Central Trades Council. 1921. 257 US 184.

Atkins, G. Douglas. 2000a. "Art and Anger—Upon Taking Up the Pen Again: On Self(e)-Expression." *JAC: A Journal of Composition Theory* 20: 414–26.

———. 2000b. "On Writing Well: Or, Springing the Genie from the Inkpot." *JAC: A Journal of Composition Theory* 20: 73–85.

Baehr, Ninia. 1990. *Abortion Without Apology: A Radical History for the 1990s.* Boston: South End.

Ballif, Michelle, D. Diane Davis, and Roxanne Mountford. 2000. "Toward an Ethic of Listening." *JAC: A Journal of Composition Theory* 20: 931–42.

Balmer, Randall. 2004. *Encyclopedia of Evangelicalism*. Waco, TX: Baylor University Press.

Barber, Benjamin. 1988. *The Conquest of Politics: Liberal Philosophy in Democratic Times*. Princeton, NJ: Princeton University Press.

Barton, Ellen. 1997. "Literacy in (Inter)Action." *College English* 59: 408–37.

Bell, Daniel. 1976. *The Cultural Contradictions of Capitalism*. New York: Basic Books.

Benhabib, Seyla. 1998. "Models of Public Space: Hannah Arendt, the Liberal Tradition and Jürgen Habermas." In *Feminism, the Public and the Private*. Ed. Joan B. Landes. Oxford: Oxford University Press, 65–99.

Berlin, James. 1994. "Revisionary Histories of Rhetoric." In *Writing Histories of Rhetoric*. Ed. Victor J. Vitanza. Carbondale, IL: Southern Illinois University Press, 112–27.

Blackmun, Harry A. 1994. Taped interview with Harold Koh. 6 July. Quoted in Suarez, Ray. "The Blackmun Tapes." *Newshour with Jim Lehrer*. 4 March 2004. Washington DC: MacNeil/Lehrer Productions.

Blakely, Edward J., and Mary Gail Snyder. 1997. *Fortress America: Gated Communities in the United States*. Washington, DC: Brookings Institute.

Bloom, Lynn Z. 1996. "Freshman Composition as a Middle-Class Enterprise." *College English* 58: 654–75.

Boquet, Elizabeth. 2002. *Noise from the Writing Center*. Logan, UT: Utah State University Press.

Bourdieu, Pierre. 1998. "The Protest Movement of the Unemployed, a Social Miracle." *Acts of Resistance: Against the Tyranny of the Market*. Trans. Richard Nice. New York: New Press.

Bourne, Jenny. 2002. "Racism, Postmodernism and the Flight from Class." In *Marxism Against Postmodernism in Educational Theory*. Ed. Dave Hill, Peter McLaren, Mike Cole, and Glenn Rikowski. Lanham, MD: Lexington Books, 195–210.

Bowers v. Hardwick. 1986. 478 US 186.

Bradshaw, Larry, and Lorrie Beth Slonsky. 2005. "The Real Heroes and Sheroes of New Orleans." *Socialist Worker* 9 September: 4–5.

Brandt, Deborah. 2001a. "Protecting the Personal." In "The Politics of the Personal: Storying Our Lives Against the Grain." The Symposium Collective. *College English* 64: 41–62.

———. 2001b. *Literacy in American Lives*. Cambridge: Cambridge University Press.

Brecher, Jeremy. 1997. *Strike!* Cambridge, MA: South End Press.

Buhle, Paul, and Mike Alewitz. 2002. *Insurgent Images: The Agitprop Murals of Mike Alewitz*. New York: Monthly Review Press.

Bunker, Matthew D., and Charles N. Davis. 2000. "When Government 'Contracts Out': Privatization, Accountability, and Constitutional Doctrine." *Access Denied: Freedom of Information in the Information Age*. Ames, IA: Iowa State University Press.

Burnham, Gilbert, Rhyadh Lafta, Shannon Doocy, and Les Roberts. 2006. "Mortality After the 2003 Invasion of Iraq: A Cross-Sectional Cluster Sample Survey." *The Lancet*. 11 October.

Butler, Judith. 1997. *Gender Trouble: Feminism and the Subversion of Identity*. New York: Routledge.

Campbell, JoAnn. 1992. "Controlling Voices: The Legacy of English A at Radcliffe College 1883–1917." *College Composition and Communication* 43: 472–85.

Carter, David. 2004. *Stonewall: The Riots that Sparked the Gay Revolution*. New York: St. Martin's.

Castillo, Ana. 1994. *Massacre of the Dreamers: Essays on Xicanisma*. Albuquerque: New Mexico University Press.

CBS v. DNC. 1973. 412 US 94.

Chang, Nancy. 2002. *Silencing Political Dissent: How Post–September 11 Anti-Terrorism Measures Threaten Our Civil Liberties*. New York: Seven Stories.

Cicero, Marcus Tulius. 2001 (ca. 70 B.C.E.). *De Oratore*. In *The Rhetorical Tradition: Readings from Classical Times to the Present*, 2d ed. Ed. Patricia Bizzell and Bruce Herzberg. Boston: Bedford/St. Martin's, 289–339.

Cockburn, Alexander, and Jeffrey St. Claire. 2002. "Strikers as Terrorists? Ridge Calls Longshoreman's Chief." *Counterpunch* 27 June. www.counterpunch.org/Cockburn0627.html

Collins, Chuck. 2003. "Shrink, Shift, and Shaft." 12 August. www.tom paine.com/Archive/scontent/8608.html

Connors, Robert J. 1996a. "Comment and Response." *College English* 58: 968–74.

———. 1996b. "Teaching and Learning as a Man." *College English* 58: 137–57.

Crowley, Sharon, and Debra Hawhee. 1999. *Ancient Rhetorics for Contemporary Students*, 2d ed. New York: Longman.

Cushman, Ellen. 1999. "Opinion: The Public Intellectual." *College English* 61: 328–36.

———. 1998. *The Struggle and the Tools: Oral and Literate Strategies in an Inner-City Community*. New York: State University of Albany, NY: State University of New York Press.

Davies, James B., Susanna Sandstrom, Anthony Shorrocks, and Edward N. Wolff. 2006. "The World Distribution of Household Wealth." Helsinki: United Nations University/World Institute for Development Economics Research. www.wider.unu.edu

Davis, D. Diane. 2001. "Finitude's Clamor; or, Notes Toward a Communi-tarian Literacy." *College Composition and Communication* 53: 119–45.

———. 2000. *Breaking Up [at] Totality: A Rhetoric of Laughter.* Carbondale, IL: Southern Illinois University Press.

Davis, Mike. 1998. *Ecology of Fear: Los Angeles and the Imagination of Disaster.* New York: Metropolitan Books.

———. 1992. "Fortress Los Angeles: The Militarization of Urban Space." In *Variations on a Theme Park: The New American City and the End of Public Space.* Ed. Michael Sorkin. New York: Hill and Wang. 154–80.

Debs, Eugene. 1918. "The Canton, Ohio, Speech." 16 June. In *Voices of a People's History of the United States.* 2004. Ed. Howard Zinn and Anthony Arnove. New York: Seven Stories. 295–97.

D'Emilio, John, and Estelle B. Freedman. 1997. *Intimate Matters: A History of Sexuality in America,* 2d ed. Chicago: University of Chicago Press.

Dobbs, Farrell. 1972. *Teamster Rebellion.* New York: Pathfinder.

Draper, Hal. 2004. *Socialism from Below,* 2d ed. Alameda, CA: Center for Socialist History.

Duberman, Martin. 1994. *Stonewall.* New York: Plume.

Eagleton, Terry. 1997. "Where Do Postmodernists Come From?" In *In Defense of History: Marxism and the Postmodern Agenda.* Ed. Ellen Meiksins Wood and John Bellamy Foster. New York: Monthly Review Press, 17–25.

Eisenstadt v. Baird. 1972. 405 US 438.

Erwin, Elizabeth. 2006. "Teaching Public Literacy: The Partisanship Problem." *College English* 68: 407–21.

Eschle, Catherine. 2001. *Global Democracy, Social Movements, and Feminism.* Boulder, CO: Westview.

Evans, Sara. 1980. *Personal Politics: The Roots of Women's Liberation in the Civil Rights Movement and the New Left.* New York: Vintage.

Evces, Mike. 2001. "Public Rhetoric for Academic Workers: Tips from the Front Lines." *Forum: A Newsletter of the Non-Tenure-Track Faculty Special Interest Group* 5.1 in *College Composition and Communication* 53: A3–A5.

Ferguson, Sarah. 2003. "In Shock and Awe: New York Will March in the Face of War." *The Village Voice* 19–25 March. www.villagevoice.com/news/ 0312,ferguson, 42680,1.html

Finally Got the News. 1970. Produced by Stewart Bird, Rene Lichtman, and Peter Gessner in association with the League of Revolutionary Black Workers. 55 minutes. First Run/Icarus Films. Videocassette.

Finner, Lawrence B., and Stanley K. Henshaw. 2003. "Abortion Incidence and Services in the United States in 2000." Alan Guttmacher Institute. www.guttmacher.org/pubs/journals/3500603.html

Flynn, Elizabeth. 1988. "Composing as a Woman." *College Composition and Communication* 39: 423–35.

Frank, Dana. 2001. "Girl Strikers Occupy Chain Store, Win Big: The Detroit Woolworth's Strike of 1937." In *Three Strikes: Miners, Musicians, Salesgirls, and the Fighting Spirit of Labor's Last Century.* Ed. Howard Zinn, Dana Frank, and Robin D. G. Kelly. Boston: Beacon Press, 58–118.

Franzen, Jonathan. 2001. *The Corrections.* New York: Farrar, Straus and Giroux.

Fraser, Nancy. 1997. *Justice Interruptus: Critical Reflections on the "Postsocialist" Condition.* New York and London: Routledge.

———. 1992. "Rethinking the Public Sphere: A Contribution to the Critique of Actually Existing Democracy." In *Habermas and the Public Sphere.* Ed. Craig Calhoun. Cambridge, MA: MIT Press. 109–142.

———. 1989. *Unruly Practices: Power, Discourse, and Gender in Contemp-orary Social Theory.* Minneapolis: University of Minnesota Press.

Frey, Olivia. 1990. "Beyond Literary Darwinism: Women's Voices and Critical Discourse." *College English* 52: 507–26.

Gannon, James P. 1968. "UAW Troubles: Resurgent Racism. . . ." *Wall Street Journal* 10 May: 16.

Garrison, Ruth. 1992. "Feminism and the Public/Private Distinction." *Stanford Law Review* 45: 1–45.

Gee, James Paul. 1999. "Learning Language as a Matter of Learning Social Languages within Discourses." Annual Conference on College Composition and Communication. Atlanta, GA.

———. 1996. *Social Linguistics and Literacy: Ideology in Discourses.* Bristol, PA: Taylor & Francis.

Georgakas, Dan. 2002. "Revolutionary Struggles of Black Workers in the 1960s." *International Socialist Review* 22 (March–April): 59–64.

Georgakas, Dan, and Marvin Surkin. 1998. *Detroit: I Do Mind Dying,* 2d ed. Cambridge, MA: South End.

George, Diana. 2002. "From Analysis to Design: Visual Communication in the Teaching of Writing." *College Composition and Communication* 54: 11–39.

George, Susan. 2001a. "Clusters of Crisis and a Planetary Contract." *Sand in the Wheels* 105 (21 November): 1–4.

———. 2001b. "Neo-liberalism and the New World Order." Globalization and Resistance Conference. November 16–17, New York, NY.

Gere, Anne Ruggles. 1994. "Kitchen Tables and Rented Rooms: The Extracurriculum of Composition." *College Composition and Communication* 45: 75–91.

Gilbert, James L., Francis H. Hare, Jr., and Stuart A. Ollanik. 1994. "Negotiation and Settlement: The Price of Silence." *Trial* 30 (June): 17–21.

Gilyard, Keith. 2003. "Composition and the Critical Moment." In *Composition Studies in the New Millennium: Reading the Past, Rewriting the Future*. Ed. Lynn Z. Bloom, Donald A. Daiker, and Edward M. White. Carbondale, IL: Southern Illinois University Press.

Giroux, Henry. 2000. *Stealing Innocence: Youth, Corporate Power, and the Politics of Culture*. New York: St. Martin's.

Giroux, Susan Searls. 2002. "The Post-9/11 University and the Project of Democracy." *JAC: A Journal of Composition Theory* 22: 57–91.

Gorz, Andre. 1982. *Farewell to the Working Class: An Essay on Post-Industrial Socialism*. Boston: South End.

Green, Duncan. 1995. *Silent Revolution: The Rise of Market Economies in Latin America*. London: Cassell and LAB.

Greenbaum, Andrea. 2001. "Bitch Pedagogy: Agonistic Discourse and the Politics of Resistance." In *Insurrections: Approaches to Resistance in Composition Studies*. Ed. Andrea Greenbaum. Albany NY: State University of New York Press, 151–68.

Greer, Jane. 1999. "'No Smiling Madonna': Marian Wharton and the Struggle to Construct a Critical Pedagogy for the Working Class, 1914–1917." *College Composition and Communication* 51: 248–271.

Griswold v. Connecticut. 1965. 381 US 479.

Guerrera, Francesco, and David Wighton. 2006. "US Set for Record Run of Profits." *Financial Times* 5 July 15.

Halloran, S. Michael. 1996 (1982). "Rhetoric in the American College Curriculum: The Decline of Public Discourse." In *Composition in the Four Keys: Inquiring into the Field*. Ed. Mark Wiley, Barbara Gleason, and Louise Wetherbee Phelps. Mountain View, CA: Mayfield, 184–197.

Hans, Valerie P. 2000. *Business on Trial: The Civil Jury and Corporate Responsibility*. New Haven: Yale University Press.

Hardt, Michael, and Antonio Negri. 2000. *Empire*. Cambridge, MA: Harvard University Press.

Harris v. McRae. 1980. 448 US 297.

Hasian, Marouf, Jr. 2001. "Vernacular Legal Discourse: Revisiting the Public Acceptance of the 'Right to Privacy' in the 1960s." *Political Communication* 18: 89–105.

Hass, Amira. 1999. *Drinking the Sea at Gaza: Days and Nights in a Land Under Siege*. Trans. Elana Wesley and Maxine Kaufman-Lacusta. New York: Metropolitan Books.

Healy, Patrick. 2005. "Clinton Seeking Shared Ground Over Abortions." *New York Times* 25 January: A1.

Heath, Shirley Brice. 1983. *Ways with Words: Language, Life, and Work in Communities and Classrooms*. New York: Cambridge University Press.

Henshaw, Stanley K., and Lawrence B. Finner. 2003. "The Accessibility of Abortion Services in the United States, 2001." *Perspectives on Sexual and Reproductive Health* 35 (January–February). www.guttmacher.org/pubs/journals/3500603.html

Herrington, Anne. 2001. "When Is My Business Your Business?" In "The Politics of the Personal: Storying Our Lives Against the Grain." The Symposium Collective. *College English* 64: 41–62.

Hill, Laban Carrick. 2003. *Harlem Stomp! A Cultural History of the Harlem Renaissance*. New York: Little Brown.

Himmelstein, David, and Steffie Woolhandler. 2001. *Bleeding the Patient: The Consequences of Corporate Health Care*. With Ida Hellander. Monroe, ME: Common Courage Press.

Horton, Miles. 1997. *The Long Haul: An Autobiography*. New York: Teachers College Press.

Howell, Jeremy, and Alan Ingham. 2001. "From Social Problem to Personal Issue: The Language of Lifestyle." *Cultural Studies* 15: 326–351.

Ignatieff, Michael. 2002. "How to Keep Afghanistan from Falling Apart: The Case for a Committed American Imperialism." *New York Times Magazine* 28 July: 26–31, 54, 57, 59.

Iraq Veterans Against the War. 2007. "Iraq Veterans Use Street Theater to Show the True Reality of War." www.ivaw.org/node/559

Jarratt, Susan C. 1991a. *Rereading the Sophists: Classical Rhetoric Refigured*. Carbondale, IL: University of Southern Illinois Press.

———. 1991b. "Feminism and Composition: The Case for Conflict." In *Contending with Words: Composition and Rhetoric in a Postmodern Age*. Ed. Patricia Harkin and John Schilb. New York: MLA, 105–24.

Johnson, Haynes, and Nick Kotz. 1972. *The Unions: The Washington Post National Report*. New York: Pocket Books.

Johnson, Paul. 2001. "The Answer to Terrorism? Colonialism." *Wall Street Journal* 9 October. www.opinionjournal.com/extra/?id=95001283

Jordan, June. 1989. "Civil Wars." *Moving Towards Home: Political Essays*. London: Virago.

———. 1985. *Living Room*. New York: Thunder's Mouth Press.

Kirsch, Gesa. 1996. "Comment and Response." *College English* 58: 966–68.

Kohl, Herbert. 2005. *She Would Not Be Moved: How We Tell the Story of Rosa Parks and the Montgomery Bus Boycott.* New York: New Press.

Koppel, Barbara. 1993. *American Dream.* New York: HBO Videos/Prestige Films.

Kozol, Jonathan. 2006. *The Shame of the Nation: The Restoration of Apartheid Schooling in America.* New York: Three Rivers Press.

Kumar, Deepa. 2006. *Outside the Box: Corporate Media, Globalization, and the UPS Strike.* Urbana and Chicago: University of Illinois Press.

Kundera, Milan. 1984. *The Unbearable Lightness of Being.* Trans. Michael Henry Heim. New York: Harper.

Kunin, Madeleine. 2003. "Images and Sounds of War." Vermont Public Radio. 7 April.

Laclau, Ernesto, and Chantal Mouffe. 1985. *Hegemony and Socialist Strategy: Towards a Radical Democratic Politics.* London: Verso.

Lafer, Gordon. 2002. *The Job Training Charade.* Ithaca, NY: Cornell University Press.

Lamb, Catherine. 1991. "Beyond Argument in Feminist Composition." *College Composition and Communication* 42: 11–24.

Lens, Sidney. 1973. *The Labor Wars: From the Molly Maguires to the Sitdowns.* New York: Doubleday.

Leonhardt, David. 2004. "Growth in Jobs Is Still Sluggish Despite Forecast." *New York Times* 6 March: A1.

Lewis, John. 1963. "Original Text of Speech to Be Delivered at the Lincoln Memorial (August 28, 1963)." In *Voices of a People's History of the United States.* 2004. Ed. Howard Zinn and Anthony Arnove. New York: Seven Stories, 398–99.

Lindorff, David. 2003. "Against War at Ground Zero." *Counterpunch* 24 March. www.counterpunch.org/lindorff03252003.html

Lovibond, Sabina. 1994. "Maternalist Ethics: A Feminist Assessment." *The South Atlantic Quarterly* 93: 779–902.

Lukács, Georg. 1997. *History and Class Consciousness.* Trans. Rodney Livingstone. Cambridge, MA: MIT Press.

Lynch, Dennis A., Diana George, and Marilyn M. Cooper. 1997. "Moments of Argument: Agonistic Inquiry and Confrontational Cooperation." *College Composition and Communication* 48: 61–85.

Madsen et al. v. Women's Health Center, Inc. 1994. 114 S. Ct. 2516.

Mahiri, Jabari. 1998. *Shooting for Excellence: African American and Youth Culture in New Century Schools.* Urbana, IL: National Council of Teachers of English.

Malinowitz, Harriet. 2003. "The Uses of Literacy in a Globalized, Post–September 11 World." In *Composition Studies in the New Millennium: Reading the Past, Rewriting the Future*. Ed. Lynn Z. Bloom, Donald A. Daiker, and Edward M. White. Carbondale, IL: Southern Illinois University Press.

Mann, Brian. 2003. "N.Y. Activists Back Pakistani Detainee." *All Things Considered*. 5 August. Washington, DC: National Public Radio.

Marcuse, Herbert. 1964. *One-Dimensional Man*. Boston: Beacon Press.

Marmor, Theodore R. 1994. *Understanding Health Care Reform*. New Haven: Yale University Press.

McChesney, Robert. 2004. *The Problem of the Media: U.S. Communication Politics in the Twenty-First Century*. New York: Monthly Review Press.

McKinnon, Catherine A. 1989. *Toward a Feminist Theory of State*. Cambridge, MA: Harvard University Press.

McLaren, Peter, and Ramin Farahmandpur. 2002. "Breaking Signifying Chains: Marxist Position on Postmodernism." In *Marxism Against Postmodernism in Educational Theory*. Ed. Dave Hill, Peter McLaren, Mike Cole, and Glenn Rikowski. Lanham, MD: Lexington Books. 35–66.

Meiksins Wood, Ellen, and Neal Wood. 1978. *Class Ideology and Ancient Political Theory: Socrates, Plato, and Aristotle in Social Context*. New York: Oxford University Press.

Mill, John Stuart. 1863. *On Liberty*. Boston: Ticknor and Fields.

Mitchell, Don. 2003. *The Right to the City: Social Justice and the Fight for Public Space*. New York: Guilford.

Moody, Anne. 1968. *Coming of Age in Mississippi*. New York: Dial.

Moody, Kim. 1997. *Workers in a Lean World: Unions in the International Economy*. New York: Verso.

Navarro, Vicente. 1994. *The Politics of Health Policy: The US Reforms, 1980–1994*. Cambridge, MA: Blackwell.

———. 1993. *Dangerous to Your Health: Capitalism in Health Care*. New York: Monthly Review Press.

"Negro Rally Seen as Threat to Rights Bill." 1963. *New York Times*. 15 July. 19.

Negt, Oskar, and Alexander Kluge. 1993. *Public Sphere and Experience*. Minneapolis: University of Minnesota Press.

Nelson, Cary. 2001. *Revolutionary Memory: Recovering the Poetry of the American Left*. New York: Routledge.

Nguyen, Tram. 2006. *We Are All Suspects Now: Untold Stories from Immigrant Communities After 9/11*. Boston: Beacon Press.

Nopper, Katherine. 2006. "Student Labor Action Project: A Two Year Retrospective." Vermont Workers' Center. 26 June. vwcsolidarity.blogspot.com/2006_06_01_archive.html

Norris, Michele. 2006. "Spellings Announces Plans to Improve Higher Ed." *All Things Considered*. 26 September. Washington, DC: National Public Radio.

Novack, George. 1965. *The Origins of Materialism*. New York: Pathfinder.

O'Dair, Sharon. 2003. "Class Work: Site of Egalitarian Activism or Site of Embourgeoisement?" *College English* 65: 593–606.

Olson, Gary. 1999. "Toward a Post-Process Composition: Abandoning the Rhetoric of Assertion." In *Beyond the Writing Process Paradigm: Post-Process Theory*. Ed. Thomas Kent. Carbondale, IL: Southern Illinois University Press, 7–15.

Pough, Gwendolyn D. 2002. "Empowering Rhetoric: Black Students Writing Black Panthers." *College Composition and Communication* 53: 466–86.

Ramsey, Maja, Justine Durrell, and Timothy W. Ahearn. 1998. "Keeping Secrets with Confidentiality Agreements." *Trial* 34 (August): 38–43.

Reagan, Leslie J. 1998. *When Abortion Was a Crime: Women, Medicine, and Law in the United States, 1867–1973*. Berkeley: University of California Press.

Rees, John. 1998. *The Algebra of Revolution: The Dialectic and the Classical Marxist Tradition*. London and New York: Routledge.

Richardson, Elaine, and Sean Lewis. 1999. "'Flippin' the Script'/'Blowin' Up the Spot': Puttin' Hip-Hop Online in (African) America and South Africa." In *Global Literacies and the World-Wide Web*. Ed. Gail E. Hawisher and Cynthia L. Selfe. London and New York: Routledge.

"Right Goal; Wrong Method." 1963. *New York Times* 23 July: 28.

Roe v. Wade. 1973. 410 US 113.

Ronell, Avital. 1994. *Finitude's Score: Essays for the End of the Millennium*. Lincoln: University of Nebraska Press.

Rose. Mike. 1989. *Lives on the Boundary: The Struggles and Achievements of America's Underprepared*. New York: Free Press.

Rosen, Stephen Peter. 2002. "The Future of War and the American Military." *Harvard Magazine* 104 (May-June): 29–31.Rowbotham, Sheila. 1973. *Woman's Consciousness, Man's World*. London: Penguin.

Rowbotham, Sheila. 1973. *Woman's Conciousness, Man's World*. London: Penguin.

Roy, Arundhati. 2001. *Power Politics*. Cambridge, MA: South End Press.

Royster, Jacqueline Jones, and Jean C. Williams. 1999. "History in the Spaces Left: African American Presence and Narratives of Composition Studies." *College Composition and Communication* 50: 563–84.

Ruddick, Sara. 1989. *Maternal Thinking: Towards a Politics of Peace.* Boston: Beacon.

Ste. Croix, G. E. M. de. 1981. *The Class Struggle in the Ancient Greek World: From the Archaic Age to the Arab Conquests.* Ithaca, NY: Cornel University Press.

Schacter, Aaron. 2001. "Comfort Retailers." *Marketplace Morning Report.* 9 October. Minneapolis: Minnesota Public Radio/Public Radio International.

Schenck v. United States. 1919. 249 US 47.

Selfe, Cynthia L. 2000. "To His Nibs, G. Douglas Atkins—Just in Case You're Serious About Your Not-So-Modest Proposal." *JAC: A Journal of Composition Theory* 20: 405–13.

Singer, Daniel. 1999. *Whose Millenium? Theirs or Ours?* New York: Monthly Review Press.

"The Sleeping Giant." 2006. *New York Times* 29 April: A10.

Smith, Dorothy E. 1987. *The Everyday World as Problematic: A Feminist Sociology.* Boston: Northeastern University Press.

Smith, Sharon. 2006. *A Subterranean Fire: A History of Working-Class Radicalism in the United States.* Chicago: Haymarket Books.

———. 1992. "Twilight of the American Dream." *International Socialism* 54: 3–43.

Sorg, Lisa. 2005. "Scratching a Niche: Indie, Progressive Presses Target Audiences Looking for the Stories Behind the Headlines." *San Antonio Current.* 26 May.

Starhawk. 2001. "Only Poetry Can Address Grief: Moving Forward after 911." *Sand in the Wheels* 101 (24 October): 6–12.

Sustar, Lee. 2002. "Bush and the Bosses Target Dockworkers." *Counterpunch* 18 October. www.counterpunch.org/sustar1018.html

Tackett, Michael. 2006. "Angry Electorate Says 'No' to Bush." *Chicago Tribune.* 8 November. A1.

Taylor, Denny, and Catherine Dorsey-Gaines. 1988. *Growing Up Literate: Learning from Inner-City Families.* Portsmouth, NH: Heinemann.

Thomas, Helen. 2006. "Give Voters a Choice About War." *Common Dreams* 1 September. www.commondreams.org/views06/0901-23.htm

Tickner, J. Ann. 2001. *Gendering World Politics: Issues and Approaches in the Post-Cold War Era.* New York: Columbia University Press.

Tompkins, Jane. 1987. "Me and My Shadow." *New Literary History* 19: 169–78.

Totten, Shay. 2006. "Vermont Soldier Offers Troops Baked Goods, Way to Speak Out Against War." *Vermont Guardian* 19 December. vermontguardian.com/local/122006/MilitaryCare.shtml

Toussaint, Eric. 2005 (1999). *Your Money or Your Life: The Tyranny of Global Finance.* Chicago: Haymarket Books.

Trimbur, John. 1994. "Taking the Social Turn: Teaching Writing Post-Process." *College Composition and Communication* 45: 108–118.

Tropico. 2001. CD-ROM. PopTop Software. In *MacAddict* 66 (February 2002).

Trotsky, Leon. 1970. *Women and the Family.* New York: Pathfinder.

Trotsky, Leon, John Dewey, and George Novack. 1969. *Their Morals and Ours: The Class Foundations of Moral Practice.* New York: Pathfinder.

Turl, Adam. 2007. "Is the U.S. Becoming Post-Industrial?" *International Socialist Review* March–April.

Tyler, Patrick E. 2003. "A New Power in the Streets." *New York Times* 17 February: A1.

"U.S. Policy on Iraq Draws Fire in Ohio." 1998. CNN Interactive. 18 February. www.cnn.com/WORLD/9802/18/town.meeting.folo/#2

USA Today/Gallup Poll. 2006. "Question 24: Here Are Four Different Plans the U.S. Could Follow in Dealing with War in Iraq. Which One Do You Prefer?" June. Princeton, NJ: The Gallup Organization.

UVM Student Labor Action Project. 2006. "Move in to Tent City!" 12 April. http://uvmslap.wordpress.com/page/2/

University of Vermont. 2006. Office of Institutional Studies. Survey of 2005 Graduates. 5 September. www.uvm.edu/~isis/gs05/gs05hr.pdf

Warren, Charles, and Louis Brandeis. 1890. "The Right of Privacy." *Harvard Law Review* 4: 194-221.

Webster v. Reproductive Health Services. 1989. 492 US 490.

Weisser, Christian R. 2002. *Moving Beyond Academic Discourse: Composition Studies and the Public Sphere.* Carbondale, IL: Southern Illinois University Press.

Welch, Kathleen. 1999. *Electric Rhetoric: Classical Rhetoric, Oralism, and a New Literacy.* Cambridge, MA: MIT University Press.

———. 1994. "Reconfiguring Writing and Delivery in Secondary Orality." In *Rhetorical Memory and Delivery: Classical Concepts for Contemporary Composition and Communication.* Ed. John Frederick Reynolds. Hillsdale, NJ: Lawrence Erlbaum. 17–30.

————. 1990. "Electrifying Classical Rhetoric: Ancient Media, Modern Technology, and Contemporary Composition." *Journal of Advanced Composition* 10 (1990): 22–38.

Welch, Nancy. 1999. "Playing with Reality: Writing Centers After the Mirror Stage." *College Composition and Communication* 51: 51–69.

————. 1998. "Sideshadowing Teacher Response." *College English* 60: 374–39.

————. 1997. *Getting Restless: Rethinking Revision in Writing Instruction.* Portsmouth, NH: Boynton/Cook.

Wells, Susan. 1996. "Rogue Cops and Health Care: What Do We Want from Public Writing?" *College Composition and Communication* 47: 325–41.

White, E. B. 1982 (1941). "On a Florida Key." *One Man's Meat.* New York: Harper Colophon.

Williams, Patricia J. 1991. *The Alchemy of Race and Rights: Diary of a Law Professor.* Cambridge, MA: Harvard University Press.

Willis, Ellen. 2001. "The U.S., Islam, and Terrorism." Globalization and Resistance Conference. November 16–17, New York, NY.

Wypijewski, JoAnn. 1999. "Pounding Out a DRUM Beat." *New Left Review* I/234 (March–April): 141–159

Yancey, Kathleen Blake. 2004. "Made Not Only in Words: Composition in a New Key." *College Composition and Communication* 56: 297–328.

Young, Iris. 1990. *Justice and the Politics of Difference.* Princeton, NJ: Princeton University Press.

Zinn, Howard. 1968. *Vietnam: The Logic of Withdrawal.* Boston: Beacon Press.

Zinn, Howard, and Anthony Arnove, ed. 2004. *Voices of a People's History of the United States.* New York: Seven Stories.

Žižek, Slovoj. 2002. "Shadows of the Real: Why the 20th Century Is Worth Fighting For." University of Vermont. 8 April.

————. 1993. *Tarrying with the Negative: Kant, Hegel, and the Critique of Ideology.* Durham, NC: Duke University Press.

Zweig, Michael. 2001. *The Working Class Majority: American's Best Kept Secret.* Ithaca, NY: ILR Press.